Recreational Tourism

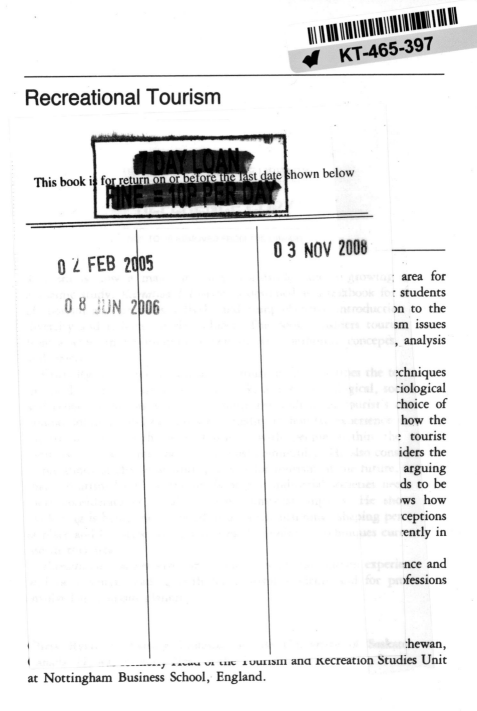

... growing area for ... textbook for students ... introduction to the ... tourism issues ... concepts, analysis

... the techniques ... ... gical, sociological ... tourist's choice of ... ... how the ... this the tourist ... ... also considers the ... ... of the future, arguing ... ... tourist needs to be ... ... He shows how ... ... shaping perceptions ... ... currently in ...

... experience and ... ... for professions

... Saskatchewan, ... formerly Head of the Tourism and Recreation Studies Unit at Nottingham Business School, England.

Recreational Tourism

A social science perspective

Chris Ryan

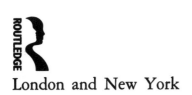

London and New York

First published in 1991
by Routledge
11 New Fetter Lane, London EC4P 4EE

Simultaneously published in the USA and Canada
by Routledge
29 West 35th Street, New York, NY 10001

Reprinted 1993

© 1991 Chris Ryan

Disc conversion by
Columns Typesetters of Reading
Printed and bound in Great Britain
by Mackays of Chatham PLC, Chatham, Kent

British Library Cataloguing in Publication Data
Ryan, Chris
    Recreational tourism: a social science perspective.
    1. Tourism. Socio-economic aspects
    I. Title
    338.4791

Library of Congress Cataloging in Publication Data
Ryan, Chris, 1945-
    Recreational tourism: a social science perspective / Chris Ryan.
        p.   cm.
    Includes bibliographical references and index.
    1. Tourist trade.   I. Title.
    G155.A1R9 1991   91-46815
    338.4'791-dc20   CIP

ISBN 0-415-05423-0
        0-415-05424-9 pbk

Thank you, Mum and Dad, Anca and Mark

Contents

Figures and tables

FIGURES

TABLES

Preface

There has been an increased recognition of tourism as not only a major industry, but as a valid area for undergraduate and postgraduate study. This is evidenced by the increasing number of courses that are now being offered not only in British universities, but also in North America and Australasia. As an area of academic study tourism possesses an interest which is both accessible and stimulating. Accessible in the sense that the great majority of students have been, and will become, tourists yet again and hence should perhaps be aware of the implications of their actions. Stimulating, because it requires an integration of all the main social sciences with their disciplines of economics, psychology and sociology, with the humanities as represented by history and geography combined with those parts of the physical sciences that relate to the environment. If this seems to be a recipe for a veritable 'hotch-potch' of skills and attitudes, then let this indeed be the case, and welcome it, for it enables the student to develop a holistic viewpoint towards what is a major activity in the developed and developing worlds. Equally, however, the difficulties involved for the teacher and the student should not be under-estimated. To be successful the tools of analysis have to be honed and sharpened; and hence considerable expertise is required. To read studies which, for example, refer to perceptions of place, or economic impacts of tourism, without knowing how an attitude may be defined or measured, or what exactly is the multiplier, or what are the deficiencies related to the concepts, is rather akin to driving a car without knowing how the car works. It can be done, but just as at least some mechanical knowledge helps in improving driving skills, so too, it is hoped, that understanding the concepts used in analysing tourism will further help the student to appreciate the subject.

Like many books, this work is not simply the result of the three months it has taken to type out the text. Rather, it is a compilation of experiences of working with colleagues and students, and of practical experience of tourism issues and past work undertaken on behalf of hoteliers, regional tourist authorities, stately homes, restaurateurs, parks authorities and other tourist attractions. There are, thus, many to thank, and if I have inadvertently omitted the name of someone, please accept my apologies. Amongst those to whom I must give public thanks is Brian Wheeller, now at the Centre for Urban and Rural Studies, Birmingham University. Brian and I taught tourism courses at the Nottingham Business School over the period 1980–1988, and whilst I must formally thank him for notes he has lent me on his studies of multiplier effects in Wales, I must also thank him for his stimulating criticisms over the years. Equally, I must thank Dr Myra Shackley and Professor Peter Franklin for the encouragement, support and freedom they have given me at the Nottingham Business School; to Professor Farouk Saleh of the University of Kuwait and Professor Jack Dart at the University of Saskatchewan, for permitting me to 'experiment' on their students; to Professors Ed Mayo (University of Western Michigan), Stephen Smith and Geoff Wall (University of Waterloo) who initially influenced me through their written works, and who subsequently I found to be helpful and friendly when I met them at conferences in the USA and Canada; and to staff at the offices of the East Midlands Tourist Board, Economic Development and Tourism, Saskatchewan, and the Meewasin Valley Authority, who, over time, have always provided friendly support. I must also thank colleagues who have helped me devise tourism courses at the Nottingham Business School, and in doing so have made me aware of new facets of the subject. There remain but three groups of people to thank. Firstly, Elisabeth Tribe of Routledge, who, as is the role of most editors, acted as 'god-parent' to the text, and without whom this book would not have been published. Secondly, to all of my past students who have not simply listened to me, but have criticised, questioned, and come up with new ideas, and to my family – my mum and dad who wondered what their son was up to now, and to my loving wife, Anca, who has always told me to go ahead, to write, to study, and who has thus often borne the unfair costs of such endeavours. To all of you, thank you.

Chris Ryan
Saskatchewan
June 1990

Acknowledgements

The author would like to thank the following for permission to use the tables and figures in the text, Methuen and Co. for Table 5.2 taken from Murphy, *Tourism – A Community Approach*, The British Tourist Authority for Table 5.3, Edwards, the National Trust and Pergamon Journals for Table 6.1, Prentice Hall and Ontario Ministry of Tourism and Recreation for Table 6.2, the *Independent* newspaper for the map used as Figure 6.1, the Meewasin Valley Authority and *Star Phoenix*, Saskatoon for the map used as Figure 6.2, *Chronicle Features* and the *Toronto Globe and Mail* for the Bizzaro cartoon. If any unknowing use has been made of copyright material could owners please contact the author via the publishers.

Chapter 1

Objectives and aims

This is a textbook for students studying tourism. A simple sentence to write, a difficult task to fulfil well. You, the student, should be aware that no one book can completely cover the field, and that this book, like most textbooks, is the result of a series of compromises and value judgements. There are therefore, a number of omissions in what you are going to read, and you need to be aware of these. A geographer will tell you that the treatment of spatial modelling is incomplete; that, for example, it does not cover the Lakshmanan-Hansen Model. The psychologist will remark that the theories of motivation are not fully explained, and perhaps more treatment might have been given to perceptual mapping. The economist may argue that more consideration might have been given to input-output analysis, and so the list continues. An author might respond that space is limited, and give a series of technical reasons why something was not covered in detail. For example, with reference to input-output analysis, different countries adopt different conventions with reference to the compilation of national income statistics, and to give a complete treatment of this is a book in itself. In short, authors are often the people who are most aware of what is lacking.

On the other hand, a textbook should seek to fulfil a series of functions. It should serve as an introduction to the diversity and richness of a subject, and tourism certainly possesses those attributes. It should retain the student's interest, which means that its style should convey enthusiasm and a love of the topic, but at the same time indicate further readings that a student can undertake. If contentions are made, there should be some attempt to support those contentions. Yet, ideally, it also should provoke thought and pose questions. It should indicate to the student not only the parts of the subject, but also how those parts relate to each other. It should also seek to explain issues and concepts, but not simply stop at the conceptual level, but also seek to, at least in part, explain some of the practical, functional problems which these issues pose, and means of solving these problems. Now, it can be seen why a textbook is so difficult to write!

What does this textbook attempt to do? Firstly it attempts to combine the social sciences and some of the humanities to develop a holistic view of tourism and the problems associated with it. Yet, even whilst attempting to provide a gestalt viewpoint, it seeks to examine the component parts of the tourism experience and the way that experience affects all parties concerned. Secondly it seeks to incorporate in its explanation some analytical techniques. Of necessity, a selective process of techniques has taken place, and the book describes those techniques that relate to the conceptual issues raised. At times, this, it must be admitted, reduces some aspects of the text to a listing of factors. Yet, this is in itself part of the process of problem and potential solution identification. In short the book attempts to combine concepts, analysis and a degree of functional practice that is suitable for students commencing their study of tourism in higher education.

However, the book is written from a specific viewpoint. Essentially tourism is about an experience of place. The tourism 'product' is not the tourist destination, but it is about experience of that place and what happens there. And, what happens there is a series of internal and external interactions. Images, impressions, stereotypes of people and place are either changed, or confirmed. The tourists' own perceptions of not simply the location, but of themselves may change. If personality is, in part, the compilation of experience, then the leisure, tourist experience is an important part of the formation of our personalities. The tourist interacts with other tourists, with people serving the tourist industry, and with others of the host community. This book is written from a humanistic, eclectic viewpoint for it is concerned with the quality of that experience. But, the process of interactions does not stop at the psychological. Economic consequences flow from the movements of people, and so too do environmental impacts. Hence, these factors must also be explored.

There is another theme which is implicit within the text, and that within the western world there is a greater segmentation of life styles emerging. Even within a world that is increasingly concerned with environmental problems, people are still increasingly adopting life styles that suit their way of doing things, and within their leisure and recreational pursuits are finding activities which fulfil specific needs. This process has implications for tourism, and increasingly market segmentation is expected to emerge with consequent decisions on matching tourist 'products' to tourist types. Yet, the 'tourist' is not consistent in the sense that one need does not continually dominate. The tourist may, at one moment seek to explore new destinations in unspoilt places, but, on their next holiday, may seek to fulfil other needs. Equally it must be said that tourist destinations are not static. However, it is argued within this book, that this process of changing life styles must be recognised along with the recognition of fragility of tourist resources, and hence marketing considerations must be incorporated within tourist planning in a way in which it has not always been done in the past. 'Societal marketing' must be considered more fully.

The book thus commences with a consideration of the demand for tourism from three perspectives. The first is to consider the economic determinants of demand from both a micro- and macro-economic viewpoint. However, it is argued that economic variables do not successfully explain the whole of tourism flows, and even within the micro-economic models the variable, 'taste', is a recognition of the importance of psychological determinants. Since our perceptions are in part based upon our social experiences, this leads to a consideration of both psychological and social determinants of demand.

The second chapter moves from the framework of demand to consider whether that demand is met — what in fact is the nature of the tourist experience and what factors may account for satisfaction or dissatisfaction? Since, as has already been noted, the tourist experience is within the context of a tourist environment, this leads to a consideration of the tourist zone, and this forms the concern of the third chapter.

Chapters four, five and six are concerned with the consequences of the tourist interactions within the tourist zone. Economic consequences emerge, and this necessitates a review of those types of consequences and means by which flows on income and costs can be assessed. Increasingly it is being recognised that economic costs include environmental costs, whilst at the same time the nature of the environment is important in determining the quality of the tourist experience. Chapter five links these concerns in an examination of the ecological impacts of tourism. Chapter six considers in more detail the contention that an important part of the tourist experience is an interaction with the host community, and examines the impacts of tourism upon societies and cultures. Essentially the viewpoint adopted here is that the potential impact of tourism upon a society is very dependent upon the internal strength of the norms of that society, and the context of the impact. Urbanisation and industrialisation may cause considerably more impacts than tourism, yet, perhaps because of the fact that tourism, unlike other exports, is an industry where the user is 'imported' to the point of supply, significant concern has been expressed in the literature about the role of tourism as an agent of change. These concerns are noted and discussed in this chapter.

The final chapter discusses the 'hidden agenda' that in a world of change, of increased segmentation of life styles, marketing is important, and needs to be incorporated into tourism planning as it shapes perceptions of place, types of usage and usage rates of tourist zones, and hence impacts on 'carrying capacities'. However, if this is the case, there is also a need to understand how perceptions may be measured, life styles described and potential tourists reached, and hence this chapter also introduces the student to some of the techniques currently being utilised.

Thus, on completion of the book, it is hoped that the student will have gained an overall view of the nature of the tourism experience, an experience that is not confined to the tourist alone, but to those people and places that the tourist comes into contact with. Inevitably, in such a topic, value judgements are being made, and on the whole it is hoped that the text reflects a humanistic, optimistic and environmentally aware ethic.

Chapter 2

The determinants of demand for tourism

DEFINITIONS OF TOURISM

To paraphrase the great English playwright, William Shakespeare, if indeed all the world is a stage, and men and women have their exits and their entrances, then perhaps in the late twentieth century the tourist is the audience. Perhaps the tourist does not always comprehend what it is that he or she sees, perhaps at times the tourist enters upon the stage as either the figure of fun, or the catalyst of change, but increasingly the tourist cannot be ignored. The numbers of tourists swell, as if in response to some pressing need to see the world, to view it as if it contains some truth that would otherwise be denied to them. What is the nature of this phenomenom, and what is it then that leads to this need? In analysing the nature of tourism a number of approaches may be taken. The first is to view it as an economic activity, and thus recognise that tourism is an industry. Such an approach is inherent in a definition which refers to tourism as:

> a study of the demand for and supply of accommodation and supportive services for those staying away from home, and the resultant patterns of expenditure, income creation and employment.

Yet, whilst this may in turn lead to a series of technical definitions that are needed for the collection of data, it seems to lack the 'fun' that is associated with the tourist experience. An example of a technical definition is that used by the British Tourist Authority for the collection of statistics for the Home Tourism Survey, where, for example, a tourist trip is defined as:

> a stay of one or more nights away from home for holidays, visits to friends or relatives, business conferences or any other purpose, except such things as boarding education or semi-permanent employment.

The fun and excitement of tourism is perhaps caught by the holistic approach taken by the Tourism Steering Group to Stratford-upon-Avon District Council, when in its report in 1978 it spoke of:

> day trippers from the cities of the Midlands, evening theatre-goers from

London, coach tour passengers from all over the world hurtling through the country, conference delegates and longer stay customers of the whole price range of serviced and unserviced accommodation . . . a visitor to the District for whatever reason he or she comes, for however long he or she may stay, and by whatever means he or she may come.

Equally, the psychological impacts of tourism may be recognised, for a major component of tourism is holiday travel, and the prime motivations for such travel are ones of rest, discovery and pleasure. From this viewpoint holiday tourism may be defined as:

the means by which people seek psychological benefits that arise from experiencing new places, and new situations that are of a temporary duration, whilst free from the constraints of work, or normal patterns of daily life at home.

It thus becomes possible to define tourism from at least four viewpoints, the economic, technical, holistic and experiential. In turn these considerations can be used to analyse the demand for tourism, and three separate, albeit related approaches can be undertaken. The first is to view tourism as a service or a product like any other, a demand determined by economic variables, and hence subjected to the economic 'laws' of demand. A second approach might be to view tourism and the nature of its demand as a reflection of social change. As Krippendorf (1987) comments, 'Sick societies generate sick tourists'. Further there is the feeling that as one reads econometric studies relating flows of tourist movement to exchange rates and changes in income, or theories of tourism as a means of escape from the pressures of work, that in some respect these variables do not actually apply to us, the individual tourist, particularly well. Hence there is a need for a further approach, and that is to examine the psychological roots of tourism demand.

ECONOMIC DETERMINANTS OF DEMAND

a) The role of income

In micro-economic theory the demand for a particular product can be expressed as being:

1) $D_t = f(P_t, P_1 \ldots P_n, Y, T)$

$$\text{where } \begin{aligned} D_t &= \text{ the demand for tourism} \\ P_t &= \text{ the price of tourism} \\ P_1 \ldots P_n & \text{ are the prices of other goods} \\ Y &= \text{ income} \\ \text{and } T &= \text{ taste.} \end{aligned}$$

It can be easily hypothesised that as incomes increase, so the demand for tourism is likely to increase. However, increasingly studies would seem to show that in the developed world, the demand for tourism has actually increased faster than the growth of national income. For example, expenditure on tourism proved remarkably resistant to the recession that occurred in the early 1970s following the oil crisis, and it would seem that in fact the demand for tourism is income elastic and price inelastic. In other words, for any given percentage increase in income, tourism demand grows faster. On the other hand, in a downward direction, tourism demand would appear to be income inelastic, that is, if there is a reduction in income (or more likely in a practical sense, incomes rise less quickly than expected), the demand for tourism does not slacken. Equally, it can be claimed that tourism continues to grow, even if prices increase. However, as with all generalisations, care needs to be taken, and attempts to forecast future growth of tourism by using economic models have proven that in practice income alone explains little of the variance in changes in tourism flows. Partly this may arise from technical reasons. From a macro-economic viewpoint in the use of national income data, and average wage rates and their movements, the analyst will often use what is in effect a long-term tourist demand function. For example, if the growth in total tourism expenditure, or some other measure of tourism activity such as the number of trips or the number of tourist nights was plotted against income, the diagram in Figure 2.1 might result.

However, within each of these different years, a cross-sectional analysis would show that of course not everyone earns the average income figure, and people with different levels of income might have different propensities to spend any increase in income on travel and tourism. Therefore there is a need to impose on the original diagram the annual cross-sectional distribution of incomes within society as is illustrated in Figure 2.2. There are hence a number of questions that arise about such 'consumption functions'. For example, as lower income groups attain higher income levels, how does this influence their spending patterns? Do they spend the total of their additional income, and at what time do they begin to increase their savings? Other similar questions would relate to the use of credit. This distinction between longitudinal income patterns and cross-sectional distribution of income may in part help to explain why studies that concentrate on annual movements of income and tourist expenditure do not always show the expected high correlation.

In addition, from the viewpoint of tourism analysis, an additional question relates to the definition of income. It might be that the relationship between tourism expenditure and gross personal income is indirect, and the links between 'discretionary' income and tourism spending are more pertinent. The relationship may be defined in the following manner:

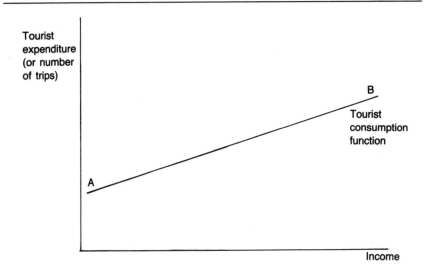

Figure 2.1   The tourist consumption function

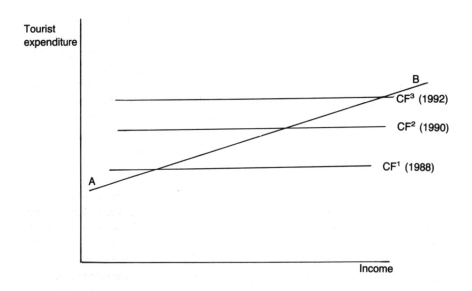

Figure 2.2   The long-run consumption function and cross-sectional analysis

2) $E_t = f(Y_{dis}) = f[(Y_d) - (E_b), S]$

   where E_t = Expenditure on tourism
         Y_{dis} = Discretionary income
         Y_d = Disposable income
         E_b = Expenditure on non-leisure activities
         S = Savings

and $Y_d = f(Y - T)$
and $E_b = f(P_1 . . ._n, i)$

   where Y = Gross income
         T = Taxation
         $P_1 . . ._n$ = Prices of non-leisure items
         i = Interest rates

From this viewpoint discretionary income is determined by the level of gross income minus taxation (i.e. disposable income). However, every householder has to meet certain bills and expenditures. For example, there is the need to pay for food, heating, lighting, travel to and from work, and mortgages on household properties or rents. Only then is there sufficient money left for either saving or spending on leisure pursuits. It can therefore be seen that such discretionary income can be affected by variables such as increases in the cost of food, travel to work and other inflationary pressures. Interest rates may also have an important role to play as was possibly indicated in the British economy in 1989. In order to dampen down demand, the then British government sought to reduce consumer spending by increasing interest rates. Following, as it did, a significant increase in house prices and high levels of home buying, this meant for many families a significant rise in mortgage repayments, thus reducing their discretionary income. This factor was partially thought to be a cause of a reduction in demand for foreign package holidays from approximately 14 million in 1988 to 12 million in 1989. However, other variables intrude in such an analysis, for 1989 also saw a significant increase in holiday bookings by the British within Britain – holidays which were not necessarily cheaper than the holidays offered by the British tour operators. Hence this may have also had elements of not a reduction in demand *per se*, but of demand switching due to disillusionment with the overseas package holiday. For many Britons, 1988 had been an experience of long delays in airports on both outward and return flights; a feature that had been reported widely by both press and TV media. In passing, it might also be commented that if mortgage interest rates are to be effective in determining holiday demand, then it is being assumed that large numbers of people are becoming recent home buyers, and are primarily financing such purchases by mortgages rather than past savings or the realising of family assets such as selling homes of equal value, or using inherited wealth. With an ageing population that increasingly has access to inherited wealth, as is symptomatic of many western developed nations of northern America and northern Europe, such assumptions may become less valid, and hence mortgage interest rates will have a weaker effect upon determining the demand for tourist expenditure.

From the above it can be argued that any attempt to relate tourism flows to income movements must therefore take into account not only gross income changes, but also changes in taxation, general inflation and interest rates. In addition, it might also be noted that increasing interest rates may not only affect leisure expenditure by increasing the price of necessities either directly or indirectly, but might also encourage a shift in the savings ratio (savings/income), which in turn impinges on possible expenditure on leisure. In addition, it must be noted that expenditure on tourism also competes with expenditure on other leisure pursuits, a factor that is further examined below.

b) The cost of travel

Expression 1) also indicates that a possible economic determinant of demand for tourism is the price of the holiday. The price that the tourist pays for the holiday might be said to cover three components:

a) cost of travel,
b) cost of accommodation,
c) cost of the activities undertaken by the tourist at the destination area.

With reference to an ITC (Inclusive Tour Charter), or independent travel requiring a flight, the main components of the cost of travel could be hypothesised as being:

3) $$C_t = f(F,O) + f(R)$$

where C_t = Cost of travel
F = Cost of fuel
O = Other travel costs including administration
R = Profitability of airlines.

In the case of holiday costs, approximately 40 per cent of the price of a package holiday offered by British tour operators arises from the flight. Of the flight costs an important variable is the fuel cost. Fuel costs are subjected to significant causes of uncertainty due to two factors. The first is that past history has shown that petroleum product prices are far from stable, inspite of efforts by the OPEC countries to control oil prices, and fluctuations can occur not only from year to year but from month to month. One way to overcome the risks involved for airlines and tour operators is by establishing a futures market in aviation fuel. A second uncertain variable is that aviation fuel is priced in US dollars, and thus prices are affected by exchange price movements. In practice, this may in fact be a simplifying and stabilising element inasmuch as any alternative position could pose major problems for airlines. The thought of having to pay for aviation fuel in the currency of the country of embarkation would create a highly complex movement of prices and could affect the willingness of airlines to fly to any given destination. Nonetheless, even the current situation can mean that as currencies move against the dollar, costs for fuel may fall or rise for any given airline.

Under these circumstances, it may very much be a matter of swings and roundabouts. In some cases favourable movements in exchange rates may be offset by increases in prices of fuel, in other cases both variables may move together, either favourably or unfavourably. Under some situations they may be less influential than might otherwise be the case. For example, in the period 1982 to 1984, neither currency nor fuel price movements were particularly favourable for British tour operators, yet the costs of holidays and flights were highly competitive. This was a reflection of the market place, where an expansion of supply dictated a need to fill aircraft, and the utilisation of marginal pricing techniques where discounted seats meant that the sale of a seat obtained at least some revenue, whereas empty seats of course meant no revenue. Thus in the above formula (3) profit (as reflecting organisational difficulties) is the variable that may reflect this situation.

c) The cost of accommodation

With reference to the cost of accommodation, exchange rates can yet again play an important role. For example an American tourist may have visited Britain in 1964, and paid £10 for a hotel room. At that time the exchange rate was $2.79 to the £1 and hence from the American's viewpoint the price was $27.90. If it is assumed that 20 years later the American wishes to return to Britain, and that hotel prices have now increased to £30 per room, the American will not in fact be faced with a 300 per cent increase in costs. In 1984 the exchange rate was $1.23 to the £1, and hence the room will be perceived as costing $36.90, an increase of only 32 per cent.

4) $C_a = f(H, X)$

where C_a = Costs of accommodation
   H = Hoteliers' costs
   X = Exchange rate

Our American would then probably conclude that Britain was a 'cheap location'. Expression 4) indicates the factors involved as a further component of the costs of the holiday. The same processes could apply to the third element of the tourist's cost of a holiday. In this instance it might be said that:

5)
$$Cac = f\left(X, \frac{\Delta Ph}{\Delta t} \middle/ \frac{\Delta Pg}{\Delta t}\right)$$

where Cac = Cost of tourist's activity in the tourist destination
  X = Exchange rate

$\dfrac{\Delta Ph}{\Delta t} \middle/ \dfrac{\Delta Pg}{\Delta t}$ = rate of inflation in the host country divided by the rate of inflation in the tourist generating country; a measure of the differential inflation between host and generating countries.

For example, in 1982 the £1 equalled 200 pesetas, whereas in 1983 a British visitor to Spain would have obtained 220 pesetas for their £1. Would therefore, the British visitors have found that the cost of their sightseeing and other activities was 10 per cent less in 1983 as against one year earlier? In practice this was not the case, because the rate of inflation in Spain in that period was approximately 15 per cent per annum. Nonetheless the British tourist would have had some protection against the Spanish inflation. An item which cost 200 pesetas in 1982, would have cost 230 pesetas in 1983, but for the British tourist the cost in terms of pounds sterling would have been £1.05, an increase of 5 per cent. As this would have been comparable to the rate of inflation in the UK this would have probably been acceptable to the British tourist. However, in 1984 the £1 was equal to 206 pesetas, and assuming an inflation of a further 15 per cent in Spain, the British tourist would, in 1984, be paying 264.5 pesetas for the same item, which represented £1.28 for the British tourist, an increase in price of 23 per cent. As this was much higher than inflation in the UK Spain would, logically, be perceived as an expensive destination, and hence it would be expected that the level of tourist demand for Spain would fall.

Hence, the previous paragraphs can be summarised as stating that the economic determinants of demand for tourism are:

a) total income;
b) prices of other factors that determine 'discretionary income';
c) economic structure of industries relevant to tourism and their profitability;
d) inflation in the host and tourist generating countries;
e) rates of exchange.

d) A review of evidence

It thus can be seen that a series of potential testable economic relationships can be hypothesised, and indeed the literature contains many examples of attempts to explain tourist flows by the use of econometric modelling. However the results are far from conclusive. For example Witt and Martin (1987) conclude that income is an explanatory variable in 38 of 39 cases, but noted differences between nationalities, in that the lagged variable was important in explaining British holiday-taking behaviour that contained a degree of destination loyalty which was missing from the German market. However, in his original thesis Witt warns of the enormous difficulty of undertaking such work, for such models require significant inputs of data. Thus in examining British visitor numbers to Italy it was found that the statistics from 'Centro per la Statistica Aziendale' were incomplete. Witt (1978) also concluded that

> a one per cent increase in real personal disposable income per capita results in a 0.518 per cent increase in the number of foreign holiday trips per capita.

This compares with later findings which show that tourism is income elastic (Witt and Martin 1987, Martin and Witt 1988, 1989). It might, however, be argued that people are reluctant to forgo their annual holiday, and in periods of recession, or when economic growth has slowed down, the holiday will be financed from changes in either spending patterns, or more probably from a reduction in savings. Consequently, during such periods, tourism will appear to be income inelastic as falls (or reductions in economic growth) do not cause diminution in tourism demand. However, in periods of economic growth characterised by feelings of confidence, tourism demand may be income elastic, in that for any given increase in growth of income, there may be a faster percentage growth in tourism demand.

Such problems are compounded further when tourist demand functions for smaller areas are attempted. For example Quayson and Var (1982) consider demand functions for tourists visiting the Okanagan, British Columbia, and suggest that 'a 1% increase in income will generally be associated with a less than proportionate increase (0.623) in tourism receipts in the Okanagan'. However, for visitors from California, tourist trips to British Columbia were in fact income elastic, implying that tourist trips to destinations further from home, and hence by implication being more expensive, are more readily determined by rising income.

This brief review might lead to a number of likely conclusions. The first is that economic forecasting may be able to indicate, within constraints, potential demand for tourism activities, but may be poorer at predicting actual flows in terms of where people go. Secondly, it might be contended that economics is based on a concept of the rational economic man, and tourism is concerned with motivations other than rationality. Guitart (1982) comments that:

> The Briton is essentially, a great traveller; he retains his old habits even in an unfavourable domestic economic climate. . . . It might have been expected that . . . relating numbers of passengers using ITC flights to per capita private direct consumption in constant terms would provide a high correlation coefficient. But this was not the case in the UK's case. One might equally have expected a certain amount of economic rationality by UK tourists, changing or modifying their decisions in the election of their destination as the prices changed in the Mediterranean areas. But this was not always true.

Thirdly, it might be concluded that perhaps econometric techniques are not appropriate in analysing tourism patterns of expenditure. Rebecca Summary (1987) in discussing a demand function for Kenya's sunlust tourists concludes that:

> typical multivariant demand functions estimated by the ordinary least squares regression may not represent the optimal technique to use in all tourism studies . . . perhaps the best solution as Uysal and Compton suggest is to use qualitative and quantitative models to provide the best possible tourism-demand analysis.

THE SOCIAL DETERMINANTS OF DEMAND

a) An overall view

It is suggested by Guitart (1982), Pearce (1982), Mayo and Jarvis (1981) and many others, that attempts to explain determinants of tourism demand without reference to motivations or social change can only yield at best incomplete forecasts of tourism movements. The implications of social change can be discussed with reference to the tourism/work and tourism/leisure ratios. These can be defined as being:

$$\text{Tourism/work ratio} = \frac{\text{Percentage change in hours spent on tourism}}{\text{Percentage change in hours spent on work}}$$

$$\text{Tourism/leisure ratio} = \frac{\text{Percentage change in hours spent on tourism}}{\text{Percentage change in hours spent on other forms of leisure}}$$

The growth of tourism demand has been fuelled in part by a combination of growth in income and increases in leisure time permitted by, in the earlier part of the twentieth century, increases in paid holiday time and free weekends. In addition, the introduction of flexible working patterns permits people to plan and take extended weekend breaks more easily than in the past. Thus the tourism/work ratio has swung towards tourism as the number of hours of holidays have increased and the number of hours worked decreased. However, as the number of hours of leisure available to people increase, so too, arguably, the tourism/leisure ratio may also change, as possibly other forms of leisure begin to compete with tourism. There are also linkages with economic factors in a micro-economic sense. People may obtain increases in leisure time, but if those increases in leisure time are not accompanied by proportionate increases in income, then the available discretionary income per unit of available leisure time will fall, thus inhibiting a greater use of leisure time for holiday purposes. To take an obvious example, the worker made redundant has obvious increases in leisure time, but not necessarily the income which permits expenditure on increased travel. Equally, the person who receives additional holiday entitlement from work without an increase in pay also has less available income per unit of leisure time, and thus the additional holiday time might be spent on leisure pursuits within or around the home. The factor of discretionary income and available time might therefore indicate potential inhibiting factors on the growth of tourism. In 1982 the Economist Intelligence Unit sought to assess growth in tourism to 1990 by assessing the changes in leisure time, and population changes, to estimate the total weeks available for tourist activity. The study concluded that, whereas for a country such as the UK, 87 per cent of the potential market was already being penetrated, different habits in other countries such as Canada meant that there only 39 per cent of the possible tourist market had been penetrated.

The tourism/leisure ratio can also be determined by other factors.

a) Firstly, there might be a growth in the popularity of other leisure activities that rival tourism in competing for the valuable hours of leisure time. It is true that the holiday always offers one thing that other forms of activity based at home do not have, and that is the chance to experience a new environment; and the motivation to experience novelty is strong in us all to a greater or lesser extent. However, if somebody is finding significant degrees of fulfilment in their hobbies and interests practised in their home area, then the escape motivations that prompt travel are weakened.

b) Secondly, there may be diminishing satisfaction per additional unit of tourism experience consumed. This is an application of the economist's concept of diminishing marginal utility. Can it be argued that continued increases in travel produce yet further wants or needs to travel, or does there occur at some point a form of world-weariness which makes the traveller appreciate if not actually yearn for the peace and luxuries of home? If holiday travel becomes synonymous with experiences of delays at airports, traffic jams, queues for entrance, being subjected to abuse from drunken fellow travellers, and the transfer of the ills of the city into the countryside, then indeed the tourist may feel that 'home is best'.

c) Thirdly, the motivations of our forbears in seeking holidays may be less valid in the last part of the twentieth century. Amongst the factors that induced a growth in travel was the wish of working people to escape from the everyday noise and bustle of work and large cities. The countryside not only offered peace and tranquillity, or scenic beauty, but also a chance to recover from daily toil. But if the nature of the daily task changes, perhaps our requirements of the holiday also change.

In examining this relationship between work and leisure four hypotheses can be examined (Zuzanek and Mannell 1983). These are:

a) The trade-off hypothesis, where people choose between work and leisure time.
b) The compensation hypothesis, where holidays and leisure compensate for the boredom or troubles of everyday life.
c) The spin-off hypothesis, where the nature of work produces not contrary but similar patterns of leisure activity.
d) The neutralist hypothesis, where there is no relationship between work and leisure.

b) The trade-off hypothesis

From this viewpoint there is an inverse relationship between work and leisure time. Consequently there is a choice between working longer hours and generating more income, or working fewer hours and having less income. This situation is demonstrated in Figure 2.3. Hence it could be argued that a choice has to be made between selecting Oa level of income and Oc hours of leisure. However, the concept can be refined further. It might be that the person concerned may find it difficult to choose between the two options, in that both have attractions and hence would yield equal degrees of satisfaction. However, what is known is that a combination which represents Oa of income and a higher level of leisure time is more agreeable than the combinations represented on the curve I^1. Consequently it may be possible to draw a whole series of such indifference curves, where the further from the origin the curve lies, the greater is the satisfaction associated with that combination of choices.

The question is then, what stops the selection of the curve generating the highest levels of satisfaction? Two constraints obviously exist. The first is the limited amount of time available, and the second is the need to

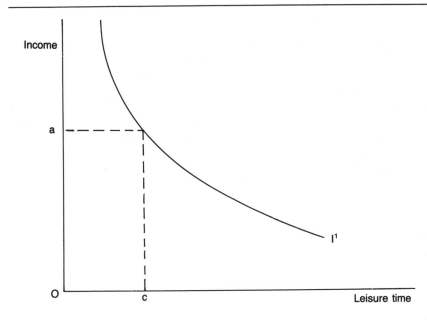

Figure 2.3   The work-leisure 'trade-off'

obtain at least some minimal level of income. Hence a constraint line representing time may be drawn. This line, XY, is imposed on the map of curves in Figure 2.4, where X represents the maximum amount of income that could be earned if all suitable available time was spent in work, and Y represents the maximum amount of leisure that might exist. Hence, the actual choice made by the person concerned will be that combination of income and leisure made possible by the point where the constraint line touches the highest satisfaction value curve, that is the point at which it is tangential to the curve. This is represented in Figure 2.4 at the point A, thus producing Oa of income and Oc of leisure.

With increases in productivity made possible by increased investment, for any given amount of hours worked, over time the income per hour worked will increase. Therefore the constraint line, XY, will pivot about the point Y, for at point Y if no hours are worked, income will remain at zero. This now produces a new combination of hours worked and hours taken in leisure. This enables us to derive a demand curve for leisure.

In the first instance, if the combination selected is Oa of income, and Oc of leisure, then the 'price' of that leisure is the income lost whilst taking that leisure, i.e. Xa. Hence the price of the leisure is Xa/Oc per leisure time unit (hour). As the constraint line changes, so too does the price of the leisure time taken. Economists would refer to the income lost as the 'opportunity cost', that is in this instance, it is the income forgone in order

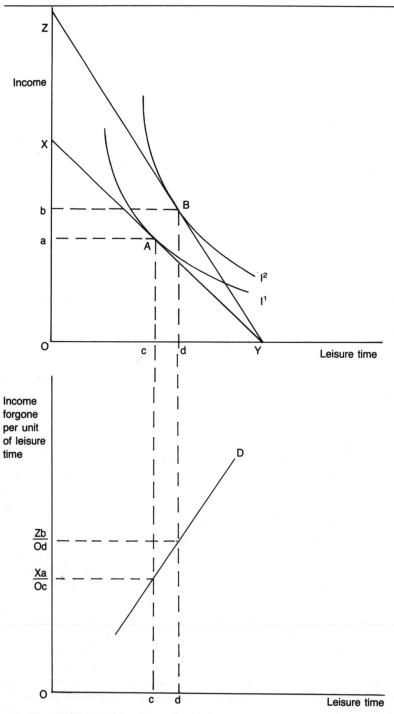

Figure 2.4   Deriving a demand curve for tourism

to spend time on leisure. The original point of Xa/Oc can be joined to the subsequent point of Zb/Od, and by joining these points a demand curve for leisure time can be derived.

The above analysis does have technical problems associated with it. A major one is that the pivoting of the time constraint curve around point Y may not be as smooth as is drawn. As drawn, it implies that the increase in productivity leads to increases in income whereby those selecting a higher income receive larger increases than those selecting an option of lower income and more leisure time. This might appear plausible, but such factors may actually change the shape of the initial indifference curves.

This approach indicates that whilst increases in income actually permit an expansion of leisure time, the increase in such leisure time taking is a movement along the demand curve rather than a move of the demand curve itself. Hence in interpreting the past expansion of tourism demand this simple model does indicate that in part the increase in demand is a function of movements along an income/leisure time demand curve, rather than a move of the relationship itself. Therefore, if it is found that economic variables become less effective in predicting tourism demand, then it may be because there are other variables at work that are causing the income/leisure time demand curve to shift over time. One of these factors may be the relationship between work and leisure. The most obvious implication of Figure 2.4 is that the trade-off hypothesis seems to indicate that the demand for tourism/leisure actually increases the greater the cost of that leisure in terms of forgone income. A number of comments may be made about this hypothesis. The first is that there is some evidence to suggest that this may indeed be the case, in that, as has already been argued, there is evidence that the demand for tourism is income elastic. In other words, as incomes increase, the demand for tourism increases at a faster rate. Even when incomes grow less slowly, the demand for tourism may increase faster than disposable incomes. Thus for example, in 1990 the Conference Board of Canada predicted that for 1991, even whilst Canadians' disposable income would increase by 1 per cent, tourist expenditure on foreign travel would increase by 3.2 per cent. Therefore, the real cost (or opportunity cost) of the holiday increases in that to finance a 3.2 per cent increase in expenditure when disposable income increases by 1 per cent means that other items are not being consumed, or interest earned from savings is being forgone. Hypothetically, as society moves into the post-industrial world characterised by flexible working patterns and more frequent occupational change as envisaged by Toffler (1970) and others, for higher income groups the decision to take time off from work becomes costly in both financial and temporal terms. However, because high pay is earned from time that is spent working, the financial cost can be borne. It is important to remember that the upward sloping demand curve results from the constraint line pivoting due to increased productivity. Hence professional people, who in effect contract out their skill to an employer or client during their time working, are able, due to that experience, to charge a higher fee on subsequent periods when they work. The decision not to work thus implies a higher opportunity cost for leisure/tourism. It can be postulated that this scenario becomes more common in the emerging post-industrial world, and is not restricted to young urban professionals ('yuppies').

c) The compensation hypothesis

The compensation hypothesis argues that leisure is the means by which people compensate for the deficiencies in their work. If work is boring, repetitive, dictated by the speed of the machine, subdivided into smaller tasks so that the worker never sees the whole, then leisure is the means by which the worker *re-creates* the sense of being human. This theme of the worker as an appendage of the machine is common in both films (for example Charlie Chaplin's *Modern Times*) and literature. The historical social evidence for such a thesis is provided by the examples of the late nineteenth and early twentieth centuries where the mining communities of South Wales and Yorkshire developed their traditions of choral singing and brass bands, and the textile workers of Lancashire and Yorkshire were founder members of hiking and cycling clubs. The implications for holidays is that the desired holiday is determined by an *escape* motivation. The holiday becomes a means of escaping the daily routine of toil of not only work but also the home. In consequence the holiday offers fulfilment of a fantasy, often based on a concept of the life of the 'idle rich'. The holiday is where the round of cooking and washing need not be done; the hotel offers a standard of accommodation higher than that experienced at home, and it is a place where waiters come to serve drinks as you take your place in a sun lounger by the side of the pool. Also, in a work environment where communication with fellow workers becomes well nigh impossible over the din, cacophony and noise of machinery, the holiday offers communication with like-minded people. The resultant holiday becomes hotel based, and actual destination is of secondary importance.

However, if the hypothesis is consistent, it must also work in the opposite direction. In other words, those with interesting work will seek peace and monotony at home and at leisure. Whilst there is some truth in the caricature of the manager who returns home to converse with his or her spouse only in grunts as he or she collapses in front of the television set, it would appear from the evidence, (Parker 1971, Pennings 1976, and Zuzanek and Mannell 1983), that this is generally not the case.

d) The spill-over hypothesis

The spill-over hypothesis shares with the compensation hypothesis a recognition of the importance of work and an assumption that it affects the way in which we spend our non-work time. However, unlike the compensation theory, it argues that there is not a contrast between work and leisure, but rather a complementary relationship. For the worker who fills a role subservient to machine dictated routine, leisure becomes a passive affair. Thus the major leisure pursuit will be watching television, and the role normally adopted is that of spectator rather than participant. Thus the traditional package holiday represents a continuation of this process. The holidaymaker is taken from aircraft to hotel, from hotel to day-trip and back again. Even decisions about where and when, and indeed what to eat, are removed from the holidaymaker. The holiday itself becomes as much a production line process as the industrial work left behind. Holidays become industrialised in form.

On the other hand for those involved in interesting work, leisure also is characterised by participation in doing things. People are generators of action, be it do-it-yourself, amateur dramatics or playing sports.

The above situation descriptions are caricatures, but for a purpose. Many, for example Alvin Toffler (*Future Shock* 1970, *The Third Wave* 1981), have argued that as developed societies move into a post-industrial period, the nature of work changes. This is evidenced by the growth of the service sector which is characterised not by human/machine relationships, but personal relationships supported by the machine (computer). Such work patterns have a potential to create more self-fulfilment. Emery (1981) adds to this argument. Not only does the work/leisure relationship change, but so too does the home/travel relationship. As people adopt more fulfilling work patterns, so too, due to increasing incomes, are their home patterns offering more opportunities for leisure. People have their windsurfers and boats, they have accessibility to their golf, leisure and sports clubs from home. Pursuits previously undertaken perhaps only whilst on holiday, are now a normal part of home life. In addition, increasingly hotels no longer offer a style of accommodation that is more comfortable than home. When a hotel advertises it has satellite or cable television it is not a boast that it is offering more than the holidaymaker is used to, but rather a reassurance that normal home television viewing will not be interrupted due to a loss of facilities. In short, increases in participation levels in various leisure and recreation pursuits might be expected. However, various constraints have emerged (Jackson and Dunn 1987, 1988) whilst it has also been noted that one characteristic of modern society is an apparent lack of time. Shaw (1990) has coined the expression 'time famine' to describe this phenomenon. However, it has been noted that those with the highest participation rates in leisure tend to note the constraint of time most (Kay and Jackson 1990), whilst Shaw's findings are in part dependent upon the definitions of leisure that are used. For example, is engaging in a 3-mile jog a leisure activity or part of a keep fit programme which the respondent sees as essential.

The consequence of both changing work patterns, and changing leisure opportunities around and within the home environment, is a change in what is sought from the holiday. Holidaymakers become more selective in their choice. Escape motivations are undermined, and pull factors become more important. The pull factors include not only the nature of the destination and accommodation, but also the activities undertaken whilst on holiday. The evidence for this is represented by the growth of demand for self-catering holidays. This is not motivated by a wish for cheaper accommodation, but for the freedom that it represents. Similarly amongst the fastest growth sectors of the holiday market are seat-only sales where people increasingly make their own independent arrangements, seeking smaller, more personal hotels, and holidays based on an extension of hobbies. Many now require of their holiday that it extends the mind, and hence holistic holidays such as the *Skyros Experience* can attract holidaymakers. Ryan and Groves (1987) found, for example, that high income holidaymakers valued flexibility and independence within their holiday arrangements. Emery (1981) argues that in the future the relationship between the home setting and that of the holiday destination will change with the result that tourists will be more selective about their choice of destination. However he warns against laying too much stress upon the concept of self-actualisation as a holiday motivator, writing:

> Self-actualisation and self-expression are too limited to the era of self liberation in the sixties and seventies. In the longer haul, and over the broad reaches of human society, I do not think that self-actualisation will be found adaptive if it is not also an active concern to nurture the self-actualisation of others.

One implication of this concept of nurturance of others is if it becomes possible through a freedom from self-denying labour made possible in emergent post-industrial processes, then tourists will become more concerned about the impact that their tourism makes on host societies and cultures; which in turn will change the nature of tourist activity.

Apart from these potential changes, what can be said is that the tourism/leisure ratio changes. Tourism faces increased competition from other uses of leisure time, although many of these may require some travel, but not accommodation. It may therefore be assumed that increased daytrip activity will occur.

e) The neutralist hypothesis

Both the compensation and spill-over hypotheses have a common viewpoint in that human behaviour has an underlying entity. The work experience either drives people to seek compensatory action, or drives them to adopt leisure patterns similar to their work experience. It assumes an ascendancy of work, and implies a causal relationship, with work being the determining factor. It is true that the arguments of Emery and Toffler can be re-interpreted to imply a reversal of this last contention. If, in post-industrial societies, work becomes not only interesting, but it also becomes possible to opt into and out of work in flexible working patterns as dictated by the wish to adopt different positions on the leisure time/income indifference curve postulated by the trade-off hypothesis, then it can be argued that the leisure component of the desired life style will begin to determine the work pattern to be adopted. Nonetheless, even this position still maintains a work/leisure relationship. The neutralist hypothesis rejects such linkages, arguing that there is no relationship between work and leisure – both are separate components of our lives, and people can distinguish between the two, and act differently in each. Ironically, this separation is made possible by the very same processes that Toffler and Emery describe. As Bacon (1975) records: 'Work has lost its former hegemony and centrality in most people's lives and has become a much more marginal experience.'

If this is the case, then the emergent holiday trends referred to above are not so much a product of the changing nature of work in terms of work becoming more fulfilling, but simply that with work becoming less important, individual choice over the use of non-work time becomes increasingly more a reflection of individual needs and inherent psychological drives. Hence there is a need to assess the psychological motivations for tourism.

However, before leaving the general social framework that may dictate the demand for particular types of holidays, and indeed the overall demand for holidays, it can be noted that to some extent all four hypotheses are not mutually exclusive in the sense that only one must explain all behaviour at any one time. Just as when discussing the role of income it was suggested that both a longitudinal and cross-sectional analysis needs to be conducted to assess the role of income, so too, the same may be true of the social forces. It is tempting, albeit dangerous, to see a temporal progression in society from the compensation to spill-over hypothesis, and hence to possibly the neutralist stance, but equally it must be said that within society different social segments or groups might adopt one pattern of work/leisure/holiday relationships, even whilst another group adopts different behaviour patterns.

Zuzanek and Mannell (1983) discuss the evidence for each of the theories and comment, in approaching this topic, that whilst there are methodological and operational deficiencies, it can only be concluded that there is a 'multi-faceted and multi-dimensional nature of the work-leisure relationship'. What certainly must not be forgotten is that work in itself can be a source of satisfaction, and the work-place is an important source of social interaction for many people. A survey of 3,600 men and women conducted by the University of Michigan found that work rated as the fourth most preferable activity out of a list of 25 (Rodale 1989). From the viewpoint of tourism, what is of interest is that there does appear to be some ceiling to continued growth of demand that is operated by social factors. For example, examination of the data for holiday-taking activities of British tourists, as published in the British Tourist Authority's *Home Tourism Survey*, indicates that consistently about 20 per cent of AB (professional and managerial) social group do not appear to take a holiday of four or more nights away from home. For such a group it is not a lack of income that affects this decision. Part of the group may be accounted for by ill-health, and for others intensive work schedules may also account for not taking such holidays, but it can be contended that for some there is a deliberate choice not to take a holiday. Equally, for other parts of the AB group, whilst they tend to take more holidays than their C1C2 (skilled manual and clerical/lower administrative) counterparts, there has not been a drastic growth in additional long-stay (over four nights away from home) holiday taking. Overall, inspite of increases in income, there is still about one-third of the British population which does not take a holiday. Equally, in other European countries, the same phenomenon of a slow down in the growth of numbers of people taking holidays is seemingly occurring. For example, Mazanec (1981) examined the German holiday market and, using factor analysis, postulated a number of life styles, some of which were conducive to tourism, some of which were not. He concluded:

> the leisure type mapping endorses the view that leisure life style barriers to continuous market penetration of travel and tourism are real: some incompatibility exists with certain leisure life styles. It becomes particularly pronounced if 'home-orientedness' combines with low cultural/educational aspiration level.

A further factor in assessing the changing relationship between leisure and tourism is that of a growing desire for quality of tourism experience which may actually reduce the total amount of tourism travel below that which would otherwise take place. Sarbin (1981) records a survey of American tourists where:

> the proportion of respondents who stated they like to travel but were engaging in other activities instead because of the 'hassle' of travelling had recently increased from 13 percent to 24 percent. Forty percent of

respondents to a national survey said they did not visit parks and recreation areas because of crowding, and 25 percent said the areas were too polluted.

THE PSYCHOLOGICAL DETERMINANTS OF DEMAND

Brief mention has been made of the fact that tourism as a 'product' represents either an escape from daily reality, or a means of self-fulfilment. Whilst in fact tourism can offer more than this, it does highlight one particular characteristic of the 'product' which differentiates it from many other purchases. Essentially tourism is not a purchase of the physical, but a means by which the holidaymaker acquires experiences and fulfils dreams. It possesses the very essence of intangibility, for at the end of the holiday the purchaser has little in the way of physical possessions. And those that do exist, the souvenirs and the photographs, have as their main purpose the evocation of memory. There are further 'odd' aspects which distinguish the holiday from other purchases. There is a substantial outlay without, in many cases, a previous sight of the destination. Even if the tourist has previously visited that destination, there is no guarantee that the second experience will replicate the first. The holiday is looked forward to − it is seen as the culmination of a year's work. People make purchases 'for the holiday'. New swimsuits and beach wear are purchased. Anticipation becomes part of the product. After the holiday, it becomes part of experience which can be evoked to help get the tourist through the dark days of winter, and past memories are refreshed by the anticipation of new holiday experiences. The holiday is often not a spontaneous decision. It is perhaps a joint decision between family and friends. Part of the pleasure is the comparison of brochures. It can be seen that the holiday experience is not simply an experience of place, it has a time dimension as well.

It can also be argued that the holiday meets a series of deep psychological needs. Amongst the motivations Cohen and Taylor (1976), Crompton (1979), and Mathieson and Wall (1982) have identified are the following:

a) The escape motivation

This has already been described in some detail, and is essentially a wish to get away from a perceived mundane environment.

b) Relaxation

Partly related to the escape motivation, this is a wish for recuperation.

c) Play

This is a wish to indulge in activities associated with childhood. Play on holiday is culturally sanctioned. Adults indulge in games not otherwise permitted (except perhaps on TV game-shows!). There is a regression into the carefree state of childhood.

d) Strengthening family bonds

In the common situation where both partners are working full-time, the holiday represents a time when both can renew their relationship. However, there is a reverse side to this. Relate, the British Marriage Advisory Council, has reported that holidays are an occasion when both parties realise that they have grown apart. Daily life has been led with each doing their 'own thing', and the enforced sharing of each other's company for 24 hours per day provides too high a strain upon the marriage. More happily, holidays can provide a time when fathers can spend time with their young children, and so strengthen paternal bonding.

e) Prestige

Status and social enhancement amongst one's peers can be temporarily gained on the basis of the destination chosen for the holiday. Certain destinations are fashionable, whilst others are not. The selection of a fashionable, or unusual and hence seen as exotic, destination will serve to confirm an impression about the holidaymaker. Holiday destination choice becomes yet another statement about 'life style', a confirmation of self-identity and role amongst one's peers. It is also not simply a question about destination, but also about the form of accommodation and activity. To stay at a hotel on the Costa del Sol says one thing about you, whilst to stay in your own villa makes another kind of statement.

The desire for status enhancement need not necessarily be confined to one's peers back home. It can also be met by the role within the group of holidaymakers, or by the group creating a group identity whereby they perceive themselves as being superior to other groups of tourists, or the members of the host society.

f) Social interaction

The holiday represents an important social forum for individuals where the normal conventions can be disregarded. For a fortnight a group meets with a common experience, and without past knowledge of each other's backgrounds. The dynamics of such groups can be a powerful determinant of the success or failure of the holiday. Holiday companies which specialise in holidays based on hobby or leisure interests such as painting or sailing, or outdoor activity centres, recognise that one of the major determinants of the success of their holidays is that it creates a group of like-minded people with a common interest all sharing an experience. Other holidays are actually being designed for single people so that they can become part of a group and not feel isolated amongst the traditional family orientated package holiday.

g) Sexual opportunity

One aspect of social interaction is the opportunity for sexual relationships. This can be overt or implied, physical or romantic. One of the traditional appeals of the cross-Atlantic ships of the 1930s was the possibility of a romance. The popular characterisation of the 18-30 holiday market as sometimes displayed by the tabloid press, is that it represents an opportunity for 'bonking', or whatever the current jargon is. However, in certain cases the rationale of the holiday is simply an opportunity for sexual activity, as is demonstrated in the sex tourism of the Far East in Thailand or the Philippines.

To some extent there is in both this case and the opportunity of play a common theme in that the holiday offers an opportunity to be free from the normal constraints of home. The holiday may be a period of a loosening of a sense of responsibility. The clerical workers on the 18–30 year olds holiday who drink too much, eat too much, create too much noise in rowdy games and disco all night long return home to their 9.00 to 5.00 jobs and their respectability. Behaviour which at home might threaten a loss of job, on holiday, far from home, becomes, if not excusable, tolerated to a degree, and indeed, is in part expected.

h) Educational opportunity

At the heart of tourism is the concept of travel; a chance to see new and strange sights, to learn about the other places of the world, and to talk to others with different cultures and viewpoints. No matter that the cynical may agree with Ogden Nash that 'Travel does not broaden the mind, only the bottom', or that in the process of creating the global village the Coca-Cola sign is to be found everywhere, and that one hotel complex looks like another, there is still an opportunity to discover differences. Equally there is a chance to see the sites of history, or to see the original great works of art instead of their reproductions. For many people seeking a cultural return from their travel the educational opportunity is a real motivation for their touristic perambulation.

i) Self-fulfilment

The voyage of discovery may not be simply a discovery of new places and people, but also the opportunity or catalyst of self-discovery. In the medieval world it may have been called the pilgrimage to the holy places. A secular age permits individuals to create their own holy places, which may be places of natural beauty, or areas where they challenge their own sporting skills or body. The search for self-discovery may be directed and purposeful as the tourist specifically seeks a type of holiday experience, or it might come unsuspecting as a thief in the night. It is not unknown for people to return from holiday with either a changed life or a changed perspective. It might be the knowledge, as indicated above, that the marriage is now sterile, or indeed reborn. It might be that some respond to the siren call of summer sun and return to give up their jobs and become sailing instructors under Mediterranean skies. Others may return to their previous existence, but with some experience that gives an inner strength. For such people the full sense of the word, recreation, is indeed a reality. If this is read as being poetic licence, then the promoters of holidays based on events such as outdoor activities, sailing or hiking can generally cite examples of such conversions.

j) Wish fulfilment

For some the holiday is the answer to a dream, a dream which has perhaps sustained a long period of saving. The naturalist may feel a thrill as he or she visits the Galapagos Islands and has indeed prepared by reading about Charles Darwin's visit upon the *Beagle*. Increasingly the experience may be the translation of a pretence into a reality. How else can one explain the popularity of theme parks, except that they are an escape into a fantasy? The film, *WestWorld*, where holidaymakers travelled into a 'themed' existence where robots permitted them to act out their fantasies, was but an extension of the common experience of the theme park carried through to a logical conclusion. Already one might journey upon the Shuttle Missions by attending the IMAX cinema, or experience the white waters of the Amazon, or indeed use nature itself as the 'themed' experience by hunting with historical weapons in North American parks, or replicate the pioneer experience by travelling by wagon train or raft. History provides us with many themes that permit a realisation of the dream of time travel as visitors mix with the costumed inhabitants of Colonial Williamsburg or the Beamish Museum.

k) Shopping

Although this may seem a prosaic reason, shopping is not only one of the most common tourist activities, but it can also, at least under certain circumstances, be the motivating factor for travel away from home, and indeed for international travel. An example is provided by the aftermath of the signing of the free-trade agreement between Canada and the USA, combined with, in 1987, the growing strength of the Canadian dollar. The firm of accountants, Ernst and Young, recorded a 31 per cent increase in 1988 in automobile traffic over the year at 31 Canada/US border points, and at Pigeon River alone an increase of $19 million (Canadian) of goods were brought into Canada in the year ending July 1988. The number of custom filings for imported goods rose by 133 per cent in the same period for Canadians buying goods in the USA and bringing them back home. The same phenomena can be observed at many other border communities, for example, between Eire and Northern Ireland, and Switzerland and Italy. As all of these trips are cross-border trips, they may be counted in the official statistics as tourist trips.

These, then, are some of the psychological motivations that may initiate the type of holiday chosen. Whatever type of holiday is selected may in fact be a statement about our self-identity; a statement about a set of priorities felt at the time of decision taking. However, in the diversity of both choice and needs, it would be dangerous to read too much into the actual choice, for many people will undertake more than one type of holiday over time, thereby perhaps delaying the meeting of one particular need in order to meet another.

However, built on the concept that different motivations differentiate between categories of tourists, a number of profiles of tourist types have been created. One of the earliest, and still much quoted, was that described by Cohen (1972). Cohen described four types of tourist based on the degree of institutionalisation of the tourist and the nature of the impact upon the host community. Briefly stated his four categories were:

The organised mass tourist

These are the least adventurous tourists, who on buying their package holiday remain encapsulated in an 'environmental bubble', divorced from the host community as they remain primarily in the hotel complex. They adhere to an itinerary fixed by the tour operators, and even their trips out of the complex are organised tours. They make few decisions about their holiday.

The individual mass tourist

They are similar to the organised mass tourist in that they utilise the facilities made available by the tour operator, but they have some control over their own itinerary. They may use the hotel as a base and hire a car for their own trips. However, many will tend to visit the same places as the mass organised tourist in that they will visit the 'sights'.

The explorer

The explorers arrange their own trip alone, and attempt to get off the beaten track. Yet they will still have recourse to comfortable tourist accommodation. However, much of their travel will be prompted by a motivation to associate with the people, and they will often speak the language of the host community. Nonetheless, the explorers retain many of the basic routines of their own life style.

The drifters

The drifters will shun contact with the tourist and tourist establishments, and identify with the host community. They will live with the locals and adopt many of the practices of that community. Income is generated by working within the community, but often through low skilled work, which creates a tendency to mix with the lower socio-economic groups.

One problem with this categorisation is that whilst it creates easily recognised types, does it actually reflect the complexities of tourist behaviour? These categories are observations of behaviour without reference to the reasons for the adoption of that behaviour. Many behaviour patterns may be the result of constraints rather than specific preference, as the tourist indulges in a series of exercises to optimise the return upon limited time. Equally, as previously observed, with the taking of more than one holiday a year by several sectors of our society, such holidaymakers may adopt different styles of holidays. In short, there is no consistency of behaviour. Pearce (1982) reviews many of the categories of tourists as described by Chadwick (1981), Cohen (1972), and Smith (1977), and indeed advances his own categorisation based upon factor analysis in which he distinguishes between 15 types based on 5 role-related behaviour patterns. Witt and Wright (1990) argue that multi-motivational models are necessary to understand tourism motivation.

One way in which these tourist classifications have a value is to relate it to the destination that the tourist type will prefer. Plog (1972) was one of the first to do this. Essentially Plog argued that there was a continuum between types of tourists from the allocentric to the psychocentric tourist. The allocentric is akin to Cohen's explorers in that they seek new destinations, and are prepared to take risks in searching for new cultures and places. On the other hand the psychocentric tourists seek the familiar, and are happier in an environment where there are many tourists who are like-minded. They are not risk takers and adhere to the proven product, being conservative in choice. Plog hence identified that these types of tourists would be drawn to a particular destination. This is illustrated in Figure 2.5, which indicates the destinations as originally identified by Plog.

As will be discussed with regard to the social impact of tourism this has some important implications in terms of the types of tourists destinations attract. An additional implication is that there is a time element associated to the links between tourist type and destination. Destinations are originally 'discovered' by allocentrics, but subsequently they search out other destinations and are followed by the near allocentrics, and thus through the tourist types until a destination becomes a psychocentric destination. For example, Palma de Mallorca is now a psychocentric destination and in danger of being perceived as a down market destination, whereas in the 1950s it could have been typified as a near allocentric or mid-centric destination as far as British tourists were concerned.

In many cases, however, these descriptions of tourists are based upon behavioural patterns and motivations are imputed to them. It might also be that in many cases the lists of motivations have perhaps two essential drives. These may be described crudely as a 'push' motivation, that is a wish to get away from a place, and a 'pull' motivation, a desire to see some other area. Iso-Ahola (1982) clarifies this latter motivation as 'a desire to obtain psychological [intrinsic] rewards through travel in a contrasting world'. The 'pull-push' factors can also be held to operate upon humans in two dimensions, man as the social animal seeking inter-personal relationships, and man as the solitary person seeking either refuge from others or solitude. Accordingly a matrix of four segments is suggested by

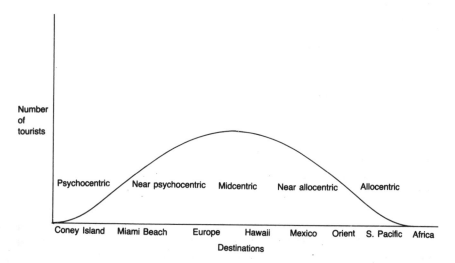

Figure 2.5 Plog's categorisation of tourists and destinations

		SEEK INTRINSIC REWARD	
		Personal	*Inter-Personal*
DESIRE TO LEAVE BEHIND ENVIRONMENT	Personal	Ego-enhancement Escape from responsibility Aesthetics	Strengthen kinship
	Inter-personal	Status enhancement Prestige	Meet new people in new places Play

Figure 2.6   Motivations of holidaymakers

Iso-Ahola (Figure 2.6), in which it becomes possible to locate the series of different motivations that other writers have identified.

This approach has other advantages. The listing of types of tourists does produce recognisable types, but evidence increasingly shows that tourists are not consistent in their wants, and hence the type of holiday selected. Gyte (1988) found in his survey of tourists in Majorca that some perceived their package holiday as not only a second holiday in terms of numbers, but also in type. In Plog's terminology, the holidaymaker may engage in allocentric behaviour at one time, and in psychocentric behaviour at another. Given increased incomes and leisure time people can increasingly meet a series of needs. Iso-Ahola's model recognises the dialectical process that exists between wishes for escape, and desires for intrinsic reward. It is thus possible that not only over different holidays, but indeed within the same holiday, people will switch from one cell to another within the matrix. It is a recognition that although the holiday may satisfy a prime need, a 'good' holiday also has the ability to satisfy a series of secondary needs. These secondary needs may become more pressing upon the satisfaction of the prime need. For example, if the primary need is for relaxation, a few days of idleness might well meet that requirement, and the holidaymaker will then indulge in other forms of behaviour such as seeking out new places.

It must however be remembered that the holidaymaker is continually making a series of choices on the use of a constrained resource, namely time. The role of time must not be understated when examining tourist motivation. This is illustrated by Lyon (1982) with reference to timeshare holidays (Figure 2.7). He postulates that the concept of timeshare implies an identification with a particular location by the holidaymaker, or a motivation to own property, and this distinguishes the timeshare

		NEED TO IDENTIFY WITH A SPECIFIC LOCATION	
		HIGH	LOW
	HIGH	Property ownership in holiday destination	Holiday property bonds
TIME FLEXIBILITY	LOW	Timeshare	Package holiday?

Figure 2.7 Motivations for holiday types

holidaymaker from others. However, the ownership of timeshare implies a lack of flexibility in time. Subsequently the dimensions of time and identification with location give rise to a four cell model, within which different holiday products can be located. As with Plog's approach this implies a linkage between holiday motivation and type of holiday undertaken.

Whilst, intellectually, the idea of linkages between motivation, holiday types and destinations is attractive, in practice the linkage may be subtle, exposed as it is to a lack of consistency of behaviour as the tourist changes holiday types from one holiday to another, and to the fact that, for many, family holidays may in fact be compromise decisions that attempt to reflect the differing interests of family members. One must also again refer to the nature of the holiday decision. As previously stated, it is the purchase of, in most instances, a previously unseen intangible, and it might be that false images created by the marketing departments of tour operators actually lead the holidaymaker to make a wrong decision. Crompton (1979) makes this warning statement:

> to expect motivation to account for a large variance in tourist behaviour is probably asking too much since there may be other inter-related forces operating.

Those other forces have been identified as being both economic and social as well as psychological. In isolation each seems unable to forecast tourist behaviour; together the variables are perhaps too many to permit an easy explanation of complex behaviour patterns. However, together they point to not simply a growth of demand for tourism, but a realisation that such growth cannot simply be taken for granted. The very increases in income that made tourism possible, now generate opportunities for an improved quality of life within the home environment which undermines the escape motivation. Concern with quality of life may make people wonder if travel is necessary. Tourists may travel, but continually they take themselves. Escape from daily routine is possible, escape from self is not. If there is a relationship between income, recreational opportunity and concern about quality of life with the attributes of self-actualisation as described by Abraham Maslow, then the question can be asked, does self-actualised man require travel? The answer to the question might depend upon the quality of the travel and touristic experience.

SUMMARY

The demand for tourism is determined by a number of economic, psychological and social factors. These include the factors such as income, taxation, interest rates, attitudes to saving, available time, prices of holidays and other factors. In consequence, the potential holidaymaker has a discretionary income that permits holidaying behaviour, but the type of holiday to be taken is decided not in isolation, but within a set of behaviour patterns which reflect allotted values to competing demands upon leisure time. People may wish to use holidays as a means of escape, or of fulfilment, but in many cases holidays are prompted by more than one motive, whilst being subjected to income constraints and the demands of other family members. Simple uni-casual theories are inadequate in explaining holiday-taking behaviour, and complex models incorporating economic, psychological and sociological factors would be required to develop more meaningful explanations.

Chapter 3

The tourist experience

TOURIST, OR BEING A GUEST!

The irony of tourism is that for many tourists they achieve the highest levels of satisfaction when they feel that they have ceased to be a 'tourist'. They do not necessarily want to be a full member of the host society, for to do so means they lose the privileges accorded to a guest. They seek the status of a guest, because in being such they are welcomed into what McCannell (1976) calls the 'backroom', the area not normally seen by the outsider. McCannell describes this feeling as follows:

> Tourists are not criticised by Boorstin and others for leaving home to see the sights. They are reproached for being satisfied with superficial experiences of other peoples and other places . . . [but] touristic shame is not based on being a tourist but in not being a tourist enough, on a failure to see everything the way it 'ought' to be seen. The touristic critique of tourism is based on a desire to go beyond the other 'mere' tourists to a more profound appreciation of society and culture, and it is by no means limited to intellectual statements. All tourists desire this deeper involvement with society and culture to some degree; it is a basic component of their motivation to travel.

But in this desire the tourist may be defeated by a combination of factors. The first is that the tourists may have this wish to understand the host society, but it is only one of a number of wishes, and relaxation and other motivations may have priority. Secondly, the tourist has usually but a limited amount of time, and hence must use the intermediaries available to him or her, and such intermediaries may promise understanding of the host society and culture, but may themselves be tangential to it. Thirdly, the tourist is caught up in what Pearce (1982) has termed, a 'tourist environment'. Pearce argues that the characteristics of the tourist environment are that they have high transient populations, have been physically modified to facilitate inspection of the locale, and have a structure to control visitor accessibility. These physical attributes foster the feeling of being a tourist. Essentially what is this feeling? It can be argued that it consists of sensing that one is an 'outsider', and being immediately recognised as being such. In consequence the sense of being a tourist is not, arguably, strongly felt in the mass tourism centres such as Torremolinos or Benidorm, but is in fact more keenly sensed in the less crowded areas, in the areas perhaps visited by few tourists. Perversely, in the mass touristic areas, especially those popular with one's own nationality, the sense of being an outsider may only be marginally felt. The shops, places of entertainment, and accommodation are filled with people with whom communication is easy, and with whom there are shared conventions and sets of expectations. In such cases the tourist only experiences the sense of being an 'outsider' if something goes wrong and they come into contact with the legal or medical systems of the host community.

It can be argued that there is a continuum which moves from being a 'tourist' to being a 'guest' and potentially a 'friend'. This is demonstrated in Figure 3.1. The sense of being a tourist is engendered within the context of Cohen's Mass Tourist. The tourist is but one in a coach party, but one in a hotel. Tourists seek to establish their identity as is evidenced by the need to strike up a relationship with the waiter who usually serves their table, but the waiter has seen such attempts for every week of the summer. Accordingly, identity is often established with other members of the holidaying group, and thus the sources of satisfaction are found in communication with fellow holidaymakers and not from contact with the host community. The wish, if it was at all strong in the first place, to relate to the host society is displaced by this activity to meet the needs of belonging.

From the viewpoint of those who serve the tourist, the tourist is but part of an anonymous, amorphous mass. The situation begins to improve when the tourist does manage to establish some identity. With this process the tourist becomes a customer; there is a recognition of individuality albeit on a formal basis. Some tourist environments permit this. The hotel waiter can get to know those he serves, the receptionist can recognise the hotel guests and call them by name. Those who serve in local shops recognise their customers. On the other hand those who receive tourists at tourist attractions by the bus load will have little opportunity to relate to their visitors in such a way. Indeed, a criterion of success of such visits is whether or not the tourist feels that a relationship has been created by the tour guide. At the same time, as tourists go shopping, use local transport, perhaps go to the theatre or cinema, use a restaurant, they indulge in the same type of activities as many of the host society. In consequence, those that serve these activities, whilst they may treat tourists differently from local people, have constraints imposed upon them by the fact that both tourist and local person intermingle more closely by sharing the same physical space.

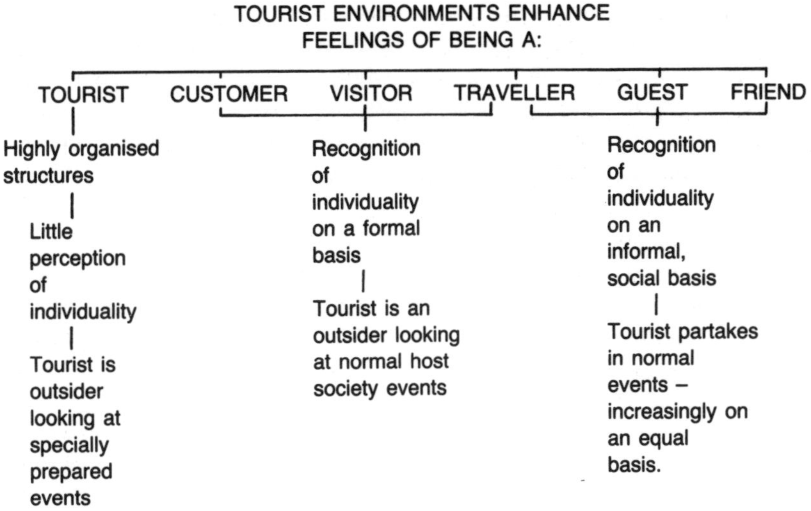

TOURIST ENVIRONMENTS ENHANCE
FEELINGS OF BEING A:

TOURIST	CUSTOMER	VISITOR	TRAVELLER	GUEST	FRIEND

Highly organised structures	Recognition of individuality on a formal basis	Recognition of individuality on an informal, social basis
Little perception of individuality	Tourist is an outsider looking at normal host society events	Tourist partakes in normal events – increasingly on an equal basis.
Tourist is outsider looking at specially prepared events		

Figure 3.1   The tourist-friend continuum

For many tourists a reason for continuing to return to a given destination is because they have established a relationship with local people and a friendship is developed. Increasingly they become part of a local community, even if for a short time. It might be said they are part of, but not from, the host community. For many tourists a highlight of the holiday is talking with 'local people'. A perverse phenomenon may be observed about such contacts. The middle-class tourist frequents a bar and is drawn into conversation with a 'local', who often is a manual worker. Upon returning home the tourist will talk of the conversation and the insights that it gave him or her into the host society, and perhaps even into 'life' itself. The irony is that whilst at home that person would not normally frequent the company of manual workers.

As is the case of any experience, the events do not take place in isolation from other events. The tourists experience results from a set of behaviours, which behaviours themselves may be dictated by a set of antecedent conditions interleaving with intervening variables. The tourists have arrived with a set of expectations and motivations shaped by socio-economic variables and their knowledge and perception of the area. The location itself is an information transmitter with its infrastructure of facilities, transport networks and contact points with others affecting wishes, desires and hence behaviour. Equally, the time constraint and abruptness of changed circumstances have their role to play in determining the tourist experience. The holiday has been long anticipated and there is an excitement about the travel and the arrival. This may be tempered by a tiredness. Upon arrival in a new location there is a process of recovery from the journey, learning, discovery and exploring of the immediate vicinity. Whilst this process of learning and discovery may last the whole of the holiday it tends to be greatest during the initial holiday stages, and thus a process of adjustment takes place during the latter stages of the holiday. Towards the end of the holiday, thoughts of the return occur, and other emotions are felt.

TOURIST LEARNING BEHAVIOUR

From this simple description, a number of hypotheses can be constructed about patterns of behaviour.

a) There is a pattern of exploratory behaviour by the tourist.
b) Stress may be associated with the process of adjustment.
c) Environmental learning of that thought to be important by the tourist occurs relatively quickly.
d) Behaviour is determined in part by anticipation of enjoyment.

The first simple observation is that the initial anticipation and the time constraint can create on the one hand an eagerness to learn, to explore, whilst on the other it can generate an intolerance of what is perceived as inferior service. Both perhaps are aspects of a desire for immediate gratification of wishes. The first couple of days of the traditional package holiday are often characterised by certain sets of behaviour. The first day is spent in both recovering from the journey and checking the immediate environment. During this checking a process of comparison takes place, a comparison between the expectation as shaped by past experience, hearsay or the travel agent's brochure. Expectations may be met, surpassed or disappointed. Often the first night of the stay is characterised by a group discussing initial impressions, and these might not always be favourable, compounded as they are by the remnants of tiredness from the journey and the process of adjustment. This adjustment process is not simply one of a change of venue, but a change, however temporary, of life style. With the second and third day it can be hypothesised that in many cases a misplaced confidence can occur, and it is during this time that the holidaymaker can lie in the sun too long, and so become sunburnt, or eat or drink too much, and therefore suffer from upset stomach, or hangovers. Past travel experience can of course inhibit such negative practices, but such behaviour patterns would be easily recognisable by many travel couriers. After a few days, exploratory behaviour takes the tourist further afield, and by the beginning of the second week of the typical two-week or ten-day holiday, favourite venues are being established, whether they be tavernas, scenic spots, restaurants or discos. Thus, by the end of the holiday, greater predictability of travel patterns might be established.

Is there evidence to support this type of observation? Evidence of the predisposition for minor illnesses comes from Pearce's (1982) study of Australian holidaymakers on the islands of the Great Barrier Reef. The sample group was asked to record minor illnesses for the fortnight prior to the holiday, and then those that occurred during the holiday. These he divided into three categories. Tension symptoms were felt by a third of the sample prior to the holiday, but these symptoms (as evidenced by feelings of anxiety, headaches, nervous irritability and the like), declined through the holiday so that by the fourth, fifth and sixth days only 8.6 per cent of the sample of 300 recorded such feelings. On the other hand there was an increase in 'viral symptoms' (colds, coughs, stomach upsets, etc.) so that by the same period a third complained of these, and just over 60 per cent complained about stings, insect bites, skin rash, sunburn and similar 'environment shock symptoms' by the end of the first week's holiday. The nature of such illnesses will be in part determined by the age and social characteristics of the tourist, and the degree of difference between the physical components of the holiday environment and that of the tourist's home. Nonetheless, the reality for many holidays is that they are indeed characterised by minor complaints, usually associated with food, sun or drink, that can mar enjoyment. However, in recounting the story of their holiday to friends and peers upon return (which process is itself part of the enjoyment of the holiday), such illnesses are either conveniently forgotten, or become part of the story of adventure. Few will actually admit to not enjoying their holiday.

Evidence for the exploratory patterns of tourist travel also exists. For example Cooper (1981) plots the patterns of tourists to the island of Jersey. Within the first day the great majority of visits (75 per cent approximately) toured St Helier, the capital and the hotel base for the sample. Only a small proportion went touring on their first day. On the second day St Brelade's Bay became a popular destination, and it was not until the fifth day that the group was reaching Plemont. Also by this stage of the holiday travel patterns were becoming more dispersed. Similarly, Elson (1976) traces the 'recreation activity space' of visitors to the south coast of Sussex, England. The coastal resorts of Brighton and others account for 90 per cent of the reported visits, whilst only 20 per cent visited the northern parts of the county. In consequence, travel patterns by visitors can be established, and it does appear that there are temporal aspects to such travel activities.

Guy and Curtis (1986) studied the speed with which tourists make perceptual maps of the holiday destination by observing tourists visiting the town of Würzburg, West Germany. The results were scored on four variables, the number of items mentioned, the correct identification by name and the correct function and location. The researchers concluded that:

1) 'Overall, the results of the exploratory research parallel expected

patterns. First, it appears that environmental learning takes place relatively quickly. Fewer tourist sites were added to maps over time than business or retail items suggesting that perhaps most touring activities occurred early in the visit. Shopping and retail commerce activities evidently remain stable or increased as the tourists' stays lengthened.

2) Experience did indeed function as the primary correlate of environmental learning in terms of scope, accuracy and detail.'

One of the factors that may influence travel patterns in terms of determining the number of sites visited is social class. Cooper (1981) in an analysis of numbers of sites visited found that professional classes were more likely to visit a greater number of sites on a holiday trip in that over 40 per cent of social group AB visited more than 9 sites compared with 34 per cent of C1C2 and less than 28 per cent of group D in his sample. Various hypotheses can be put forward as to why this is the case, but it can be stated that in part the travel pattern is the result of an interaction between motivation, expectation, accessibility and promotion, and the recording of such travel behaviour is not in itself a measure of the strength of any one of these individual factors, but rather of the synergy arising from combining these variables.

THE ROLE OF EXPECTATIONS

Expectation and perception can be powerful determinants of satisfaction, but the direction between these two variables and satisfaction is not entirely predictable. Saleh and Ryan (1990) observe with regard to guests' perceptions of hotels that 'it is imperative that guests' expectations be realistic and possible for the firm to deliver, otherwise an obvious gap in service quality is created'. The question arises as to how the tourist deals with the gap. The tourist may either feel dissatisfied by the short-fall between reality and expectation, so that the holiday or trip experience is perceived as having negative components, or on the other hand a process akin to cognitive dissonance occurs. What takes place in many cases is a shifting of evaluation of aspects of the location. Holiday destinations have spatial components, and hence the holidaymaker can escape the immediate cause of dissatisfaction in two ways. The first is simply a geographic move away from hotel, beach or resort or source of dissatisfaction and the second is an associated activity change. Coupled with cognitive dissonance whereby the unsatisfactory hotel may now be perceived as being unimportant in the holiday mix because compensating activities have been initiated, the holiday may be perceived as being successful. The determining factor as to which path is selected may be the commitment to the success of the holiday. As Kelly (1955) comments, behaviour is an anticipatory as well as reactive factor. An example of this is shown by Adams (1973) in a study of beach users in New England. When the weather forecast was one of 60 per cent chance of rain it was noted that this information was interpreted differently by separate behavioural groups. Of those on the beach, 46 per cent interpreted the forecast as meaning that it was likely or almost certain to rain. Of those that cancelled their trip, 86 per cent interpreted the same data as being likely or very likely to rain, as against two-thirds of a control group who interpreted the forecast in the same way. Commitment to a course of action meant reinterpretation of data. The reluctance to let unsatisfactory factors interfere with the enjoyment of the holiday is perhaps reinforced by the process of anticipation of enjoyment prior to departure. The anticipation shapes the behaviour, the behaviour changes the perception.

THE QUALITY OF EXPERIENCE

The experience of both 1988 and 1989 for European and particularly British package holidaymakers does add another dimension to this discussion. This is the aspect of the timing of the dissatisfactory event, and its relevance to the overall satisfaction level. Both years were characterised by long delays at airports as crowded air schedules came into conflict with antiquated air control procedures, strikes by European air controllers, and the lack of a European wide air control system. The results were long queues and delays at airports as aircraft missed their take-off slots, and accumulated examples arose of aircraft simply being in the wrong place at the wrong time. This caused high levels of dissatisfaction at two key points in the holiday process. The first is that there is a delay at the very outset of the holiday. The expectations are not being met. However, the very press coverage of the issue actually meant holidaymakers arrived at the airports expecting a delay, and hence 'small' delays of up to two hours were regarded as 'acceptable'. For those experiencing longer delays, encroachments were being made upon valuable holiday time and hence dissatisfaction was being created. This was particularly the case if only one week's holiday was booked. However, upon arrival at the holiday destination, the pattern of the holiday would mitigate the initial bad impressions. However, the return was characterised by the same delays, and in many cases this was worse. One requirement returning holidaymakers want is certainty of time of arrival in order to meet family, travel perhaps for several hours back home from the airport, and a need to get back to work. If delays are long the very benefits of the holiday in terms of relaxation are being undermined. Not only was the British press reporting delays, but also the risks that holidaymakers faced from other directions. The holidaymakers may be shot in 'exotic' destinations such as Thailand or Kenya, be 'mugged' and have their bags stolen from their shoulders by young Mediterranean males on scooters, or run the risk of being assaulted by fellow holidaymakers. Reports of new policies on airlines refusing to carry drunken passengers occurred in the trade press throughout 1988 and 1989. Davison (1989) reporting on the fortieth anniversary of the British package holiday saw fit to repeat Eric Idle's observations from a Monty Python sketch that:

> Herded into endless hotel Miramars, Bellevues and Continentals with their modern international luxury roomettes and Watney's Red Barrel and swimming pools full of fat German businessmen pretending they're acrobats. Adenoidal typists from Birmingham with flabby white legs and diarrhoea trying to pick up hairy bandy-legged wop waiters called Manuel. So-called typical restaurants with local colour and atmosphere and you sit next to a party from Rhyl who keep singing 'Torremolinos, Torremolinos' and keep complaining about the food.

The truth of such observations is that the resorts that attracted the initial expansion of the Mediterranean package holiday are perceived by many to be drifting down market, offering tacky accommodation and risks of interruption by boisterous if not drunken 'lager louts'. In such resorts as Torremolinos, at the height of the tourist season, it is not uncommon for 200 British youths to spend the night in a Spanish jail due to drunken and disorderly behaviour. Many are fined and released (*Sunday Times* 30 July 1989).

Cohen (1987) explored the relationship of tourist and the law by pointing out that the tourist is in an ambiguous position. The tourist is not simply a stranger, but is a *temporary* stranger. To a greater or lesser extent they are a guest, but an impersonal guest. The result is that, given the context of the state of tourism development in the host community and the types of tourists being attracted, the tourist may be victimised as being a highly visible stranger ignorant of laws and customs, or be given preferential treatment with ignorance being treated as an extenuating circumstance for minor infringements of the law. Cohen also argues that the mass organised tourist will be less exposed to the local criminals and enjoy the protection of the tourist establishment and the law enforcing agencies, whereas the drifter may be more exposed to the local criminals but enjoy protection from the local community, even whilst however subjected to suspicion from the legal agencies.

An important component of the tourist experience is the quality of the encounter with the provider of a service, and in other industries this has increasingly been studied. Bitner *et al.* (1990) explore the 'service encounter' through the use of critical incident analysis in three situations – hotels, restaurants and airlines – in the United States and concluded that degrees of satisfaction and dissatisfaction arose within three groups of incidents, namely, employee response to service delivery failure, employee response to customer needs and requests, and the nature of unprompted and unsolicited employee actions. There were industry differences between the incidence of each of these incident types – for example most of the incidents in the restaurant industry were of the third type. Arguably, within tourism as a whole, it is this third type of incident that will be the greatest source of satisfaction or dissatisfaction, as tourists find what is to them out of the ordinary concern for them as individuals, or possibly the opposite, marked rudeness because of the tourist being perceived as an 'outsider'. Parasuraman *et al.* (1985) draw attention to the gap between expectation and perception of the reality of the service as a source of satisfaction or dissatisfaction, and this model, the SERVQUAL model, based on the dimensions of tangible components of the service, reliability, responsiveness, assurance and empathy, probably has application to the tourist industry in terms of explaining the causes of tourist satisfaction or dissatisfaction.

An alternative approach can be recognised in the work of Csikszentmihalyi and Csikszentmihalyi (1988) and Voelkl and Ellis (1990) who argue that in recreational pursuits the degrees of satisfaction to be obtained are determined by the dimensions of challenge and skill. If the challenge exceeds the level of skill, dissatisfaction results with a reduction in participation. If skill exceeds challenge, then boredom results. In fact the model has been extended to form an eight-channel model as indicated in Figure 3.2. This model has immediate application to not only certain types of holiday activities based on hobbies, but could be adapted to cover certain components of the travel experience. For example, passengers delayed in air terminals might be observed as passing through a process of arousal, to anxiety, to worry, to apathy, as they become initially frustrated by delays which eventually reaches apathy because of an inability to control events (i.e. their 'skills' are not appropriate to the situation). Certainly these approaches do open new avenues for research into the nature of the tourist experience.

THE QUALITY OF THE TOURIST EVENT

One of the major activities undertaken by tourists is that of seeing the sights. The quality of this activity has attracted criticism by a number of writers such as Boorstin (1961), Turner and Ash (1975), and Fussell (1982). Thus, Boorstin writes:

> The multiplication, improvement and cheapening of travel facilities have carried many more people to distant places. But the experience of going there, the experiences of being there and what is brought back from there are all very different. The experience has become diluted, contrived, prefabricated.

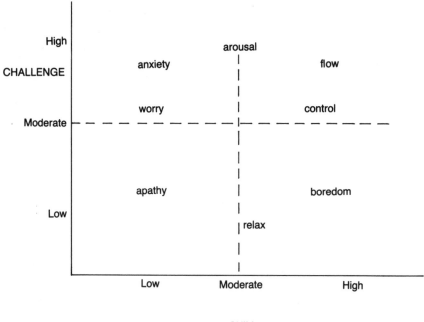

Figure 3.2   The travel experience on challenge-skill dimensions

To some extent these and other writers, such as Morris (1987) and Rivers (1974a), decry the current tourist experience as not having value compared to the days of 'travel'. Adverse comparisons are made with the past where the motivation for travel is perceived as being one of education and self-enlightenment. To some extent this view of the past may in part be a misconception, for as Christopher Hibbert (1987) shows in his history of the Grand Tour, for many young men the highlight of the tour of Europe was not the culture of Classical Rome, but the adventure, spice and thrill of Venice, the brothel of the eighteenth century. The emptiness of the modern tourist experience is reputedly shown by what Boorstin termed the 'pseudo-event'. Thus it can be asked, what is the value of the visit to, for example, the 'Spanish Fiesta', where coaches bring several hundred guests from high-rise hotels to eat chickens barbecued and served with chips, to sing the anthem of the package holiday, 'Viva Espana', and to carouse with fellow holidaymakers of one's own nationality. The Spanish influence is served and packaged without risk as dancers meet the desired stereotype, and the long wail of the *saeta* is not heard. For Boorstin this is a 'pseudo-event', a drama packaged for the tourist with little reference to reality. But just as Boorstin perceives that it has little to do with a cultural experience of Spain, so too do many of the tourists. It has much more to do with different sets of values and norms; the norms of group consciousness and relaxation. The occasion is a pretence designed not to meet educational purposes, but designed to generate a 'good time', which parts the tourists from their money but leaves them feeling euphoric and good tempered. Perhaps more of a pseudo-event are the very items celebrated by the middle-class tourists in their search for 'reality'. As McCannell (1976) provocatively states:

> Modern museums and parks are anti-historical and unnatural . . . not in the sense of their destroying the past or nature because, to the contrary, they preserve them, but as they preserve, they automatically separate modernity from its past and from nature and elevate it above them. Nature and the past are made a part of the present, not in the form of [an] unreflected inner spirit, a mysterious soul, but rather as revealed objects, as tourist attractions.

But it may be argued that the value of the tourist experience is not that of the academic writer imputing a set of normative judgements to the situation, but what is felt by the tourist him or herself. As has been argued, the tourist brings to the situation and to the site, a set of expectations that interact with the site. The site itself is also not a constant with reference to the physical attributes of the situation. Part of the site is the weather conditions, and other conditions within which the tourist sees it. Thus, for the visitor to, say, the Alhambra, in early spring, on a clear morning early in the day, there is a magic, which the visitor would not find in the month of August at 5.00 p.m. when there are large numbers of other visitors. Equally, the busiest hotel on the popular Costas can create different experiences for the tourist dependent on the mix of people present, or the time of year. Cohen (1979) sets out a model of interaction between scene and expectation with reference to the authenticity of the event viewed. Essentially there are two dimensions, the tourist who views the event as either being staged or real, and the nature of the event itself, as being staged or real. This gives rise to a four-cell matrix as shown in Figure 3.3. This relates to tourists with a high tourist for authenticity. Consequently tourists with both an expectation and need for authenticity will be dissatisfied if they find an inauthentic event and they perceive it as being such. Equally, if they feel an event to be staged, even where this is not the case, then low levels of satisfaction will occur. Cohen then develops the model for the tourist with a low need for authenticity, and indeed such a tourist, it may be cynically observed, has a higher chance of moderate degrees of satisfaction. But what are the clues that lead to the perceptions being formed, either correctly or incorrectly? Further, it has been argued that as expectation shapes behaviour, tourists may indeed find themselves in the situation of obtaining high levels of satisfaction through having failed to identify the proceedings of a 'pseudo-event'! And what if the tourists, although having a need for authenticity, perceive the event to be false, but suspend disbelief and enjoy the spectacle on its own terms? This form of behaviour is found in many other areas of human behaviour, so why should it stop when the person becomes a tourist?

It is right to be concerned with quality of tourist experience, but the quality of that experience is not dictated by whether or not the event has an elitist meaning as seems to be implied by writers such as Fussell, Boorstin and others. Their viewpoint has had a significant impact on the literature of tourism, and to discuss the 'authenticity' of the tourist experience is in itself a reflection of their impact for it discusses the issues upon the terms they espouse. The quality of the experience is dictated by the need of a tourist and the quality of the provision of the service and management of the tourist area. There would appear to be nothing intrinsically wrong with a desire for relaxation. The tourist can enjoy the experience of the fantasy as portrayed at theme parks, and can equally enjoy the packaged insight into native culture as carefully sanitised by native groups performing in the bars of multi-national hotels. In both cases tourists do not leave behind their critical faculties, and recognise that both are forms of 'show business'.

There are undoubtedly problems. As Krippendorf (1987) observes, the holiday experience itself exhausts. The holiday resort is just a backdrop, often the tourist is surrounded by the familiar – the same people, the same nationality. More importantly, 'we drag with us the problems of our towns and present them to our hosts – the traffic problems, air pollution, noise, metropolitan architecture, alienation'. Whilst the packaged show of culture can be rationalised in that its objectives are limited to simply those of entertainment and awareness generation of the traditions of a culture, it no longer achieves those limited purposes where it distorts the hosts' culture to

| | | TOURISTS IMPRESSION OF THE SCENE | |
		REAL	STAGED
	REAL	Authentic and recognised as such. High satisfaction	Suspicion of staging. Low Satisfaction
NATURE OF THE EVENT			
	STAGED	Failure to recognise event as staged. High satisfaction	Lack of authenticity recognised. Low satisfaction

Figure 3.3   The link between authenticity and satisfaction

fit tourists' stereotyped images of a place. To show bare-breasted African female dancers in Muslim areas of Africa is a reflection of the tourists' cultures, not those of Africa (Pettifer 1987).

The perversity of such tourist provision is that increasingly it is not what tourists themselves want. Tourists are now experienced at being tourists. They have seen the peep shows, the imitations, and now, especially as they are not limited to one holiday a year, are clearer in their expectations and wants. In particular they want well-managed tourist resorts that permit them choice and flexibility of arrangements. The need for such management is also a two-sided need, for the host environment also needs similar care if it is to maintain the qualities that attracted the tourists in the first place.

THE PROCESS OF GENERATING TOURIST SATISFACTION

Are there any possible linkages between the elements of the above discussion? What is being implied is that there is a process between initial expectation and satisfaction through the interaction between the intervening variables presented by the location, and the way the tourist responds to these variables. The response is a two-stage process. There is initially a series of conscious and unconscious adaptations to the destination which are subsequently expressed through sets of behaviour. The behaviour is generally directed by a wish to achieve satisfaction, but the ability to adapt to the gaps that might exist between the original perception and the actual experience becomes a determinant of eventual satisfaction or dissatisfaction. The antecedents prior to the trip of expectation creation are based upon an interaction of personality and other attributes of consumer behaviour as they respond to the images that are created of the destination based on past knowledge, experience and the marketing efforts of the destination promoter. The nature of the travel experience may, at least in the initial stages of the holiday, colour perception, whilst the tourist learns about the resort and what it has to offer. Gaps may then exist between expectation and reality, but the nature and seriousness of the gap depends upon both perception of the problem and the internal processes of adjustment. Part of this process depends upon the possession of certain skills, for example social and adaptive skills. The result is that a series of behaviours are engaged in which have as their objective the creation of a satisfactory feeling about the holiday. The level of satisfaction achieved then in turn becomes feedback in the system in that it shapes knowledge for the next holiday.

This process is reflected in Figure 3.4, which highlights the role of personality of the tourist. Personality is a factor that helps formulate motivation and sets of expectations as indicated on the left of the figure. The interpretation of the travel experience and the nature of the resort area with the personality generates both perceptions of gaps between the resort

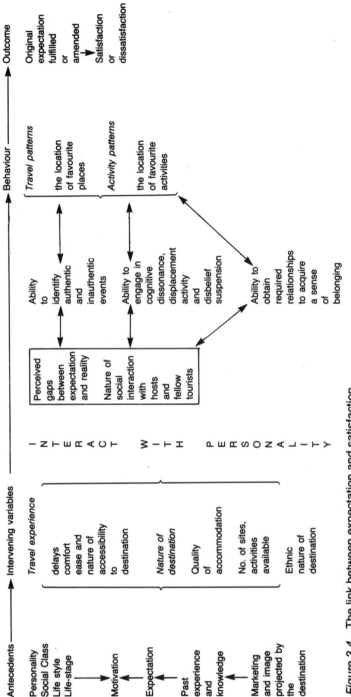

Figure 3.4 The link between expectation and satisfaction

zone and expectations, and governs the nature of interactions with others, but then certain social and psychological skills also come into play in the sense of being able to perceive authenticity, suspend disbelief when required, and conduct positive sets of relationships. These attributes help shape travel and activity patterns which permit the fulfilment of the original or amended expectations and hence create satisfaction. The tourists do not therefore assume a passive role, but utilise all the social and psychological skills that they normally exercise within their home setting, and actually engage in goal seeking, purposive behaviour – the goal being the generation of a satisfactory experience. Indeed, the cynic might say that it is this ability to generate a 'good time' out of sometimes sub-standard accommodation provided by tour operators in the past that has in fact produced the high satisfaction rates recorded by Lewis and Outram (1986). Thus, they record that the flight was only on time in 27 per cent of cases, in 23 per cent of cases good food was not available, and the courier was not readily available in 30 per cent of recorded cases. On the other hand, the weather was good on 95 per cent of occasions! In total, 54 per cent of the respondents agreed that there were some disadvantages to their holiday, and yet 69 per cent also agreed with a statement that they would advise their friends to go on the same package holiday. The authors conclude that 'the data analysis has indicated a high level of overall satisfaction among the respondents with regard to their package holidays', which, in view of late flights, a high chance of poor food, and experiences of some drawbacks, indicates a high value placed on convenience and, it may be argued, a strong level of determination to enjoy the holiday.

SUMMARY

It can be seen that the nature of the tourist experience is dependent upon many factors, including:

a) needs of the tourist for authenticity;
b) needs of the tourist to be accepted by the host community;
c) the ability of the tourist to learn and to adapt to the 'tourist environment';
d) the gap between expectations and perceived reality.

Chapter 4

The tourist resort area

In seeking to analyse the tourist resort area it can be said that four approaches exist. These are:

a) The descriptive approach

Essentially this consists of creating an inventory of facilities and assets possessed by the tourist area and describing them. The description might also extend to a description of the tourists' perceptions of the area.

b) An explanatory approach

This considers the patterns of travel and usage rates of facilities within the area, and attempts to explain them. It notes the nodal points within the area, the routes taken by tourists between these points, and the mode of travel used. It seeks to establish the patterns of tourist travel behaviour within the area.

c) The predictive approach

If it becomes possible to establish patterns of usage within the tourist area, then by definition it could become possible to make predictions as to not only future patterns of use, but also the future shape of the tourist zone. The predictive studies of an area are thus concerned with trend analysis and the spatial interaction between attractions within the zone.

d) The prescriptive approach

Forecasts in themselves are of little purpose unless used for management strategies in establishing priorities of use. The establishment of priorities requires a series of normative judgements in the case of tourism, for the assets that are being used are habitats and social groups; possibly fragile, non-renewable assets with limited carrying capacities. In consequence, the structure plans of planning authorities contain prescriptions as to use in terms of zoning levels of activity within the tourist resort.

It will be obvious that in practice these are overlapping approaches, for the descriptive should lead to the explanatory, and so on, and thus the techniques may serve more than one purpose. It will be argued that analysis of tourist resort areas is a complex task, for the tourist zone is not static in either spatial or temporal terms, and in addition there exists an inter-relationship between the attributes of tourist attractions and the types of tourists being attracted.

In describing the tourist area there is a need to undertake an audit of the attributes of the area, and Gunn (1979, 1982) suggests a cartographic approach in his studies of Texas and Canada. Nine variables were identified; water resources, flora distribution, climate, topography, history, aesthetics, visitor attractions, service centres and route network. Each of the nine variables was mapped, and the relative importance of each aspect for an area was assessed by distributing 100 points between the variables. The process can be simply completed by creating a series of overlay maps which then highlight areas or features with the scores indicating highest importance for tourism. Two immediate problems arise with this approach. The first is the boundaries of the area. Usually a political or administrative area is studied, but of course tourist use does not always recognise such boundaries and the tourist zone may overlap the administrative area. In consequence, a second approach may be adopted, and that is to undertake some perceptual or cognitive mapping which consists of asking tourists to draw maps indicating the tourist attractions as they seem to them, and the spatial relationship between these facilities. Whilst both approaches establish boundaries, the second problem of the stability of those boundaries still remains. However, to ask tourists to undertake perceptual mapping of an area does begin to quantify an answer to the question, how strongly perceived is an area? The detail, and accuracy of answers becomes a measure of how clearly delineated the area is, and by implication, how 'mature' a tourist attraction it is.

THE CHANGING NATURE OF THE TOURIST RESORT AREA

Young (1983) and Miossec (1976) both indicate how the tourist attraction may change over time. Young, writing of the development of a Maltese village into a tourist resort, identifies a six-stage process. Initially the village is in its early traditional stage, where its traditional economic functions still provide the main sources of income for the village. Secondly, comes the late traditional stage which is characterised by the arrival of some summer homes, and in Young's model, by the arrival of a police station. In many of these models, as will be discussed in the chapter on the social impacts of tourism, there is often a supposition that one is considering the arrival of foreign tourists, but this is not necessarily the case. Indeed in many instances tourism is first developed by nationals of the same country as the location of the tourist resort, these being the first to identify tourist potential. Thus, for example, in the island of Majorca, it was the wealthy classes from the capital, Palma de Mallorca, who built their villas in the north at Alcudia and Porto de Pollensa. In Young's model therefore, it can be hypothesised that these summer homes could belong to fellow Maltese escaping from Valetta.

The third stage represents the period of initial tourism exploration where tourist rooms and guest houses are being established. The tourist area is now slowly beginning to change its shape and area. The summer homes have been built on the perimeters of the village, thus extending it. The guest houses may be creating a process of change of use of village buildings. This is certainly the case in the fourth stage, called, early tourism involvement. The village might now be showing some signs of the wealth accruing from tourism. In Young's example, a new church has been constructed, a symbol not only of new wealth, but also a continuation of traditional priorities. But the tourist complex has also arrived, based upon a new, modern, luxury hotel. The original homes that faced the harbour are being purchased, and their original use changed to become souvenir shops and other enterprises based upon the tourism trade. Hence it moves into stage five – the expanding tourism development. A 'planning zone' has now been created to cope with the increasing demands upon land, a demand from two sources. There continues to be an expansion of hotels and villas, but the village is also expanding as it needs accommodation, schools and medical facilities to meet the demand of a larger population, for the tourist industry has attracted immigrant labour. Finally, there arrives the process of 'intensive tourism consolidation'. By now there is little resemblance to the original fishing village. The very harbour itself has become subject to a 'redevelopment plan' and now, called the marina, luxury yachts replace the wooden fishing boats of the past. A casino helps to attract an international jet-set, and the rationale of the whole complex is tourism; it has no other purpose. Thus the tourist resort has developed, and as Miossec (1976) points out, the resort now has an image of its own. It is no longer perceived as being part of, in this case, Malta, with the images that tourists would associate with Malta, but now is clearly delineated in the mind of the tourist as being an area in its own right. Thus, for example, Benidorm or Torremolinos are no longer 'Spanish' in their image, but rather something else. The tourist resort area thus undergoes a change in terms of its area, its prime functions, and even its image.

In essence what has been described is a life cycle of the tourist resort area, and associated with each stage of the resort's development are different numbers and types of tourists. In the early stages the supposition could be that if foreign tourists are involved they are not only few in number, but tend to be explorers as defined by Cohen, or Plog's allocentric tourists. As the numbers grow, so the early explorers leave, to be replaced by perhaps mid-centric tourists, until in the stage of maturity these too are being replaced by psychocentric tourists.

To what extent this process is automatic and not capable of halting is discussed in Chapter seven, but a management problem is how to recognise when the resort is moving from one stage to another. With hindsight it is easy to be wise, the problem is how does one assess a situation whilst it is occurring. Haywood (1986) argues that an obvious means is to examine the change of visitor numbers from one year to another, and plotting such changes as a normal distribution with a zero mean to distinguish the stages

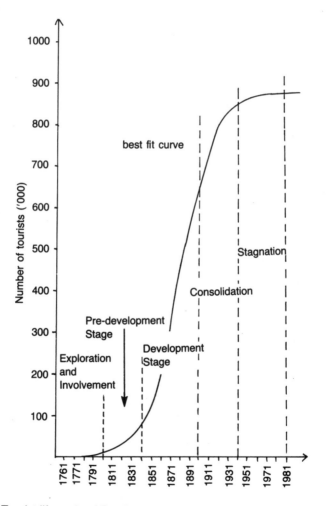

Figure 4.1   Tourist life cycle of Scarborough

of growth and decline of the resort. The technique Haywood recommended was adopted by Wilson (1989) in a study of Scarborough, a mature seaside destination in Yorkshire, England. She was able to distinguish, as Haywood suggested, six clear historical periods from 1761 to 1988 on the basis of visitor numbers kept by the resort. Figure 4.1 illustrates the patterns found.

MEASURES OF PHYSICAL ATTRACTIVENESS

One of the factors that follow from the above discussion is that in describing the resort area it is not sufficient to simply undertake an inventory of attractions, but it is also necessary to have some measure of perception. Some simple measures concentrate on the numbers of attractions as having a degree of 'uniqueness'. For example, within an area, however defined, if there is only one of something, then it might be that its uniqueness will draw tourist attention to it and thus it becomes a heavily visited attraction. Uniqueness thus becomes:

$$U = \frac{1}{\text{Number of items having listed features}}$$

where U = measure of uniqueness

The truly unique feature thus has a value of 1. This can be used to produce an aggregate uniqueness score where:

$$U = \frac{1}{F_1} + \frac{1}{F_2} + \frac{1}{F_3} + \frac{1}{F_4} + \frac{1}{F_n}$$

where $F_1 \ldots F_n$ are the number of features

The features listed may be separate features, e.g. the number of historical homes, churches etc., or they may be aspects of a particular attraction. For example, Leopold (1969) tried to create an index of uniqueness of rivers based on 46 variables representing physical, biological, and human usage of rivers. The problem is that the approach gives rise to a score which is difficult to interpret. Another approach that has sought to quantify subjective assessments of geographical features has been the use of landscape photographs where respondents have been asked to 'measure' on various evaluative scales, the attractiveness of the landscape features (Fines 1968, Smith 1983). The results of such measures are that the derived scales can then be applied to other landscapes, thereby assessing the potential attractiveness of the landscapes or other tourist features.

The problems associated with these approaches are self-evident in terms of interpreting results, but there is a purpose in the exercise. As described below, one of the ways of predicting travel patterns within, or between, tourist areas is the use of spatial modelling, or gravity models, and such models require measures of 'attractiveness'. These measures of uniqueness etc. can therefore be used within the gravitational models. Another approach, so far little used, may be to use hierarchical techniques as described by Saaty (1980). The premise behind hierarchical techniques is that it is difficult for tourists to rank or scale a series of features of attractiveness, but what is possible is for people to make comparisons, and to say that one feature or facility is more attractive than another. Thus the respondent is presented with a series of pair-wise comparisons whereby respondents state whether the two items are of equal attraction, or one is more attractive or very much more attractive than the other. It is as a result of these comparisons that a scale is developed. In his book, Saaty (1980) shows how the technique worked when asking respondents to assess the distance of cities one from another; in other words, when used to quantify a variable, distance, where respondents did not possess an exact knowledge, the technique produced an answer which corresponded highly with measured distance. By inference therefore, in cases where known measured scales do not exist, the techniques produce a value which does have an 'objective' meaning. It is these scores that can then be utilised in spatial modelling.

One problem, however, still pertains to this approach. The image of a place arguably (following Fishbein 1967, Ajzen 1988), consists of two components. The first is the belief about the place, and it is this that scales of attractiveness may be measuring. The second component is the importance of the belief. For example, it may be found that tourists rate an area as being very attractive, but still do not visit it because it is attractive on the basis of criteria that are unimportant to them. This may seem to be a perversity of human nature, in that the premise of attractiveness is that it 'attracts' people to it. But, to use Plog's typology, a psychocentric tourist may agree that the Amazonian Basin is indeed 'attractive', meaning beautiful, but he or she would not wish to visit it. Equally, an allocentric may agree Banff National Park is 'attractive', but again would not visit it. It may be that the very word 'attractive' poses problems, and hence researchers need to be careful to distinguish between properties which actually 'attract/pull' tourists to them, and those perceived as being 'beautiful' but not 'pulling' the tourists.

It might be thought that the constructs of attitude towards what makes an area attractive or otherwise is complex, but researchers utilising the methods espoused by the American psychologist George Kelly, have generally found that they are in fact comparatively few in number. Both Kelly (1955) and Allport (1961) argued that we attempt to make sense out of the situations in which we find ourselves, and in doing so create a list of elements, say, holiday destinations, and then seek to differentiate between them. This process of differentiation, 'the way in which two or more things are alike and thereby different from a third or more things' (Kelly 1955) thus forms a series of 'constructs'. Each construct is bi-polar, for the process of affirming something means that simultaneously something is denied. The third component of the attitude is the 'linking mechanism', the judgement of each element by the use of the construct, and this is essentially revealed by the form of grid that is utilised, i.e. rank, dichotomous, rate, etc.

Utilising the method is comparatively straightforward. Respondents are asked to indicate whether they like, dislike or feel unsure about certain holiday destinations. From each of the 'like' and 'dislike' lists four destinations are selected, and to these is added one 'unsure' destination. The respondent is then presented with a group of three (a triad), and these are compiled in such a way that they contain either two 'likes' and one 'dislike', or two 'dislikes' and one 'like', or one 'like', one 'dislike' and one 'unsure'. The respondent is then asked to select which is the 'odd' one out, and then to state why. The factor selected is the construct. Generally it is found that respondents will repeat themselves after a comparatively short time, and equally, any given sample will generally produce a comparatively small number of constructs. The responses can be analysed by statistical techniques to find the underlying themes.

From the viewpoint of practical research comparatively small samples are required, approximately two dozen. Gyte (1988) in a study of British tourists to Majorca, found that criteria being used to assess the attractiveness of the destination included how good the beaches were, the variety of sites, host attitudes, whether the holiday was active or peaceful, the cost of the holiday, the scenery, the history and culture of the area, facilities, whether the destination was spoilt by tourism, food and drink, and the degree to which the culture was familiar or unfamiliar. Denis (1989) on a sample of Canadian students found similar constructs, with culture, climate, the degree of commercialism, scenery, familiarity accounting for most of the responses. Bowler and Warburton (1986) utilised Kelly Grids to assess attitudes towards water resources in Leicestershire, and found that the attractiveness of the resource was assessed by scenic quality, leisure facilities, level of use, accessibility, size and the resource's 'naturalness'. The actual 'attractiveness' of the site to any given tourist, however, will depend upon the type of tourist, and the requirements of the holiday. Thus, with multiple holidaytaking occurring, the tourist may want an urban setting for one type of holiday, and an unspoilt rural setting for the next. The same destination can therefore be both 'attractive' or 'unattractive' depending on the type of holiday. In short, models that utilise measures of attractiveness cannot necessarily regard 'attractiveness' as an objective value without reference to the context of use. Nonetheless, such a measure is required when seeking to explain travel patterns.

PATTERNS OF TRAVEL BETWEEN AND WITHIN RESORT AREAS

Spatial models

One of the means of 'explaining' travel between and within locations has been the use of spatial modelling. This owes its origins to Newtonian physics, and the law of gravity can be rephrased to state, 'Two tourist areas attract trade from an intermediate [tourist generating] point in proportion to the size [attractiveness] of the centres and in inverse proportion to the square of the distances from these two tourist areas to the intermediate place'. Initially developed in the 1930s by Reilly (1931) to trace retail patterns in the southern USA, it can be expressed as:

$$\frac{Ta}{Tb} = \frac{Pa}{Pb}\left(\frac{db}{da}\right)^2$$

where Ta = the proportion of trade attracted by location a from the intermediate point

   Tb = the proportion of trade attracted by location b from the intermediate point

   Pa, Pb = populations of locations a and b

   da, db = distances from the intermediate point to locations a and b

From the viewpoint of initial work in assessing retail location, size of population was a sufficient criterion of attractiveness, but subsequent studies began to replace this with other criteria such as floor-space or retail mix. Following therefore the redefinition of the concept by Huff (1966), the basic model became:

$$T_{ij} = \frac{A_j{}^a/d_{ij}{}^b}{\sum\limits_{n=1}^{i} A_j{}^a/d_{ij}{}^b}$$

where T_{ij} = the probability of a trip from origin i to destination j

   A_j = the attractiveness of destination j

   d_{ij} = the distance between origin i and destination j

a and b are parameters to be empirically determined.

There are both practical and conceptual difficulties involved in the use of such models. The first is what measurement of attractiveness is to be used? Smith (1989) uses, for example, in the case of Canadian tourism, populations of areas on the basis that much Canadian tourism is prompted by visiting friends and relatives. In many cases the criterion of attractiveness is a quantitative one and rarely attempts to utilise measures of subjective attractiveness, although in tourism one would expect images of places to play a role in determining travel. A second practical problem is determining the values of parameters (a and b) to be used. One method is essentially a curve fitting exercise whereby the variables are applied to known data on travel movement and the values of parameters duly determined. These values can then be transferred to a new situation. Reference can obviously be made to past studies in undertaking this, and with a computer the process becomes relatively easy. The conceptual problem can be summarised as whether a law of physics, which has no reference to human behaviour or its motivation, can really be applicable to a subject such as tourism? Even if one does incorporate subjective assessments into the criteria used for measuring 'attractiveness' the question remains. Smith (1989) refers to this question, and argues:

> This criticism was historically correct but is irrelevant, and is no longer true. Stewart (1948) and Zipf (1946) . . . based their formulations explicitly on an analogy to Newton's law of gravitation. Although their models had no theoretical basis, it has been shown empirically that their models and various modifications that developed were successful or more successful in forecasting travel patterns than models derived directly from theory. Further, Niedercorn and Bechdolt (1966) have derived the gravity model from existing economic theory. They demonstrated that the gravity model is a logical and theoretically sound solution for the problem of maximising individual satisfaction subject to time or budget constraints.

A further point that needs to be borne in mind about the technique is that it has a tendency to over-predict short trips and under-predict long trips (Smith 1989, Ryan and Richardson 1983). The use of various weightings can permit adjustment of this tendency.

Mayo and Jarvis (1986) have some useful comments about the spatial/psychological dimensions of space as they relate to gravitational models. The usual assumption is that distance is an inhibiting factor in travel, but this is obviously not necessarily the case. They enumerate six factors that will influence inter- and intra-tourist destination travel.

a) gravity – a force that stimulates travel – 'pulling' people to a destination;
b) friction of distance – a force that deters travel;
c) start-up inertia – a force acting to impede travel of any length, no matter how short;
d) inertia of movement – a force acting to reduce the the effect of friction of distance (i.e. momentum);
e) subjective distance – a force stimulating travel beyond a certain point

because each additional mile is perceived to be less than a measured mile;

f) the attraction of the far off destination – some travel to a destination simply because it is far off.

They argue, on the basis of studies done of perceptual mapping, that subjective distance increases proportionately less than objective geographic distance, but that as subjective distance increases, the attraction of the destination grows for the tourist. An example of this is Fiji. For many British tourists Fiji would be an exotic destination, and they would not realise that it is in fact a built up tourist destination catering for the Australian market. One of the possible implications is that if gravitational models are being used to study movements between tourist areas, then perhaps the distance component within the formula may have to reflect the subjective distance as described by Mayo and Jarvis (1986). Another variable that may influence the pattern of travel, both within tourist areas as well as between tourist destinations is that of travel time. If, as appears to be the case, in large urban areas which are also tourist attractions, such as London, the average speed of travel is 10 m.p.h., then time becomes a consideration. It is also one of the perversities of modern flight that the time taken to travel from home to actually sitting in the aircraft may be longer than the time taken to fly several hundred if not thousands of miles. Travel time might thus be the friction in the gravitational model, not distance *per se*.

Nearest neighbour models

A related question is whether or not, in looking at a tourist area, the attractions are clustered or randomly distributed. Arguably, random distribution is an inhibiting factor in tourist travel. A planning authority might therefore be seeking to locate new attractions in places that create logical travel patterns. The word, 'logical', obviously requires careful definition in practice, but for the current purpose it might be held to mean the location of attractions in positions that help engender tourist visits, whilst indeed, they may be in positions that help protect fragile areas. Accordingly various measures of dispersal have been created. Ten patterns of dispersal can be identified; each of the ten in turn being based on combinations of patterns on linear, uniform, clustered, dispersed or randomly arranged formations. Figure 4.2 illustrates this.

Associated with each pattern is a range of values derived from various techniques such as nearest neighbourhood analysis. This approach has been used for a number of problems as diverse as measuring distribution of flowers in a field (Clark and Evans 1955, Pielo 1959), shopping patterns in Nottingham (Whysall based on cartographic analysis 1974, 1989) and the

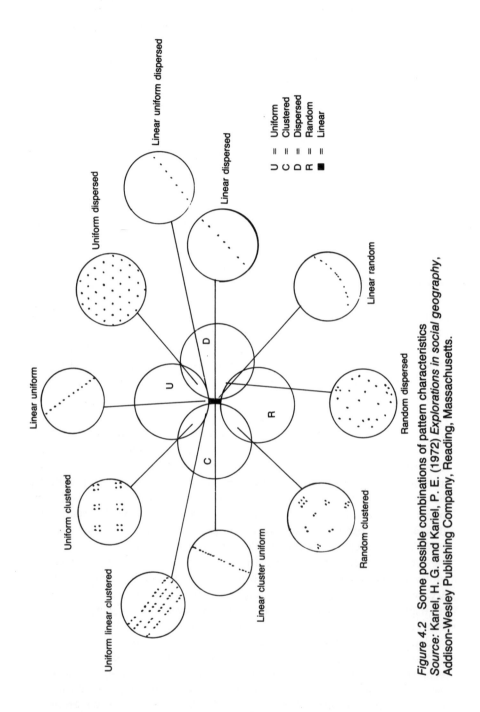

Figure 4.2 Some possible combinations of pattern characteristics
Source: Kariel, H. G. and Kariel, P. E. (1972) *Explorations in social geography*,
Addison-Wesley Publishing Company, Reading, Massachusetts.

provision of urban recreation facilities (Lovingood and Mitchell 1978, Rolfe 1964). The technique when applied to tourism seeks to assess whether or not there is any order in the location of facilities.

Essentially the nearest neighbour statistic is a ratio between the actual mean distance between neighbouring features, and the expected mean in a randomly distributed pattern of equal density. It can be expressed as:

$$R = \frac{Ra}{Re}$$

where R = nearest neighbour statistic

Ra = actual mean distance to neighbour

Re = expected mean in a random distribution of equal density

and Re in turn is the reciprocal of the square root of the density of points multiplied by 2, i.e.

$$Re = \frac{1}{2\sqrt{D}}$$

The calculation of density will in part depend on the nature of the shape of the area being considered. In looking at linear shapes Re has the value of $0.5(L/n-1)$ where L equals the length of the line and n is the number of points or attractions being considered. Smith (1983, 1989) gives examples of calculations. The resultant value of the calculation can be compared to a series of known values. Thus for example, if R = 1 then there is a random pattern, if R = 2.14 then there is a hexagonal pattern of Christaller's central place theory (1966). Should R have a value of less than 1 then a cluster is emerging, but above 1 more uniform spacing is occurring. There are some criticisms of the approach. For example, in interpreting the result some different patterns may be associated with the same value of R. Smith (1989) raises the point that where the boundaries are drawn is important in that it changes the value of Ra. It can also be questioned as to just how satisfactorily the technique deals with vacant sectors. In addition, the technique is essentially concerned with pairwise relationships within the area. Morisita (1957) and Whysall (1974) further refine the approach to overcome these objections by imposing quadrants on the area in question and looking at clusters within the quadrant. Morisita's Index of Dispersion is thus given as:

$$Id = qx$$

where $x = \dfrac{\Sigma ni(ni-1)}{N(N-1)}$

where q = number of quadrants

ni = number of quadrants containing i units

N = total number of units in the pattern.

Nearest neighbourhood analysis thus becomes a planning tool in that it can be combined with gravitational models. The planner can not only look at the forecast probability of trips between locations or attractions within the same tourist area, but can, if necessary, assess the logic of location of the new site by its spatial relationship with others. In short, nearest neighbour analysis might help in locating a 'logical' location for a new attraction, and gravity models will predict the probability of, and flows of, tourists to the new site.

Econometric models

With reference to gravity models such forecasting becomes possible by changing one of the variables within the model that relate to, say, attractiveness of the resort due to an enhancement of visitor attractions, a diminution of travel time due to increase accessibility, or the result of changes in population. On the important assumption that the parameters a and b are constant, it thus becomes possible to use the models for making a forecast. Another process with a long history of use in forecasting tourist flows to tourist areas is that of econometric modelling. Reference has already been made (in Chapter two) to some of the studies by Witt and Martin (1987) and Quayson and Var (1982). The validity and reliability of econometric models in tourism rest upon a number of requirements. Technically, problems such as multi-colinearity may have to be avoided, i.e. the variables perceived as determining variables will need to be independent of each other. This will be difficult to achieve. If, for example, exchange rates and real incomes are perceived as potential determinants of demand for tourism, there is a need to recognise that exchange rates and real income may in fact be linked variables in terms of their economic relationship. Adverse exchange rate movements may increase the rate of inflation within a country by increasing the price of imports including consumer durables and raw materials, and increased inflation reduces real incomes, even whilst increasing the cost of overseas holidays. In the absence of countervailing processes, *ceteris paribus*, it would be expected that the demand for tourism will fall. But what proportion of the reduction in demand is due to adverse exchange rates or falling real income? Apart from these problems, for which statistical techniques exist to help, it has to be recognised that econometric models for tourism require large amounts of data. Even comparatively simple models might require data on the costs of transport, travel time and departure frequency (important for business travel), the characteristics of the destinations, the relative costs of activities at the resorts, socio-economic data about consumers, income data, exchange rates, differential inflation rates between competing tourist destinations and the tourist generating countries. All these data will be required for each of the years under examination. A further problem then emerges and that is the quality of the data. There are well known problems about some tourism data. Hotel occupancy rates are a particular problem if the sample is going to be a representative one in that smaller hotels in particular may infrequently make returns. Regulations on the need to register guests may vary from one country to another. Theoretically, the quality of this data should improve with an increasing adoption of computerised reservation systems that will print out tables of occupancy rates upon demand. Data on international travel are also, in some cases, prone to what is in effect double counting. The British tourists who land at Calais and proceed to drive into Belgium, then through Germany on their way to ski in Austria may be counted four times, even though the duration of their stay in France and Belgium may be quite short. Figures of cross-boundary movements may include shoppers who, living in the locality, may simply cross the border to take advantage of cheaper prices, or tax differences. As such they nonetheless may be counted amongst the arrivals. The sampling points of cross-border traffic may be comparatively few in terms of not simply counting tourists, but seeking further data, e.g. on the purpose of the visit.

IMPLICATIONS FOR PLANNING

The above discusssion has primarily related to such questions as, what are the tourist facilities that exist, how are they to be described, what are their components, how attractive are they, what are the numbers of people likely to come, what patterns of transport might emerge and similar tactical questions. But, it is vitally important to ask the strategic question, how many tourists do we want, how many can the host environment, both physically and socially, sustain? This requires a concept of carrying capacities, and a recognition that management of tourist areas is not simply a question of tourist promotion. There is little to be gained from increasing visitor numbers if the result of such numbers is an increasing hostility to tourists, and a down grading of the very factors that attracted the tourists in the first place. The management of tourist resort areas requires that the tourist experience is enhanced even whilst the benefits to the host area are maximised and the disbenefits minimised. The product life cycle of the tourist resort area as initially described would appear to have an inbuilt logic to growth and inevitable decline. The process is not automatic. The host community may in fact choose not to permit tourist development to occur beyond a certain point. This is however difficult to achieve. It requires that the host community have some other sources of economic wealth that permit employment and income, or that the community has a strong cultural and organisational bond whereby it is able to dictate the terms upon which it permits tourism, and is able to control its own members, some of whom will want to encourage tourism development. In many instances the cycle is not completed for reasons which lie beyond the control of the community, for example if tour operators find other resort areas more willing to permit the developments they wish to foster. These issues will be discussed in more detail in Chapter seven. It does however add another dimension to what is meant by the tourism area. The tourist resort area is not only a geographical entity that may change spatially over time, but it is also a reflection of norms and attitudes that become expressed through the type of tourist development that is permitted. It is a cultural entity. The nature of the culture it shows is a reflection of the strength of the host community norms and aspirations. Yet, even this truism, as Murphy (1978) shows, needs careful assessment for it cannot be held true that the host community is homogeneous, and the tourist resort area often becomes a meeting place of different sets of values and concepts. In consequence, the tourist resort area is a catalyst of change, a physical reminder of questions about what a society wishes to achieve. The place where tourists play out their fantasies, relax, seek to satisfy their cultural curiosity about another land, travel to museums, is thus not simply a statement about the tourist, but is also a statement about the area, region or country that has permitted the tourist resort area to take place.

SUMMARY

The above discussion indicates that the tourist zone changes spatially over time, and in doing so changes the geographic dispersal of its 'attractions'. In turn, this will change the flows of traffic, both within the zone, and between the 'core' tourist area and its periphery. Key factors in the planning of the zone are therefore the identification of nodal points of traffic, and the nature of the geographic linkages between those points.

Chapter 5

The economic impacts of tourism

INTRODUCTION

This chapter will discuss a number of general issues relating to tourism in order to establish a context for a more detailed discussion of 'multiplier' processes. Having examined these processes and other issues such as the productivity of labour in tourism the chapter will then again widen the discussion by reference to a number of case studies.

Tourism has been identified as one of the fastest growing industries in the world. In both developed and developing countries government authorities have identified tourism as a means of generating employment and income in vulnerable economies. Third World countries such as the Gambia in West Africa have placed tourism as a major component of their economic strategy, whilst within North America and Europe tourism has been perceived as an important means of urban renewal in decaying waterfront and inner city areas. Major initiatives have been and continue to be generated. In Eire the government's plan for national recovery of 1987 targeted a number of key industries to generate prosperity. One of these was tourism. In the UK the English Tourist Board (ETB) in 1987 published its planning document 'Vision for England'. Under these plans a public sector investment of £570 million was planned to develop a total investment of £4 billion by 1992, with an additional 250,000 jobs to be created. In the 1970s the French government partly financed developments in the Languedoc-Roussillon region of the south not only to relieve tourism congestion on the Côte d'Azure, but also to generate employment and income in an area perceived as having a marginal economy. Such pressures for tourism development come from many different sources. Local government seeks to attract funding to support tourism development as a means of revitalising waste land and so convert it into a prosperous area that does not become a drain on local authority resources but contributes to the tax revenues through higher property taxes and other forms of tax revenues. Hoteliers and other commercial interests are also an important pressure group for tourism. Thus for example, in the 1960s, the British hotel industry continued to press government for grants similar to those given to manufacturing industry in areas of higher than national average unemployment, and indeed, partly as a result of this pressure, the government responded with the Hotel Incentive Development Scheme in 1969 which offered grants to all hotels regardless of area. Equally, in 1987 the Irish Hotels Federation sought to influence its government policy by commissioning a report which emphasised the value of tourism to Eire (Baum 1989). Local people can also exert pressure to secure tourism developments. In 1988 the people living in the area west of Paphos sought to overcome environmental pressure groups and asked the Cyprus government to permit tourism in their area so as to generate employment and income. (Paradoxically, the villagers of Ayia Nappa, in the east of the island, were preparing a new village to retreat to in the face of the 'tourism invasion'.)

Hence there is undoubted demand for tourism development, but a number of questions consequently arise. Basic questions might be said to include:

How important is tourism to the area in question?
How does one measure this importance?
Does the structure of tourism permit the creation of employment and income that can really benefit host communities?
Who benefits economically from tourism?
What are the costs as well as the benefits of tourism?

In any discussion of how important tourism is to an area, a series of further questions arises. Such questions include: What is the type of tourism being considered? What is the context of the tourism?

To take a simple example, there is a considerable difference in the types of economic, and other effects that are generated by local farmers offering bed and breakfast accommodation compared with a large multi-national organisation building a hotel, or a holiday village. Equally, the impact created by any given number of tourists is different if the context of that tourism is a large commercial city, or a rural setting.

THE DETERMINANTS OF ECONOMIC IMPACT

Even these simple examples indicate a number of key variables that must be considered when assessing the economic impacts of tourism. Before discussing in detail the nature of the impacts of tourism, it might help to indicate a general context and list the variables that may be important. Such variables include:

Level of economic development of the destination area

As indicated above, if a hotel is built and attracts visitors there is significant difference between whether or not that hotel is built in a town or a village. Within a town the spending of such tourists will represent but a small proportion of total spending, but in a village it will be a significant addition to the total income of the village, subject to the important proviso that the guests' and hotel's expenditure does take place in the village.

Nature of the tourist facilities and their attractiveness

The nature of the tourist facility helps to determine the total expenditure that takes place. As will be discussed below, it is generally true that a higher proportion of any one pound spent in farmhouse accommodation will remain in the local area than is the case if the pound is spent in a hotel. This reflects the fact that the farmer (or spouse) has a greater propensity to buy goods and services locally. However, against that fact, the visitors staying in a hotel will be more likely to be paying more for their accommodation. Although a smaller proportion of tourist expenditure in hotels finds its way into the local economy, it is nonetheless a smaller proportion of a much larger sum of money. Therefore the local economy may gain more from the hotel than the farmhouse in strict terms of revenues gained. This argument is however totally negated if the visitors do not find the hotel to their liking, and tourists are in fact demanding the experiences associated with staying with local farmers.

The degree of foreign ownership of the hotel

Although the hotel may be successful in attracting guests, the leakages of revenue away from the area in which it is located may be increased by factors other than simply where the hotel management buys its resources. One factor that has attracted attention is the ownership of the hotel. If the hotel is in the hands of foreign ownership, then the profits may be remitted back to the parent company, and thus again leave the local economy. This phenomenon is not simply restricted to hotels or retail businesses which are owned by foreign nationals, but is repeated wherever the tourist business is not owned by local proprietors. For example, in many of the Greek islands the ownership of the restaurants or shops may be in the hands of Athenians, who, at the end of the season, close their business and return to their other businesses in Athens.

Employment of non-indigenous labour

The impact of tourist expenditure in terms of generating local revenues may also be partly diminished by the employment of labour from outside the area. A number of reasons can dictate such a practice. It might be that there is insufficient local labour to meet the demands of the peak season, or local people are reluctant to be involved because their own economic base is sufficiently developed to provide employment alternative to the tourist industry, or there are social factors that inhibit their seeking jobs in tourism. If owned by large international companies, the businesses might require practices or skills not to be found in the host community, which may lack the experience of management in large-scale organisations. On the other hand, if they are small businesses owned by entrepreneurs of the same nationality, but from outside the local area, they may seek to have family members involved in the business. Finally, of course, a significant reason for the use of non-indigenous labour may be the fact that such labour is cheaper. As will be discussed, there are significant numbers of examples of tourist areas attracting labour from rural economies that are characterised as low income areas with high levels of unemployment or hidden unemployment, and thus tourism copies other examples of industries that attract migrant labour from marginal economies. Such examples of both phenomena are found in Spain, where migration has occurred from the hinterland to the coastal tourist strip. Yet, this must be placed within a context of Spain's tradition in the 1950s of being a source of emigrant labour to the industrialised northern European countries, whilst within Spain itself there had been migration from the poorer southern areas, such as Andalucia, to the industrial areas of Barcelona and Bilbao in the 1950s and 1960s.

Whatever the reasons for the use of non-local labour the consequence is that payment of wages is made to non-local people, and again it is customary that a proportion of such wages are remitted home. This is shown by Alison Lever in her study of Spanish migrant workers to Lloret de Mar (1987), and by Milligan (1989) in her study of Portuguese workers in Guernsey.

In addition to the loss of revenue to the host community, there is also a cost associated with this practice. Local workers require accommodation, medical services, transport and other services, and whilst it can be argued that the provision of such services in itself generates flows of income, the practicalities of the situation may mean that the additions to local income may be marginal and be associated with a number of social disbenefits. This point is further discussed in the chapter on social impacts.

Government provision of infrastructure

Whilst an area may have attracted those types of tourists designated by Cohen (1979) as 'explorers', should it seek to attract more tourists and move into mass tourism additional investment will have to be made by both private and public sectors. Whilst the private sector will provide the hotels, bars, restaurants, discos and many other forms of entertainment facilities, the government will have to provide a range of infrastructure support. Accessibility will be improved by the provision of roads and car parking spaces; services relating to hygiene including sewage disposal and treatment, the provision of public toilets and water treatment plants will be needed; medical facilities might be needed to treat not only the tourists but also the influx of labour that may be created, and plans relating to property development will be needed, and implemented. The provision of such services sets a complex pattern of revenues and costs into being. The building of these services is obviously a means of generating employment, and in an area of high unemployment, if local labour is utilised, the very building programme itself will be viewed as a positive economic impact. Indeed, the provision of these services will help to attract private sector investment for not only the tourism industry, but for other economic sectors such as retailing, other service industries through the provision of office accommodation, and possibly light manufacturing industry. In fact, this is the very sort of process that has characterised waterfront developments in North America, Europe and Australia. But the provision of such services requires funding, and thus a series of costs are initiated. Where central government is involved, the simple economic costs of expenditure on these investments is shared amongst the wider community, and not simply the host community in the tourist destination. The host nation considers that it will gain from factors such as earned foreign currencies and additional earnings on its balance of payments, and thus such investment is justified on these grounds. However, where investment is financed or implemented by local government, the host community bears the costs as well as the rewards. Taxes may be raised to meet either the expenditure directly, or to service the loans borrowed to finance the building. The final balance sheet of costs and revenues will thus depend upon the success of the venture, for there is no guarantee of success, particularly in the case of marginal economies (marginal in either national or world terms) for tourism is subjected to whims as to which location or type of holiday or leisure day-trip activity is in fashion. The initial euphoria of success may, after a brief period, turn sour as tastes and the market move on. Examples of such changes in fashion include the success of safari parks in the 1960s, and the more recent rapid growth of visitor numbers to Turkey by the British in 1986 and 1987, to be followed by a drastic fall in the rate of that growth.

The type of tourist

All of the above factors listed have tended to be 'supply led' in nature, that is, they indicate the economic flows that arise from the provision of services to tourists. But what of the tourists themselves? The impacts are obviously greater the higher is the number of tourists, and the higher the average expenditure per tourist. But the nature of their demand is also important. If mass tourists require items that the local community is unable to provide, the result is that a significant proportion of the revenue gained from tourism is immediately lost in terms of the need to import those items from outside the region or country. In this sense there may be a series of trade-offs for any tourist planning authority. Greater numbers of high spending tourists may, perversely, have less beneficial impact than a smaller number of lower spending tourists if the latter creates a lesser need to import. Equally, it can be argued that larger numbers of tourists generate higher social costs in terms of their impingement upon the life styles of the host community. This is particularly true if there exists wide disparities between the life styles of the tourist and the local population. It is now a cliche to say that an American tourist visiting Canada has very little impact, but that the same American tourist in, say, Bangladesh, will have a much greater influence.

In part, the economic activities associated with tourism become important when considering the purpose of tourism within a general economic framework. In the instances of waterfront or inner city tourism developments, it may be argued that the import requirements to service the tourists are themselves an important part of the overall economic objective of bringing the area back into the mainstream of economic life, and removing it from its current marginal status.

THE MEASUREMENT OF ECONOMIC IMPACTS

Therefore the question of how to measure the economic impact of tourism is both important to ask, and difficult to answer. In practice, three related techniques have been generated to calculate these impacts, and these are:

a) the use of multiplier studies taken from macro-economics;
b) the use of input-output measures, again taken from macro-economics;
c) local impact studies utilising a number of 'ad-hoc' measures.

THE MULTIPLIER PROCESS

From the 1960s there has been a series of studies undertaken throughout the world to assess the economic benefits of tourism to the host community. Many of these studies took place throughout the 1970s, but, increasingly, researchers became aware of just how difficult it was in practice to measure the flows of income and the numbers of jobs that were being created, and to some extent multiplier studies became less frequent in the 1980s. However, with the emergence of tourism as a means of helping to regenerate inner city areas in both Europe and North America there has been some renewed interest in the use of such techniques. The reasons for this are pragmatic, for local authorities have had to be able to justify the spending of public money to their own elected councillors, whilst, certainly in the United Kingdom at least, many such schemes envisage the use of public money as a 'pump priming' exercise whereby the local government funds investment which in turn attracts money from the private sector. Again, the effectiveness of such expenditure is carefully assessed. This new spirit of pragmatism has two further effects. The first is in the methods used to assess the economic impacts, because simpler methods of measurement are being used; and the second is that tourism is increasingly perceived as part of a total package of economic regeneration which includes retailing, property development and general leisure provision. The presence of these facilities is subsequently used to attract other forms of industry.

Initially, the concept of the multiplier is taken from the ideas of R. K. Kahn and John Maynard Keynes, as developed in their seminal works of the 1930s. Keynes argued that economic growth was dictated by two broad groups of flows of activity – 'leakages' from the economic systems, and 'injections' into that system. The 'injections' consisted of investment, exports and government expenditure. Investment was important for at least two reasons. The very act of creating the investment was in itself a means of creating jobs and income, whilst the investment also became a means of perpetuating employment and income for the future. Exports meant the selling of goods overseas, and thus earning money from overseas residents. Government expenditure was a means of financing investment and also a means of transferring income to individuals who could then purchase items and generate a demand for goods and services. That is, the exports and government expenditure are, what Keynes termed, 'injections', that add to economic growth. From the viewpoint of tourism, the building of the tourist attraction is thus the investment; its existence helps to attract overseas visitors and thus it is a form of export, whilst simultaneously the enhancement of tourist facilities within a country may be an import-saving investment for its citizens will holiday within their own country rather than spend their money overseas.

The 'leakages' in the system are savings, taxation and imports. The act of saving withdraws money from the economy and diminishes overall levels of demand for goods and hence employment. Savings only become 'useful' when they are used by financial intermediaries to fund investment. The same is true of taxation. By raising taxation the government withdraws money from the economic system, and so again diminishes levels of demand. It is only by government expenditure that that money is released back into the economy. Imports are a leakage in the sense that, by purchasing from overseas, the jobs associated with the production of those goods are also to be found overseas.

Keynes argued that when both the 'injections' and 'leakages' are in equilibrium, then the economy is also in equilibrium. Economic growth is generated by the 'injections' being greater than the 'leakages'.

There is another important economic flow, which is consumer expenditure, and this Keynes placed on both sides of the equation. Consumer spending is an injection in that it is the spending that fuels the demand for goods and services and thus creates employment and income. On the other hand, if the recipient of the consumer expenditure does nothing with the revenue, it is money taken out of the economic system. Accordingly, the timing and sequence of flows of consumer spending are of importance. Both Keynesians and Monetarists also recognise that money is a commodity like any other in that it has a cost, namely, interest rates. Consumer spending can therefore be affected not only by taxation, which removes or adds money to the consumer's budget, but also, in advanced economies where credit is often used, by alterations in interest rates. In addition, in societies with high levels of home ownership, and where much of that home ownership is financed by mortgages, interest rates can act like taxes. Increases in interest rates raise the value of monthly repayments by mortgage holders, and thus reduce their ability to spend on other items. Evidence of this at work was arguably present in Britain in 1989 when increases in mortgage rates to over 13 per cent following an explosion in house prices in 1988 meant that the growth in retail sales grew more slowly, and the demand for overseas package holidays fell from some 13 million package holidays to approximately 11 million. The relationship was, however, far from clear as the British summer of 1989 was one of the sunniest and warmest for decades, and holidays in Britain experienced a boom. Additionally, many holidaymakers had bitter memories of aircraft controllers' strikes and long delays at airports in the previous summer of 1988. Thus, there may have been elements of demand substitution rather than diminution of demand. However, if mortgage rates are to have the effect of taxes in controlling consumer demand it would appear that mortgages must be a significantly large proportion of household budgets, high proportions of home owners must be comparatively recent purchasers of homes with such purchases being primarily financed by a mortgage rather than past savings, and such a pattern of home ownership is widespread. It can be argued that with the passing of time this becomes diluted, particularly in an ageing population, where home ownership becomes funded by past savings, and there is a reduced dependency on mortgage financing, particularly if the housing stock is sufficient to meet demand and thus upward pressures on prices are relieved. In short, within the Keynesian context, ownership of consumer wealth, such as is represented by home ownership, is also a determinant of demand.

The above discussion can be summarised within Keynesian terms as economic growth occurring where:

$$I+X+G+C > S+M+T+C$$

where I = Investment
    X = Exports
    G = Government spending
    C = Consumer spending
    S = Savings
    M = Imports
    T = Taxation

Equally, the national or regional income can be said to be in equilibrium where:

$$I+X+G+C = S+M+T+C$$

Tourism therefore has economic effects by:

a) contributing to the balance of payments
Holidays taken overseas are imports, overseas visitors coming to the host country are counted as exports, and every time citizens take their major holiday in their own country it might be said that import substitution has taken place.

b) creating employment and income by generating the following:
 i) initial investment in tourist facilities,
 ii) creating consumer expenditure in a given location,
iii) in many cases releases flows of savings into the economic system.
The actual employment and income generated will depend upon the nature of the 'leakages' in the system, and the size of the original 'injection'.

Consider a simple example where trade into and out of an area is (conveniently) not taken into account, and where government action can also be discounted. Under these circumstances economic growth will be generated by consumer spending, savings and investment. Initially, consumers' income (Y) is disposed of by savings and spending, hence:

$$Y = C+S$$

Consider Figure 5.1. On the vertical axis is located consumption and savings. As the total of both equal income (measured on the horizontal axis), a 45° line indicates the points where $Y = C+S$. Let it be supposed that earners spend 75 per cent of any addition to their income and save 25 per cent. Therefore, if their income increases by £100 they will spend £75 of that increase and save £25. This permits a consumption line to be drawn, indicating the levels of consumption associated with any given level of income. Where the consumption line (C) crosses the 45° line, consumption equals income, and hence savings are equal to zero. To the left of this point, expenditure exceeds income, and hence savings are negative. To the right of this point, income exceeds consumption, and hence savings are positive. The savings line (S), shows this relationship. The slope of the consumption line is calculated from the relationship of the changes in expenditure divided by the changes in income, that is, the slope equals the marginal propensity to consume (MPC). MPC is that part of additions to income that are spent, i.e. the change in consumption divided by the change in income.

The initial equilibrium level of income is hence £100,000; that is the level where consumption equals income and savings is zero. Suppose that a £20,000 investment in tourism takes place. Total demand in the economy now rises by £20,000, but the new, higher level of equilibrium income is not £120,000, but £180,000. Total income has risen by £80,000, and this increase consists of two components – the initial £20,000 investment and an increase in consumer spending of £60,000. In short, a multiplier process has taken place. It will also be noted in Figure 5.1 that at the new, higher level of income, the difference between the consumption plus investment line (C+I) and the original consumption line (C) is of course £20,000, and at the point where the C+I line cuts the 45° line, the value of savings is also equal to £20,000. A new equilibrium income has established itself.

How has this come about? The answer lies in the process whereby the recipients of additional income spend part of that income, which in turn therefore forms income for others. The investment forms an initial impetus into the economy. The recipients now spend 75 per cent of this £20,000, i.e. £15,000, and save the remaining £5,000. The recipients of the £15,000 spending in turn save 25 per cent, and spend 75 per cent, i.e. £11,250. In turn, the receivers of this £11,250 spend 75 per cent of it, and save 25 per cent. Table 5.1 shows the process occurring.

In the first five 'rounds' the total additions to income are not only the initial £20,000 investment but also £15,000 + £11,250 + £8,437.5 + £6,328.1, that is, £41,015.6 of consumer spending can be added to the £20,000 investment. How is this reconciled with Figure 5.1? The figure represented the final equilibrium position of a new, higher level of income of £180,000. The flows of Table 5.1 represent the process of arriving at

Table 5.1   The flows of the multiplier process (initial injection = £20,000)

	Periods of time				
	1 £	2 £	3 £	4 £	5 £
Saved (25%)	5,000	3,750	2,812.5	2,109.4	1,582.0
Spent (75%)	15,000	11,250	8,437.5	6,328.1	4,746.1
	20,000	15,000	11,250	8,437.5	6,328.1

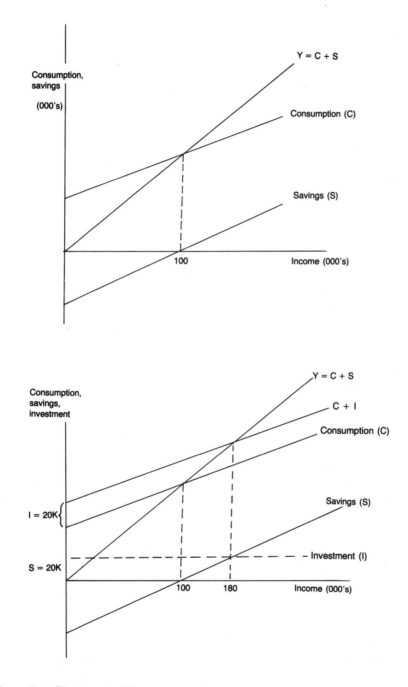

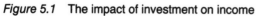

Figure 5.1 The impact of investment on income

that final position of equilibrium. It can be noticed that with the passing of time, the successive additions to income are becoming weaker. Keynes argued that the final position can be deduced from the formula:

$$\text{Value of the multiplier} = \frac{1}{\text{mps}}$$

where mps = marginal propensity to save i.e., that proportion of any addition to income that is saved.

In the example, the value of mps is 1/4 (25 per cent). Therefore, to find the new equilibrium level of income we multiply the initial injection by the multiplier. Thus:

$$
\begin{aligned}
\text{New income generated} &= £20,000 \times 1/.25 \\
&= £20,000 \times 4 \\
&= £80,000
\end{aligned}
$$

Hence, the value of the multiplier is determined by the value of the leakages. The higher the value of the leakages in the economic system, the lower is the value of the multiplier, and the lower is the resultant flow of additions to income. For example, if the marginal propensity to save was 0.50 (i.e. out of every additional £1 earned 50p was saved), the £20,000 injection in our example would have produced an addition to income of:

$$
\begin{aligned}
\text{New income generated} &= £20,000 \times 1/.50 \\
&= £20,000 \times 2 \\
&= £40,000
\end{aligned}
$$

From the example it can be seen that any injection into a local economy produces these types of flows of income. Thus, the investment referred to might be not just the building of industrial investment, but can equally well refer to the building of hotels, or the expenditure of tourists visiting an area. Economists, therefore, in the 1960s, began to adapt Keynes' concept of the multiplier for national income to regional or local economic systems to assess the economic impacts of tourism.

In assessing these impacts there are three categories that may be calculated, namely:

a) the output multiplier
   This measures the total output (or sales) induced in the economy, per unit of extra spending, and is expressed in the form of a multiplier coefficient.
b) the income multiplier
   This shows the relationship between extra spending and changes in income.
c) the employment multiplier

This indicates the relationship between the extra spending and the number of additional jobs that are created through primary and secondary employment. Primary employment would include the actual number of jobs directly generated by the tourist spending or investment, e.g. jobs in restaurants, whilst the secondary effects would, for example, include those jobs created by the spending of restaurant employees.

In the case of tourism the value of the leakages will be determined by the proportion of tourist spending that remains in the area, the proportion of tourist spending that is received by local people, and the propensity of local people to spend in their local area. The basic formulation of the Tourism Multiplier is thus:

$$\text{Tourism Multiplier} = A \left(\frac{1}{1 - BC} \right)$$

where A = the proportion of tourist expenditure remaining in the area after first round leakages

B = the proportion of income that local people spend on local goods and services — the propensity to spend locally

C = the proportion of expenditure of local people which accrues as local income.

The logic of the formulation is by reason of the fact that as most tourist regions/destinations are comparatively small, the highest element of leakages occurs in the first round when imports are undertaken, and in consequence the additions to income in the local area are felt from the second round on. However, an important determinant of the value of the tourist multiplier continues to be — who are the recipients of the income? If, in the second round, the recipients of tourist-initiated expenditure spend money outside the area, the value of the multiplier is undermined, hence the importance of values B and C in the equation.

However, this simple formulation is insufficient in practice. In the initial discussion of the concept of the multiplier some obvious questions arise. How can we be sure that recipients of income maintain the same consistent propensities to save and consume? How long are the time periods or rounds, and as money trickles through the system over time, can we again be sure of consistency of behaviour by recipients of additions to income? For example, if the farmer takes in bed and breakfast guests, is this addition to the farm's revenue perceived by the family as additions to its savings, or as money for the family to spend on itself, or a means of paying the farm's bills? Is the attitude to these sums the same at the end of the season as the beginning of the season? In short, researchers have had to disaggregate the data, often by the type of accommodation used by the tourists. As Archer and Owen (1971) showed in their studies of Anglesey, there are distinct differences in the types of expenditure patterns undertaken by those who use hotels, bed and breakfast accommodation or caravan sites for their overnight stays, whilst, equally, there are differences in spending by the recipients of the first round of tourist expenditure. It can be hypothesised, for example, that proprietors of bed and breakfast accommodation may be more prepared than hotel chains to use local suppliers. The final section of this chapter (see page 92) indicates some of Archer's work in this respect.

Murphy (1985) provides a summary of some of the findings undertaken by researchers, and his table is reproduced in part as Table 5.2. From the table it can be observed that the values of the multipliers decline the smaller is the area under study, a reflection of the greater propensity for leakages that exist in smaller areas since they are less likely to be economically self-sustaining.

Table 5.2 Tourism multipliers for various locations

Date	Location	Income multiplier
National scale		
1966	Ireland	2.7
1970	Canada	2.43
1974	United Kingdom	1.68
1964	Greece	1.2–1.4
1977	Mexico	0.97
1971	Caribbean (Commonwealth)	0.88
1974	Bahamas	0.78
Provincial		
1976	New Hampshire	1.6–1.7
1976	Hawaii	0.9–1.3
1973	SW England	0.35–0.45
Local/regional		
1976	Ely, Montana	1.67
1977	Okanagan, BC	0.73
1977	Victoria, BC	0.65
1973	Gwynedd	0.37
1975	East Anglia	0.35
1973	Greater Tayside	0.32

Source: Murphy, *Tourism – a community approach* (1985)

What can also be appreciated is the complexity of data that is required for the calculation of such multipliers. To undertake even simple calculations a number of parameters need to be defined. The first is simply that of the region under consideration. As discussed in Chapter three the concept of the tourist destination area is neither fixed spatially or temporally, for different aspects of a region will appeal to different types of tourists, and attractions change over time. It may be possible to define the tourist area by an analysis of tourist trips within the region, so identifying perhaps a 'core' tourist area. However, there is no guarantee that such an area corresponds to the administrative area used for the collection of other data. For example, the tourist area might span more than one local authority, or travel to work area; and in turn it is these latter areas which might be the basis of statistics relating to public sector expenditure or employment. Reference has also been made to the different types of tourists. Day visitors will obviously not be spending on accommodation, whilst short-break holidaytakers may have higher spend per day, but a lower total spend per holiday visit. Users of hotel accommodation tend to have higher expenditure than users of caravans.

Forms of expenditure

One interesting fact that has emerged from more recent studies is that VFR (Visiting friends and relatives) tourists may have as high an expenditure as tourists staying in hotels if the area is a well established tourist area. The evidence for this is mixed, but Vaughan (1986) indicates this in comparing expenditure patterns of tourists in Cumbria, Merseyside and Bournemouth as shown in Table 5.3.

Table 5.3 Differential patterns of tourist expenditure (daily expenditure)

Area/type of tourist	Spending on accommodation £	Other activities £	Total £
CUMBRIA			
Hotel/guest house	12.35	10.65	23.00
Rented	6.70	5.03	12.00
Caravan/camp	4.10	6.10	10.20
VFR		25.80	25.80
Day		8.75	8.75
MERSEYSIDE			
Hotel/guest house	14.35	11.50	25.85
Caravan/camp	1.25	8.60	9.85
VFR		13.30	13.30
Day		6.85	6.85
BOURNEMOUTH			
Hotel/guest house	12.90	8.35	21.25
Caravan/camp	3.95	7.00	10.95
VFR		10.25	10.25
Day		4.05	4.05

Source: Vaughan, *Estimating the level of tourism-related employment* (1986)

What Vaughan (1986), Ryan and Wheeller (1982) and many others have indicated is just how important shopping is to the tourist. Shopping for other than food and drink can easily account for 25 per cent of tourist expenditure, and in consequence the economic impacts of tourism in an area can be affected by the nature of the retail provision to be found in the host community, the ownership of the shops, and the propensity of the shops to purchase locally. It is self-evident that souvenir shops in local ownership, using local craftspeople to supply the souvenirs will have a higher economic impact upon the native population in the tourist area than nationally or foreign-owned chains which import souvenirs. In essence this last point illustrates another problem in calculation of multiplier effects, and that is the need to identify the average daily expenditure of tourists, its breakdown between different types of business and the ownership of those businesses.

The impact of ownership on businesses has been demonstrated by Sinclair in her studies of Malaga hotels (1981, 1982). The highest multiplier effects were associated with tourist miscellaneous purchases, (i.e. expenditure on items other than food, drink, entertainment and accommodation) and thus relates to those items most likely to be supplied by local suppliers. The multiplier was estimated at 0.99, and the second highest multiplier values were associated with accommodation (0.66), partly because of the employment of labour living in the area. However, there were notable differences in the levels of employment between Spanish-owned and foreign-owned hotels. Whilst foreign-owned hotels tended to employ more staff (52.2 per hotel as against the 42.3 employed in Spanish-owned hotels), this was a reflection of the fact that foreign-owned hotels tended to be larger. In terms of numbers of employees per bed-space, the average employment (for coastal areas) was marginally less in foreign-owned than Spanish-owned hotels, (0.29 as against 0.30), but in the case of hotels located in cities, the difference was far more pronounced, being 0.49 for the foreign multiple as against 0.68 for the Spanish hotel. As a general conclusion it can be hypothesised that access to economies of scale and more cost effective modes of management may produce lower multiplier effects through the process of less employees per bed-space. In the case of foreign-owned hotels the position may be further exacerbated by a tendency to remit profits. Sinclair and Sutcliffe (1982) estimated a value of first round propensity to remit profits (for the Malaga area) as being equal to 39 per cent of the long-run GNP multiplier. Does this necessarily mean that non-local and foreign ownership of assets is to be discouraged? The position is not as simple as first appears. The levels of payment to staff must be taken into account. If the large multiple takes advantage of economies of scale and management techniques not simply to save on labour per bed-space, but also to pay a higher wage per employee than their less efficient local supplier, then the initial negative multiplier effects are offset by the higher wages. But the final calculation of multiplier effects will then require an analysis of expenditure by the employees.

From this discussion it can be seen that whilst the initial concept of the multiplier is essentially clear, even when its components are disaggregated, the actual data requirements are both large and complex, and effectively have defeated many an analysis. Lea (1988) gives examples of how faulty calculations of multipliers in the Caribbean gave rise to poor policy decisions.

Nonetheless, if tourism is to be promoted by public authorities there is obviously a need to assess the possible outcome of developments. In 1986 the English Tourist Board commissioned a study to see whether or not it would be possible to devise a means of calculating not income but employment multipliers in a way that was both meaningful and comparatively straightforward. It was finally concluded that whilst there were two methods, utilising either Census of Employment data or transferring multiplier values from past studies into the area under study, neither method was ideal. Vaughan (1986) writes:

> The conclusion presented in this report is that both methods can provide broad indications of the likely size of the tourism related work force. Both methods are subject to a number of important limitations and assumptions, so neither is obviously superior to the other. The qualifications of each approach should be respected in using the estimates produced as it could defeat the object of advocacy to publish estimates which are too open to question. Neither method can fully replace a local study if qualitative information on types of jobs and types of workers is required or to provide assurances that job estimates actually reflect the particular circumstances of the local tourist industry.

Negative multiplier flows

Vaughan's warning is particularly apposite in a situation where governmental authorities at both local and national level seek to promote tourism development in the belief that economic benefits emerge. Traditionally, tourism multipliers have been found to be weak and a number of reasons can account for this. Three possible reasons are:

a) the comparatively low levels of pay;
b) costs as well as income are generated;
c) the nature of the tourist regions.

Tourism, even in advanced economies, has been associated with low levels of pay. The Low Pay Unit in the United Kingdom reported in 1986 that nearly 40 per cent of hotel and restaurant employers visited by the

Government Wage Inspectorate were found to be illegally underpaying their workers. Bland (1987) commenting on the position in Cornwall, noted:

> In Cornwall, and doubtless in other counties, no effort is made to check that hotels and restaurants who are receiving grants, publicity and facilities paid for by tax and ratepayers are paying their workers legal wages. Public funds are in effect going to support and encourage criminal employers.

If the situation is thus in advanced economies, then the position is worse in developing countries. Cater (1988) argues that in the least developed countries tourism places a high cost upon their infrastructure. The energy requirements of luxury hotels are high and place a stress upon the hosts' electricity generating capacity, and in turn load shedding, blackouts, and poor water pressure pose problems in attracting western guests. Imported managerial labour also increases leakages. In consequence, tourism in developing economies may not only have positive multiplier effects from the 'injections' of tourist spending, but there are also costs, and, indeed tourism may not generate as much additional income as is hoped. Farvar (1984), in his study of Gambian tourism, concluded that the tourist industry employed fewer Gambians than hoped for, and in addition paid wages that, whilst higher than possible earnings in alternative forms of employment, were not sufficiently high to improve their standard of living to any great extent. It would seem from many studies that local ownership and control of tourist enterprise is important in ensuring that the host community derives the highest possible tourism multipliers. However, a contrary viewpoint is that, whilst this is true, there is nonetheless an important need to obtain access to the markets which exist beyond the tourist area, and locally based businesses may not have this ability. There is therefore inevitably a need to utilise businesses located in the tourist-generating areas. Only rarely, and generally only in the cases of mature tourist regions receiving governmental backing, can businesses located in the tourist-receiving areas reach directly to consumers in the tourist-generating regions.

The problem of low wages in the industry arguably might be a reflection of low levels of productivity and added value. There is ample evidence that in advanced economies the hotel industry is characterised by high levels of staff turnover, and small units. In a survey of the tourist and leisure industry, which not only included hotels but also nightclubs, leisure facilities and museums, the Institute of Manpower Studies (1988) found that 63 per cent of the 170 businesses examined had less than 20 employees. Only 8 per cent had over 50. Because of the small size of business units, it was found that whilst the industry does have a reputation of employing part-time, seasonal labour, this was not in fact borne out by the sample, for 68 per cent of all jobs were counted as being permanent jobs. However, the permanent jobs included those of the entrepreneurs involved, and hence the picture is one of several small businesses, capable of supporting the founders of the business, or the management staff of multiples, but generally being unable to support larger numbers of workers. But the position is varied, and the report concludes that:

It was evident that the extent of use, and pattern of use, of seasonal and casual workers varied greatly within the sector as a whole, as did the employment of permanents and temporaries.

The position could be summarised as in Table 5.4.

Table 5.4 Patterns of employment in tourism

Sector	Core of permanent staff			Use of temporary staff		
	Large	Medium	Small	High	Medium	Low
Hotels, restaurants, guest houses	+				+	+
Leisure facilities		+		+	+	
Other accommodation			+	+		
Museums and galleries		+		+		
Travel agents and guides	+				+	
Nightclubs and public houses	+					+
Cinemas and theatres		+		+		

Source: Table constructed from data in Institute of Manpower Studies Report, Productivity in the leisure industry (1988)

One of the important implications of the IMS findings is that for many employed in the industry the career path is short, with limited opportunity for career enhancement as the industry is currently structured.

The overall picture is of extensive movement between companies but usually without promotion. Managers and Professionals are the only group for whom careers could be common, as promotion was reported by many establishments for recruits and leavers. This was the only group for whom internal careers appeared to be a well established feature of the employment structure. For all other occupational groups, not only was promotion reported as common by a minority of establishments only but movement out of employment entirely was not uncommon.

Tourism and levels of productivity

Recently, the conventional viewpoint that tourism is characterised by low productivity has been challenged. Medlik (1985, 1988) in particular has argued that comparisons between industries are distorted if no allowance is made for the differing proportions of full-time and part-time labour, whilst secondly he argued that in many parts of the tourism industry, increasing use of information technology meant that the conventional arguments are no longer supported by the evidence. Utilising UK data between 1979 and 1985 Medlik argued that 'the tourism sector' increased its productivity, as measured by value-added per full-time equivalent employee, from £7,200 to £7,900 compared to £8,800 to £10,000 for the whole economy. From the viewpoint of the British tourist industry, these dates are not particularly conducive to such comparisons in that 1979 represented the peak of a business cycle, and 1985 was not higher than 1979, and thus arguably the potential productivity per employee is understated, and Medlik's forecasts for the period 1985–1990 were for stronger growth. However, Medlik's work again illustrates the difficulties involved in assessing productivity and consequent economic impacts. The period of the 1980s has been one of a retailing revolution with a greater use of EPoS (electronic point of sale) systems, and a reinforcement of trends towards more economic retail operations using edge of town and purpose shopping centres. Thus, within Medlik's definition of the tourism sector there is included the retail sector to take into account the proposition that tourist expenditure involves shopping. In calculating the productivity of tourism labour the use of national retailing data poses problems. The shopping experience of the tourist will vary considerably upon destination, and whilst the retail revolution is fuelled by the multiples, for many tourists part of the holiday experience is shopping in smaller, locally owned outlets. Secondly, it may be argued that increases of productivity in retailing have little to do with tourism expenditure, but more to do with the adoption of EPoS and other factors, and thus to allocate such increases in retail productivity to tourism is slightly misleading. On the other hand, there is a movement towards a combination of retail and leisure activities as evidenced by West Edmonton Mall and the Metro Centre, and there is no doubt that some types of tourism and tourists will actively seek out the newer, more productive, forms of retailing.

It must also be recognised that the measurement of productivity in the tourism industry is itself a difficult task. Medlik (1988) uses financial measures, and hence the value of turnover is a key measure. Thus amongst the measures that might be used are:

a) the ratio between the turnover of the unit and the total payroll, i.e. wages plus pension, insurance costs etc.;

b) the value added (i.e. sales minus purchases of goods and services) divided by payroll;

c) total turnover divided by number employed;

d) total value added divided by number employed.

Under such circumstances the value added per employee might therefore be no more than a reflection of increases in prices, and not of volume of output. Hence such measures must attempt to take into account inflation, and in particular not simply a weighting by the average retail or consumers prices index, but the actual rate of inflation in tourist-related industries, for example, hotel tariffs. Equally, 'productivity' may seem to suffer, but this may be due to an increase in the cost of the hotelier's raw resources. From the viewpoint of the host community, whilst productivity may appear to suffer because wages increase, thus reducing the ratio between turnover and payroll, the additional wages being spent in the host community might in fact be beneficial. Consequently, the issues of productivity within tourism are, to put it mildly, somewhat complex. Even utilising the methods indicated above, the productivity of labour in the tourism sector would nonetheless still appear to be marginally below that of other service industries. For the economy as a whole, for the period 1979 to 1985, tourism labour productivity may be as much as 20% below the norm (Medlik, 1988).

The economic impact implications are thus relatively clear. Not only are the income multipliers reduced by reasons of comparatively low levels of pay, but the position is reinforced by most of that labour force being comparatively unqualified, and hence not able to command higher levels of wages in the labour market generally. Add to this the fact that, by reason of high levels of casual and temporary employment, it becomes more difficult for trade unions to organise themselves. Then again wage levels (and hence multipliers) are not as high as they might otherwise be. But even to this statement there are caveats. In circumstances where the tourist industry is a major employer, and a significant contributor to overall economic growth, it escapes from being marginal to becoming part of the main economic processes. Under these circumstances, it becomes possible for labour to command higher wage levels, given perhaps exceptional circumstances. An example of this occurred in Spain in the period after the death of Franco and the democratisation of the Spanish Constitution. The recognition of trade unions and the popularity and enthusiasm for democratic action led to the Spanish unions being able to increase wage levels in the hotels trading on the Spanish Costas.

To argue that wage levels are low, that labour is comparatively unskilled, and that employment may be at best seasonal may be in part an explanation for low multiplier values, but it is not in itself an argument that attempts to improve local economies might be better undertaken by means other than encouraging tourism. In many cases, whether it be in the Third World, or in the areas of higher than national averages of unemployment in advanced economies, the support structures for any industry tend to be weak. Consequently, weak multipliers from tourism may be no more than a reflection of deficiencies in such economic systems. If labour is comparatively unskilled, if there are shortages of assets and infrastructure, then almost by definition any economic activity will suffer. Evidence for this exists from work undertaken by the Tourism and Recreation Research Unit at Edinburgh University. In 1976 Brownrigg and Greig were arguing the then conventional wisdom that:

> the benefits from tourism expenditure are more apparent than real – it involves a lot of noise and activity but, at the end of the day, locals have surprisingly little to show for it.

By 1981 the Unit was reporting on the basis of work undertaken in the Exmoor National Park that whilst the multiplier from hotels was but 0.22, this actually compared well with the norm of 0.26 for mixed farming and livestock activities, and was actually higher than the 0.13 found in manufacturing processes taking place in the area. The highest multiplier of 0.70 related to bed and breakfast accommodation. Certainly in the case of rural economies, tourism is actually attracted to those regions by the very fact that they are under-developed. From this viewpoint tourism does generate flows of income that would not otherwise be forthcoming, although the social and environmental impacts of mass tourism in such areas might arguably create urban style problems (and costs) in areas still without the infrastructure of cities and towns.

In the above discussion the assumption has been made that multiplier processes are positive in nature, and that they create additional incomes. But they may also create additional costs. Hanna (1976) makes this point. He writes:

> For many practical purposes, it is crucial to appreciate that the local multiplier studies of economic gains are just that, and no more. They leave three questions unanswered. First, what are the costs? . . . But a more important question arises from the intensely narrow viewpoint of local economic analyses, whether for tourism or any other activity. The local multipliers measure the gains locally; so what will be the gains nationally? . . . Rational planning must take account of the whole benefit, not just the local benefit. The third question arises as the obverse of the second; what about the gains to an area through the secondary economic effects of tourism in other areas? Just as tourism in a small area 'leaks' benefits to other areas outside, so each small area gains the indirect benefit of 'leaks' from other areas.

In any assessment of the economic impact of tourism it must be recognised that the resources allocated to tourism are denied to other means of development, and thus the opportunity cost of tourism should be taken into account.

One says 'should', because it is a valid question to ask whether or not finances ploughed into a tourism development might not have generated a higher economic return if they had been invested into other commercial enterprises. However, the calculations of such a process might be even more complex in its data requirements than attempting to calculate the multiplier! Certainly there is evidence that tourism may have unlooked for costs. Many of these are social and environmental in nature, as discussed in Chapters six and seven, but it is possible to give a few examples here. In July 1987, the Dutch company, Sports Huis, opened its leisure centre in Sherwood Forest, having as its central feature a dome containing water amenities facilities in a constant temperature of about 80°F, and set in parkland with other sports facilities. In 1988 Councillor Carol Turner, Chair of Central Nottinghamshire Community Health Council, commenting on her Health Authority's report that in the 12 months since Center Parcs opened nearly 400 people from the complex attended Mansfield General Hospital's Accident and Emergency Department, stated:

> the County and the Districts are all pushing for tourism and Central Notts is one of the main areas because of Sherwood Forest. But they ought to be considering the likely impact. If you bring more people in, even if it is only on a daily basis, it's going to create extra demand on health services.

Murphy (1985) quotes the circumstances surrounding the building of Florida's Disney World where unskilled construction workers were attracted to the site with the result that the local Salvation Army was forced into an appeal for $400,000 to build a new shelter, the City had to employ 150 more police and build a new $6 million police station to deal with the problems of prostitution, drugs, hippies and migrants attracted to the site.

Input-output analysis

One of the means of assessing the impact of tourist expenditure on other areas of the economic system is the use of input-output analysis. This technique attempts to show the flow of economic transactions through the economy within a given time span, usually a year. It is a further refinement of the basic multiplier processes in that it seeks to show the inter-relationship between defined sectors of the economic system. Traditionally undertaken with industrial sectors, its transference to service, and in particular, tourism sectors, is partly handicapped by the lack of definition of what exactly is the tourism industry. Whilst it may be defined as a series of consumer experiences relating to leisure and recreation requiring trips away from home, in terms of a supply-led definition there is a problem from the statistical viewpoint in that, formally, there is no standard industrial classification. Smith (1989) highlights the problem thus:

> Tourism often lacks credibility in the eyes of policy analysts and decision-makers because the field is poorly defined and because the data used to substantiate many of the claims concerning the size and importance of the industry are inadequate . . . A data-collection problem even more frustrating than double-counting is the omission of data.

Within many countries there is no Standard Industrial Classification (SIC) code for the 'tourism industry', and so attempts to show the pattern of flows of expenditure between economic sectors often require the researcher to utilise sub-categories, estimate proportions of a sector or sub-sector that tourism might account for, or even ignore some activities. For example, for a restaurant located in a city, how much of its lunch-time trade might be trade to local office workers, and how much to tourists who are visiting?

Table 5.5 Employment directly and indirectly due to tourism in the UK economy

Industry group	% of employment due to tourism
Agriculture	0.22
Extractive	1.86
Food, drink, and tobacco	0.48
Chemicals and allied industries	1.13
Metals, engineering and vehicles	1.26
Textiles, leather and clothing	0.26
Other manufacturing	2.53
Construction	0.36
Gas, electricity and water	1.41
Road transport	6.89
Rail transport	12.61
Other transport	9.46
Communications	8.13
Distributive trades	2.47
Other services	9.58

Source: Richards, Tourism and the economy (1972)

Inspite of the difficulties, some attempts have been made to undertake such an analysis. Richards (1972) constructed a matrix covering 27 UK industrial sectors, and Bangor University subsequently used similar methods to develop analyses for areas of Wales. This type of approach permits estimations of the impact of tourism on other sectors of the economy, for instance, the employment that tourism generates. For example, Richards calculated that tourism accounted for 12.61 per cent of employment in the rail transport industry, and 1.13 per cent in the chemicals industry. Richards' findings are indicated in Table 5.5. It cannot however be over-emphasised just how difficult it is to undertake such estimates. Archer and Owen (1971), Murphy (1983), Mathieson and Wall (1982) and Smith (1989) all indicate the difficulties associated with such techniques. Yet there are many instances where, inspite of these difficulties, researchers have utilised findings from one area and applied them to another. Vaughan (1986) indicates the types of assumptions that researchers are thus making:

> This method, therefore, assumes that the pattern of spending, and in some cases the total amount, in the area in which the original study was conducted is the same as in the area for which the estimates are being made. It also assumes that the combinations of business types are the same.

As a result of these difficulties many authorities have sought to assess tourism impacts on a smaller scale. In addition, for many such authorities concerned with particular projects, there is more sense in concentrating on the particular rather than the general, although it becomes possible to project (albeit cautiously) to the slightly wider impact.

TOURISM AND THE BALANCE OF PAYMENTS

There is at least one further impact of tourism that requires some consideration, and that is its impact on the balance of payments. In the case of developing countries one rationale for tourism is that it is a means of earning foreign (hard) currencies, and indeed may be one of the only few means for such economies to earn export revenue. This becomes especially important at times when world prices for raw commodities such as sugar, rubber and minerals may not be high. In the case of developing countries, however, the expected earnings may not be as high as initially hoped for, especially if they are dependent upon tour operators and airlines that are based in the tourist-generating countries. In the case of package holidays, approximately 40 per cent of the cost paid by the tourist will relate to the travel to the tourist-receiving country, and that is usually paid to the airline within the tourist-generating country; an airline that may itself be a subsidiary of the tour operator. An approximation of the tour operator's cost structure indicates how little of the tourist's expenditure actually reaches the tourist-receiving country. Indeed, it may be as little as approximately one-third of the package holiday price paid by the tourist (see Table 5.6). Consequently, the importance of the expenditure by the tourist at the holiday destination on souvenirs and other elements of the holiday can be seen as being important in terms of generating income for the host society.

Table 5.6   Approximation of British tour operator's cost structure for an inclusive tour (% of total revenue received)

	%	
Cost of transport	40	Payment retained within tourist-
Commission to agent	10	generating country
Cost of printing brochures	8	
Cost of staff administration	6	
Gross margin	3	
Payment to hotelier	30	Payment received by tourist-
Payment for transfer from airport to hotel and other miscellaneous services	3	receiving country
Total	100	

In terms of payment to the hotelier, much of this is in turn used by the hotelier for the purchase of imports. Evidence for this comes from studies undertaken by the Caribbean Tourism Research Centre in its study of the linkages between tourism and local agriculture (1984). In the case of St Lucia in 1983, 58 per cent of the food consumed by tourists was estimated to have been imported. In particular, 82 per cent of the meat eaten by tourists was imported. However, Henshall-Momsen (1986) notes that in many cases hotels in the initial stages of tourism attempt to provide tourists with the diet that reflects the eating patterns of the tourist-generating country, and only subsequently introduce more local foods cooked in the local manner. To the imports of food, must also be added the importing of furniture. However, increasingly, tourists will adopt the cuisine of the host country, and indeed some types of tourists will actively seek an 'authentic' experience. The Caribbean again provides an example of this with the development since 1978 of the 'SuperClub' hotels which are owned by Jamaican businessmen. One of their hotels, 'Jamaica Jamaica' specifically seeks to reproduce a Jamaican 'experience' rather than an 'international' one.

The developing country, in its attempts to build up tourism, must also import many other commodities. In his study of the role played by the establishment of National Parks in Africa as a tourist-generating asset, Marsh (1986) notes that park lodges are often constructed with imported materials, have foreign staff, park agency vehicles such as Land Rovers are imported and National Park tours are organised by foreign companies that repatriate profits. The host country is further disadvantaged by the fact that it may not have well-established banking facilities that are located in the tourist-generating country. Tourists buy their travellers' cheques in the country of trip origin, and it is their banks who obtain the first round of commission. It is the banks in the tourist-receiving country which sustain the costs of remitting the cheques back to the original issuer. If the tourists use their credit card, it is the retailer in the tourist-receiving area who pays the fee to the card issuer, whilst the bank in the issuing country receives the interest on any loan that is made.

The high propensities to import, and the high percentage of the tourists' expenditure that actually never leaves the shores of the tourist-generating country, thus means that the net gains to the tourist-receiving country are less than might otherwise be expected. In the case of the Caribbean area the Caribbean Tourism Research Centre estimated that, in 1979, out of total earnings of US$3.3 billion, just over one-third was retained. Lea (1988) quotes the example of Fiji where approximately only 20 per cent of tourist earnings are retained.

Whilst the developing tourist-receiving countries may not gain as much as might at first sight seem possible, it is nonetheless important to remember the fact that such countries do actually receive a surplus on their tourism balance of payments. This is not the case for many developed countries, which, as the tourist generators, actually sustain deficits on their balance of payments from the tourism account. These deficits can be regarded not simply as 'leakages' within their own economies, but, possibly optimistically, as a means by which monies are transferred from the richer nations to the poorer. Whether the social costs associated with such earnings are worth the revenue is, however, a question that needs to be considered. Nor must it be seen as axiomatic that richer nations sustain deficits on their tourism balance of payments. For example, Britain has often sustained a surplus on its tourism invisibles.

Determinants of the local impact of tourism

The economic impacts of tourism are thus complex to assess. From the above, it is however possible to begin to identify some of the variables which will determine the value of the impact. These can be summarised as being:

a) the nature of the tourist facilities and their attractions
The size of the tourist destination and its context is important. Can the tourist destination absorb large numbers of tourists and does it have the necessary infrastructure, both physically and economically to not only support any given number of tourists but to also retain tourist expenditures within its own area?

b) the volume, and nature, of the tourists and their spending patterns
Can the area sustain tourists requiring overnight stays, or is it simply meeting a need for day visits? What are the forms of accommodation that are available? Are the tourists visiting all the year round, or simply at certain times of the year? Do they tend to patronise local businesses? Do they require resources from outside the host community?

c) the skills of the host community and the levels of, and numbers of, jobs held by them
Do tourist organisations import labour of all types, or can the local labour force meet the requirement of the tourist enterprises?

d) are local tourist facilities owned by members of the host community? What is the size of these businesses? To what extent are they locally financed?

TOURISM MULTIPLIERS – A FULLER STATEMENT

Archer's Tourist Expenditure Model for estimating the multiplier effects for tourist expenditure is as follows.

$$1 + \sum_{j=1}^{N} \sum_{i=1}^{n} Q_j K_{ij} V_i \times \frac{1}{1 - L \sum_{i=1}^{n} X_i Z_i V_i}$$

where: j = types of tourist accommodation, 1 . . . N
i = types of consumer outlet, 1 . . . N
Q = the proportions spent on each type of accommodation
K = the proportions spent on each type of consumer outlet
N, n = numbers of types of tourist accommodation and outlets
V = the income generation in each category of expenditure
Z = the proportion of income spent within the region by the inhabitants
L = average propensity to consume

The above gives an aggregated model for tourist expenditure, but what is important is to disaggregate data to assess the multiplier values associated with different types of accommodation and tourist activity. Archer and Owen (1971) suggest the following form.

The multiplier for a given category of accommodation is:

$$1 + \sum_{i=1}^{n} K_i V_i \times \frac{1}{1 - L \sum_{i=1}^{n} X_i Z_i V_i}$$

where K_i = the proportion spent on each type of consumer outlet
V_i = the income generation in each category of accommodation
L = the propensity to consume
X_i = the pattern of consumer spending

Z_i = the proportion of income spent within the region by the inhabitants.

Wheeller, in his study undertaken for the Wales Tourist Board, comments that the estimation procedure thereby falls into two parts, the income generation associated with each item of tourist expenditure (the direct effect) and the multiplier effect of the spending of this income within the local area by residents. To assess the income each activity needs to be separately identified, and Archer and Owen (1971) identified separate values for:

a) tourist expenditure on hotel and guest house accommodation;
b) income generation of tourist expenditure in hiring stationary caravans;
c) income generation of tourist expenditure in farmhouses and bed and breakfast houses;
d) income generation of tourist expenditure on camping;
e) income generation of expenditure in shops;
f) income generated by tourist expenditure in garages;
g) income generation from money circulating into rates and building.

In seeking to calculate the value of the multiplier, technically the calculations need to take into account the proportion of expenditure that arises from additions to income resulting from tourism, but in practice it is simpler to use the average propensity to consume, rather than the marginal propensity to consume. Arguably, within the short term, if spending patterns are consistent by the recipients of tourism expenditure, then by definition the average propensity to consume (APC) is equal to the marginal propensity to consume (MPC). Practically, the APC is a much easier figure to collect from respondents.

One of the major problems is evident, and that is the information requirements. Without surveys, there is usually little regional data that can be used. Thus, for example, in the original study undertaken on Anglesey, Archer and Owen (1971) had to use an estimated APC drawn from national data of 0.9, which itself was an estimate where the Family Expenditure Survey indicated a value of 0.84 for Rural Households, whilst National Income Tables gave a value of 0.93. Another practical problem Ryan and Connor (1981) came across was in estimating proportions of retail expenditure in areas where tourism is still developing, in that retailers have difficulty in assessing the proportion of sales that are accounted for by visitors, whilst the nature of the retail mix is also important. In practice, many multiplier studies do not go beyond the first couple of rounds of the process. It is also difficult to check the results that are obtained, although one method is to utilise input-output analysis, but again the feasibility of this will be constrained by the availability of the required data. If a multiplier study is being considered, it is also important to be able to identify the nature of the activities undertaken by tourists, and their comparative importance. For example, within a Canadian context, the role of the outfitters will be of importance, within the UK, day-trip activity will be important, within an Australian context, beach use is important. The nature of the tourist destination zone is a significant variable, and is thus another reason why the non-survey techniques described by Vaughan (1986) are of limited usefulness.

Chapter 6

The ecological impacts of tourism

It is not difficult to make the case that tourism is damaging to the environment. Mader (1988) comments that on any Sundays when the weather is fine 6,000 cars drive to Grindelwald, and in doing so consume 80,000 litres of gasoline to produce 9 tons of carbon monoxide, 1.3 tons of hydrocarbon, 1.7 litres of nitrogen and 24 lbs of lead. Examples of the potential conflict between tourism development projects and a wish to conserve and protect areas of outstanding beauty, or areas of importance to wildlife, are not uncommon. The scale and location of the tourist development might vary, but the nature of the conflict in many cases remains the same. The concern of this chapter is to examine, by giving examples, the types of conflicts that have arisen and then to argue that even whilst tourism may in places threaten the environment, equally, those factors that cause adverse changes in our bio-systems also adversely affect the quality of the tourist experience. Finally, the chapter looks at some of the ways the negative impacts of tourism might be minimised.

TOURISM AND THE ENVIRONMENT – A GENERAL INTRODUCTION

a) Tourism as a threat to the environment

The impact of the tourist upon nature can be considerable and is not restricted to the major tourist development areas. One example of significant impact can be found in the Alps (Mader 1988). Approximately 40–50 million people visit the Alps every year, and these tourists are supported by an infrastructure of more than 40,000 ski runs and 12,000 ski lifts and cable railways. Previously unvisited areas are continually being made accessible. Bulldozers reshape the mountains, and trees are felled. The result is that the drainage patterns are continually being altered. The trees are no longer present to halt the rush of melting waters; the roads, trails and hardened soil become ducts by which waters are carried further than before. In 1983, the area around Axamer Lizum, in Austria, which had been developed for the 1964 and 1976 Winter Olympics, suffered from mud slides caused, according to environmental conservationists, by the bulldozing of the area to create 68 hectares of ski runs. It would appear that landslides are becoming more common, and in 1987, 23 people were killed in a landslide at the camping site near Annecy in the French Alps, while 3 villages were buried in a landslide at Valtellina in the Italian Alps.

In the Himalayas the trek to Everest is so well established a tourist path that in 1989 a special expedition was mounted to clean up the litter that lay around base camp. To obtain hot water to meet the needs of tourists for a wash and shower after their day's trek, wood is cut down (Tuting 1989). It has been estimated that the trekking tourist burns about 14 lbs of wood per day with the result of further deforestation (Mader 1988), resulting in damage to the water drainage patterns. The Nepalese government has thus had to develop schemes of afforestation, whilst stopping local people from using wood for heating, a practice previously carried out from time immemorial. The costs of tourism thus include afforestation, and the starting of hydro-electric and other electrification schemes (Cullen 1986).

Just as the physical environment is threatened, so too is the flora and fauna. Renton (1989) describes the impact of tourism upon the breeding habits of the loggerhead turtle on the Greek island of Zakynthos thus:

> A female, on average, lays five nests a summer, and can hope that two or three of her hatchlings will survive natural predators at sea and hope to make it to adulthood. But these statistics are thrown awry on beaches where man plays.
>
> The first hazard the mother turtle faces is from motor boats and jet-skis as she approaches her ancestral breeding ground; the noise can send her back to sea . . . . Then, on the beach, plastic bags get mistaken for jellyfish, and are eaten with fatal mistakes. Should she manage to lay her eggs undisturbed, they are then at the mercy of sandcastle diggers, cars and motorbikes or even people planting beach umbrellas.
>
> But the most dangerous time is at hatching. As the young turtles scuttle to the surf, any light or noise can disorientate them. Then they can wander off to eventually die of dehydration and heat exhaustion.

The example of Zakynthos represents, in a small way, the nature of the conflict between tourism and the environment. Until 1977 the beach at Laganas was comparatively under-developed, but in 1982 it was necessary for the Greek authorities to impose a ban on building. In the following year the Sea Turtle Protection Society was formed, and in 1986 an EC funded monitoring project was commenced. By 1987 it became necessary to impose bans upon beach use between dawn and dusk and, similarly, bans were being imposed upon the use of speed boats. For those attracted to the tourism industry from the rural hinterland, and who have invested

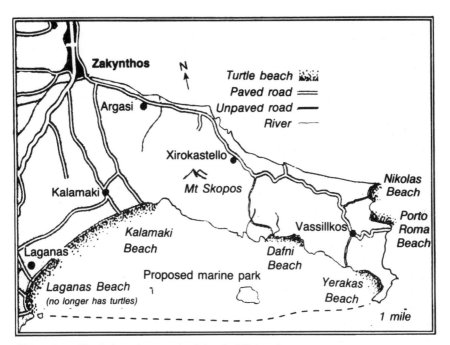

Figure 6.1   Turtle beaches on the island of Zakynthos
Reproduced from the *Independent* 5 August 1989.

family savings in the paraphernalia of the modern beach tourism industry, the turtles have become a threat. Occupancy rates in the hotels have fallen as the foreign tour operators move their business elsewhere; the landowners at Yerakas, who hoped to take advantage of the tourist, now find that their hopes will probably come to naught even whilst on other areas of the island development is still permitted. At the time of writing, the proposed solution of creating a new form of tourism upon a marine park where no motor boats will be permitted, is still being discussed by the Greek Ministry of the Environment. A similar debate continues on the island of Cyprus, where, to the west of Paphos, again lie one of the few remaining breeding locations of the loggerhead.

However, there is evidence that tourism might still threaten the wildlife that tourists come to see (Myers 1972, Reusberger 1977, Rivers 1974). The lions of the National Parks of Africa may have their feeding and breeding activities interrupted as tourist-laden Land Rovers surround them so that tourists can take photographs. Predator/prey and migratory behaviour may be disrupted (Carbyn 1974, World Tourism Organisation 1983). West, a gorilla expert based at Bristol Zoo, has expressed concern that tourism, whilst offering opportunities to save the gorillas of Rwanda, might also threaten them. He states:

Too many visits from tourists could prevent gorillas from breeding.
They live in a fragile habitat, and the damaging of footpaths and the
lighting of camp fires, will stop them from living their normal lives.
We have to regard the gorilla population in Rwanda as one that is going
extinct. [As gorillas are closely linked to humans] they can pick up
human ailments such as colds, flu, pneumonia and measles – a disease
like measles can kill a gorilla. Before tourists get close to gorillas they
ought to be screened for infection.

Nor are the examples of tourism damage restricted to 'exotic' locations.
Within Britain, the National Parks are under considerable stress. In 1979
there were approximately 90 million visits a year to the National Parks. A
decade later there were 100 million, and the Brecon Beacons, Dartmoor,
the Lake District, North York Moors, the Peak District, Snowdonia and
the Yorkshire Dales were all reporting problems of footpath erosion. The
upland environments, with their slow plant growth, are vulnerable to
damage, and the usual problem is one where people tread the top surface
away. The grass becomes worn, is unable to grow, and the result is a
muddy path. The trail then becomes wider as people make a detour from
the muddy morass, or, in dry weather, the rutted uneven path, and use the
grass borders of the path. This in turn becomes eroded, and thus the path
becomes wider over time. In 1987 a survey was undertaken of National
Trust coast line which sought to record the patterns of use and the
ecological damage arising from recreational and tourism activities. Edwards
(1987) then analysed the sensitivity of land types to recreational usage, and
found that, in effect, the damage was dependent upon the nature and
intensity of the activity and the nature of the soil. In addition, however,
the environmental impacts of tourism were both direct and indirect. Thus,
for example, there would be direct damage from wheeled traffic on grassy
areas, whilst there would be indirect damage resulting from disturbance
effects. Further, this is damage that relates solely to normal use patterns,
and does not take into account the problems that can arise from litter,
vandalism or other irresponsible behaviour.

At other times the proposed tourism-orientated developments threaten
natural habitats more directly. Apparently deserted areas may contain areas
of specific ecological value. For example, proposals for the development of a
barrage across the rivers Ely and Taff in Cardiff in 1989 directly threatened
the very existence of mudflats which were a Site of Special Scientific
Interest, and the habitat of perhaps as many as 4,200 dunlin (Davies
1988). On other occasions the threat posed is primarily an aesthetic one.
The Scottish Scenic Trust in 1989 prepared a list of housing developments,
which included a group of chalets on the island of Mull, as part of its
campaign for stronger controls on new housing in the unspoilt areas of the
highlands and islands. In many such locations housing development is for

holiday homes or the building of timeshare complexes, as has happened in the Lake District. Indeed, the Lake District, Britain's largest National Park, failed to achieve the status of a World Heritage Site, inspite of its undoubted beauty and literary connotations with Wordsworth and the other Lake District poets. This was in part due to the stresses caused on the road systems and the levels of congestion.

In other cases the sheer volume of tourism development causes a total change in landscape. Barrett (1989) compares the development of the Algarve with the onslaught of the industrial revolution in the valleys of South Wales in these terms:

> This frenzied activity is how it must have been in the South Wales valleys at the start of the industrial revolution: endless digging, building and labouring. In those days the commodities were coal, iron and steel. In the Algarve today they labour for tourism. But the results are similar. Clifftop by clifftop, beach by beach, valley by valley — the natural beauty of the countryside is being eroded. No dark satanic mills or slag heaps, perhaps, but the landscape here is being disfigured just as badly by tower blocks of hotels and apartments.

The quality of development in such resort areas is often questionable. There may be a concern with quantity rather than quality in the rush to ensure that the new crop of the post-industrial world, the tourist, is housed and fed. The result of such developments is often a tourist complex which could be located on any part of the Mediterranean coastline, so indistinguishable is it from its counterparts. Even the signposts are the same, in a mixture of Northern European languages.

Nor must it be thought that the damaging effects of tourism are restricted to the large scale. Small examples can be found in almost any location where visitors come to stare. At the site of Gabriel Dumont's grave at Batoche National Historic Park, Canada, the site of the 1885 rebellion in Canada, the effects of trampling on the grass before the grave can already be seen, for the grass is worn away. Areas with comparatively little tourism might also feel the effects of tourism, albeit perhaps as just one more component of environmental change which threatens the status quo of the existing habitat. For example, in the lakes of northern Canada increasingly strict limits are being imposed on the amount of fish that can be caught, or game that can be shot, as the tourist hunter adds to the problems being caused by wider environmental change. In 1989, the limits on fishing in the Prince Albert National Park had once again to be reduced due to a diminishing stock of fish.

This apparent sorry story of negative impacts perhaps has two underlying themes. The first is that tourism brings not only the clients to the unspoilt area, but currently also brings much of the support structure that the clients are used to in their home environment. The beauty of the

Table 6.1   The sensitivity of and ecological damage due to, recreation and tourism

	Cliff tops	Quarries	Rocky shores	Shingle	Sand dune	Salt marshes	Mud	Reed beds	Wood-land
Off road vehicles	++ $	− $	−	+++	++++ $	+	+	+	++ $
Camping caravans	+++ $	− $	−	++ $	++++ $	+	+	+	+++ $
Trampling	++ $	+ $	− $	++ $	+++ $	+ $	−	− $	− $
Path erosion	++++ $	+	++ $	++ $	+++ $	+ $	−	−	− $
Horseriding	+ $	+ $	−	++	++++ $	+	−	−	+ $
Diving	−	−	++ $	−	−	−	−	−	−
Canoeing	−	−	−	−	+	+	+*	+*	−
Powerboating	−	−	−	−	+	+	+*	+*	−
Sailing	−	−	−	+	+	+	+*	+*	−
Windsurfing	−	−	−	−	−	+*	++*	++* $	−
Rockclimbing	+ $	+	−	−	−	−	−	−	−
Wildfowling	−	−	−	−	−	++*	++*	−	−
Fishing and bait digging	−	−	−	−	−	++	++ $	−	−
National history interest	−	+ $	+ $	+* $	+ $	+ $	−	+* $	−

Key: −   little or no sensitivity
  +   slightly sensitive
  ++   moderately sensitive
  +++ highly sensitive
  *   effect due to disturbance
  $ recorded damage within heritage coasts

Source: Edwards, J. 'The UK heritage coasts – an assessment of the ecological impacts of tourism', *Annals of tourism research* vol. 14 no. 1 (1987)

unspoilt area is to be enjoyed along with all the comforts of home, modern sanitation, hot and cold running water, as well as the luxury of being on holiday. The problem then becomes intensified by the very numbers of visitors. Sax (1980) describes this process thus:

Tourism in parks today . . . is often little more than an extension of the city and its lifestyle transposed onto a scenic background. At its extreme in Yosemite Valley or at the south rim of the Grand Canyon, for example, one finds all the artefacts of urban life: traffic jams, long lines waiting in restaurants, supermarkets, taverns, fashionable shops, night life, prepared entertainments, and the unending drone of motors.

Sessa (1988) refers to this process as the development of urban tourist poles, and perceives it to be an important part in the development of the 'econo-tourism system'.

But there is yet a further added twist to this process, and that is that the imported life style is not necessarily that of the host community. The English bars dominate the southern Spanish coastline, and the Japanese signs and businesses are abundant in Banff National Park, Canada. Searle (1989) traces the growth of the 'Cineplex with 40,000 square feet of retail space soon to open, the 16 luxury condominiums available soon' at Banff, and the expansion of the township to over 10,000 permanent residents within the National Park.

b) Tourism as the ally of the environment

But there is a second important issue. Tourism is not the sole cause of environmental change. Nor is it simply an agent of negative or detrimental change upon the environment. It, too, is adversely affected by the threats to the environment caused by pollution. Again the evidence is easy to find in reports that come from around the world. It is, for example, well known that Bondi Beach is not the paradise that it has been painted to be, located as it is near one of Sydney's three sewage outlets which spills out on North Bondi. In January 1989 a clean-up operation, in which 20,000 Sydneysiders participated, produced 3,000 tons of rubbish, amongst which there were 5 cars, 3,000 hypodermic needles, 1,000 used condoms, tyres, shopping trolleys, mattresses and the body of a dead man, believed to be that of a missing Sydney fisherman (Milliken 1989). Jackman (1988) describes the north beach of Scarborough, where the resident population of 52,000 doubles in the summer, as one where:

Bacteria lie in wait — capable of causing diarrhoea, vomiting, salmonella, enteritis, hepatitis, cystitis, skin rashes, infections of the nose, ear and throat, and for unvaccinated swimmers, even typhoid and polio.

In consequence, in 1989, a £12 million scheme, which included a sewage treatment plant, was commenced by the resort to overcome the possible impacts of such sewage on its tourism trade.

Nor is the debris of the modern world to be found in highly populated zones which also happen to be major recreational and tourist resort areas. In 1988 it was reported that even on the uninhabited island of Amchitka in the Aleutians off Alaska, the US National Marine Fisheries Service found 1,375 lbs of plastic litter on a beach just a mile long (Smith 1988). In a world of linked ecological chains the potential cause for disaster may be found many miles away from the tourist resort area. In 1989 the tourist trade of the Italian Adriatic was adversely affected, and on many days the sunny coastline was empty as the media across Europe showed pictures of a mysterious algae that bloomed in the sun upon the waters of the Mediterranean. Hotel occupancies fell as the British and German holidaymaker switched to alternative destinations. The toxicity of the algae was such that it was thought to be harmless, but sun, sea and beach holidaymakers are not ones to take risks, and hence the Italian tourism industry suffered. The cause was unknown, but one theory was that it was related to the fertilisers and pesticides being used by the farmers of the North Italian plains, whilst others blamed industrial pollution, and others a mild winter (Hallenstein 1989, Sheridan 1989).

Tourism thus also suffers from the pollution of the environment that is caused by patterns of modern life and production methods. The acid rain that kills the forests of Germany, or those of Scandinavia, also indirectly threatens the tourism interests of those areas. In theory therefore, the tourism industry can become an ally of environmental conservationist groups, as there is a common cause in preserving the quality of the landscape. Examples do exist where tourist business organisations have appreciated the need to enhance landscapes so as to simultaneously enhance the quality of the tourist experience. Perhaps the most successful of these partnerships have been within the urban landscape, as property developers, local government authorities, hotel groups and others respond to a growth of interest in industrial heritage and recreational time. This has led to the development of previously derelict waterfronts, old areas of warehousing and factory plant, and also to attempts to enhance central business districts in towns to combat the move to the suburbs. An example of this type of process is provided by Salford docks on the Manchester Ship Canal. In 1980 Salford Council began a long process of renewal of the 150 acres of land and water that was characterised by rusting wrecks of old machinery, and desolate waste land inhabited by a large population of rats. Their initial attempts came to naught, but in 1982 they allocated 30 acres to a local businessman, Ted Hagan, with the mandate that he could retain the freehold on the 30 acres if in turn he could generate £9 million of investment within 3 years. With council cooperation, this target was achieved, and within five years a complex of residential homes, hotels, retail outlets and offices and workshops had replaced the devastated area. Similar examples can be found the world over. Harbourplace in Baltimore attracts 20 million visitors each year and has become a model for other developments. Toronto has changed 100 acres of under-used, derelict waterfront into an urban park. Sydney has created for itself a new asset in the Darling Harbour which has not only replaced what was formerly known as the 'City Sink' into attractive surroundings, but has also generated 10,000 permanent jobs (Collinge 1988). Ghirardelli Square in San Francisco today plays host to street theatre for both its residents and 14 million tourists, whilst Faneuil Hall has become an inherent part of Boston.

In addition, examples can be found where tourist organisations have sought to develop tourist complexes in harmony with their surroundings, and indeed to improve upon the existing scenery. Center Parcs in Nottinghamshire have developed a site within Sherwood Forest which featured the planting of several thousands of trees, the creation of a 15-acre lake, a nature reserve, a deer sanctuary and improvement of existing drainage patterns. In addition they also planned not only an existing pattern of footpaths through the forest, but also future routes, so as to avoid the problems associated with over-trampling. All this was done in what was previously 400 monotonous acres of commercial Corsican Pine (Phillips 1988). There are many schemes which attempt to develop networks of paths that permit exploration of an area without threatening wildlife, and the use of cork chips, wooden boardwalks and other techniques can minimise path erosion problems. But all too often such schemes are restricted to public-funded bodies or their like, or, if in the commercial sector, relate to the immediate environment of the commercial organisation concerned. In the case of the package holiday, the tour operator and the travel agent usually undertake little direct investment in the areas where they take the tourist. Often it is argued that they will comply with local laws and regulations, and will only use those institutions and organisations that concur with legal requirements. Until comparatively recently there was but little evidence that tour operators questioned the validity of local laws, whether they related to aspects such as the fire regulations of hotels, or the fact that tourist complexes are being built in areas of ecological value. Pfafflin (1987) quotes one speaker from the tour operator industry at the Third World Ecumenical European Conference as stating 'Development aid is not our task. Our aim is profit.' Today, however, some companies, particularly smaller tour operators, are beginning to warn their clients about fragile eco-systems and are seeking to improve matters, but such movements are still embryonic.

THE CONCEPT OF 'GREEN TOURISM'

Tourism has a potential for both good and ill, and in assessing the problems that tourism does create, such problems must be placed within the context that many other industries have far more direct impacts upon water quality, fauna and flora distribution. Can the potential situations of harm be identified? The World Tourism Organisation (1983) identifies five situations where tourism might harm the environment, these being:

a) alteration of the ecological situation of regions where the environment was previously in good condition both from the natural, cultural and human viewpoints;
b) speculative pressures leading to destruction of landscape and natural habitat;
c) the occupation of space and creation of activities producing irreconcilable land-use conflicts;
d) damage to traditional values in the zones concerned and a lowering of standards on the human scale in existing developments;
e) progressive over-capacity which drains the environmental quality of the area concerned.

In recognition of the problems posed by tourism developments some writers have sought to promote the concept of 'Green Tourism'. Amongst the foremost of these is Jost Krippendorf, who, in his book, *The Holidaymakers* (1987), argues that tourism should be consistent with its environment, and arise naturally from the activities that are natural to the area. To that end, he quotes examples from the Swiss Cantons where the host communities have sought to impose regulations that limit tourism within what might be termed the carrying capacities of the area. This viewpoint is endorsed by Phillips (1988), who, in relation to rural tourism, propounds six principles, these, briefly being:

a) The promotion of tourist enjoyment of the countryside should be primarily aimed at those activities which draw on the character of the countryside itself, its beauty, culture, history and wildlife.
b) Tourism development in the countryside should assist conservation and recreation, by bringing new uses to historic buildings, supplementing the income of farmers, and aiding the reclamation of derelict land.
c) The planning, design, siting and management of new tourist developments should be in keeping with the landscape, and wherever possible, seek to enhance it.
d) Investment in tourism should support the rural economy whilst encouraging a wider geographical and temporal spread so as to avoid problems of congestion and damage through over-use.

e) Those who benefit from rural tourism should contribute to the conservation and enhancement of the countryside.

f) The tourist industry itself should seek to develop the public's understanding and concern for the countryside and of environmental issues generally.

As will be discussed in Chapter seven, the concerns about the threat posed to the ecological environment are paralleled by similar concerns about social impacts. In both cases, the proponents of a more ecologically or socially responsible tourism are to a large degree forced upon normative arguments that seek a change of behaviour by tourists based upon changes of values. The argument is however quite logical, given Krippendorf's model of tourism being an extension of a social pattern that is itself of such a form that it denies opportunities for creativity. He argues that man is not born a tourist, but becomes one due to 'escape' needs, but 'sick societies create sick tourists'. Equally, as has been discussed in Chapter three, this argument is but an extension of the viewpoint of Boorstin, Rivers and others, which claims that tourism creates nothing more than a series of pseudo-events. To argue that tourism must change in order to preserve ecologically fragile areas that are nonetheless attractive to tourists, and to place hope in educative forces, as Krippendorf (1987) and O'Grady (1981) do, is of little immediate help to planners and those responsible for the management of tourism areas. What needs to be done is to translate the concerns into management plans. Phillips at least provides a series of possible objectives, and hence the question becomes one of how to achieve those objectives.

Before leaving this general discussion at least two further points need to be made. The first is that Krippendorf himself recognises this, and in the last sections of his book discusses practices adopted by the Swiss Cantons. Secondly, it must be said that there is an increasing recognition of the nature of the problem. Throughout the world there is at least lip service being paid to the idea that tourism needs to be developed in harmony with natural resources. There has not been uniform progress, but indicative of the progress that is being made, is the development of regional tourism strategies such as those being adopted in Australia. Thus, for example, the 1987–1989 South Australian Strategic Tourism Plan refers to strategy 14, which is to 'Manage tourism to minimise adverse impacts'; it outlines specific actions, such as the requirement that major proposals must specify environmental safeguards, whilst the appendices to the plan listing 'key issues' indicate that ' "develop at any cost" pressures' would in fact be contrary to the State's interests. Equally, the concept of environmental impact studies is being slowly adopted in other countries such as Canada, albeit such studies are not necessarily linked to tourism but to, for example, major civil engineering projects such as dams. In part, the slow acceptance of a need for such exercises is due to the educative processes desired by Krippendorf (1987), O'Grady (1981) and Wheeller (1985), as they represent a response to public concern about environmental issues, and increased interest in forms of tourism that emphasise nature.

METHODS OF MANAGING TOURISM'S ECOLOGICAL IMPACTS

a) General issues

Arguably the first stage in planning tourism is the development of an audit of resources, markets, activities and competition. It can be maintained that there is a symbiotic relationship between tourist resources within the destination zone, and the market, for as has already been examined, certain tourist types will be attracted towards certain tourism areas. Equally, however, it is known that the tourist zone is not stable, but can change, as was described by Young (1983) in his description of the touristisation of a Maltese fishing-farming village. The implication of the concept of the tourist area life cycle is that planning needs to be undertaken from the initial period of development, particularly if the developments are taking place within ecologically fragile areas. Unfortunately, the first stages of tourism may occur almost unnoticed, for at first there is but a trickle of tourists, and they are not only non-threatening either in numbers or in type, but are indeed careful and appreciative of what it is they see. At such a stage there may be felt that there is little need for planning, but both the concept of the life cycle and past history of many destinations indicates that such an attitude cannot be maintained. From the practical viewpoint, this poses severe problems for planning authorities. It may be difficult to persuade communities that restrictions need to be determined at an early stage when currently there appears to be little need for such restrictions. Charges of elitism may well be made, and perhaps not without foundation. The host community will be asked to make difficult decisions that might imply a restriction upon economic returns from tourism when the costs of future tourism flows are difficult to assess, and can be nothing more than speculative, and in the case of ecological considerations, the reasons for such restrictions may seem intangible. The problem may be further exacerbated if the self-same authorities are also responsible for the economic well-being of the community, which might be marginal to the mainstream of economic activity within its country, and is thus looking to tourism to generate income and employment. Initially, indeed, tourism can be seen as a 'lesser of two evils'. Thus, in parts of Colorado in the USA, tourism, based on skiing and mountain resorts, provided a means of revenue which compensated rural communities which had chosen this path rather than permit the mining of molybdenum deposits found in the surrounding hills, arguing that such mining would have detrimental environmental effects. However, subsequently these communities have found that tourism too has its costs in terms of stresses on water quality, impacts of tourist numbers and the other well documented ills (Nova 1990). Perhaps what is required is a recognition that natural resources are not infinite, and are as other resources, subject to disrepair. In this respect the concept of the environment being subjected to techniques, such as cost benefit analysis, in order not only to help tourism planning, but also any other form of physical development, would seem not only logical, but necessary; and such was the conclusion of the report by Professor Pearce adopted by the British Minister of the Environment, Christopher Patten, in the summer of 1989. Without such requirements, the environmental cost is in danger of simply being disregarded.

Therefore there exist very real problems in beginning the planning processes relating to tourism development, for the very process of planning in itself requires a recognition that the market forces of demand and supply are going to be subjected to restrictions. However commenced, once begun, it can be argued that a first requirement is an audit of the area. Mill and Morrison (1985) quote the methodology used by Marshall *et al.* (1980) in their study of a tourism development strategy for southern Ontario. Natural resources need to be identified, as do man developed and man controlled. They developed a basic grid which is indicated in Table 6.2. The markets to be examined in more detail may be further sub-divided into local, regional, national and international. As such, the market may be defined in terms of numbers or even types of tourists. The opportunities that exist may have to be further analysed by their duration throughout the year; some may be only possible during winter or summer months. Climatic conditions may also have to be part of the audit, as perhaps might be tourism policies, labour policies and other socio-legal aspects. The location and distribution of the resources may have to be examined, and in short the audit might well utilise the descriptive techniques examined in Chapter three.

b) Carrying capacities

An important part of the process, in terms of ecological issues, is a consideration of the carrying capacity. The concept of a carrying capacity has attracted much attention, holding out, as it does, some notion of being able to measure the ability of an area to sustain a given number of tourists that does not pose a threat to ecological or social systems. Barkham (1973) indicates that 'Carrying capacity is a phrase delightful in its simplicity, complex in its meaning and difficult to define, as in different situations and to different people it is understood in different ways'. Stankey (1981) goes on to state:

Table 6.2   Basis for a tourism audit

Region	Existing	Markets Desired	Potential
Natural resources Water-based recreation opportunies			
Land-based recreation opportunities			
Land- and water-based recreation opportunities			
Air-based recreation opportunities			
Man developed and man controlled resources Natural resource opportunities			
Historical resource opportunities			
Cultural resource opportunities			
Recreation/leisure developments			

Source: Taken from Mill and Morrison, *The tourism system* (1985) and Marshall, Macklin and Monoghan, *Tourism development strategy* (1980)

Carrying capacity is a means to an end, with the end being a set of ecological and social conditions defined as desirable. Those desired conditions, in turn, are not defined by any inherent feature of the physical setting or deterministic notion of 'highest and best use'. Rather, they are a product of a complex prescriptive process that involves participation by the citizenry, resource managers and researchers, and are specified in area management objectives.

In short, the concept that there are fixed limits is a mistaken one. The area can be 'managed' so that the limits can be changed. Getz (1983) points this out when he notes that three variations of capacity linked to costs and benefits can be discerned. The first is to determine if a limiting factor can and should be overcome in the pursuance of some goal such as economic growth. Secondly, to what degree should social and/or ecological problems be tolerated in the pursuit of the goals and finally, can an optimal balance be found between the costs and the benefits. Precisely because of these issues Wall (1983) questions the very use of the term 'carrying capacity', preferring instead to write of 'sustainable capacity'. He strongly argues that any level of capacity that results is essentially a 'transactional' process in that host communities, business interests and political authorities must appreciate that the type of tourism they wish to develop has differing needs and impacts, and it is inconsistencies between types of tourism, as much as between levels of tourist activity and physical environment which is the determinant of 'sustainable capacity'.

c) Impact studies

It follows, therefore, that after any audit of tourism resources, careful thought needs to be paid to the objectives of the tourism strategy to be adopted. Getz (1983) accordingly advances a systems model where after a prioritisation of goals and objectives, a series of strategies is evaluated, and the preferred path of action is duly selected. Incremental development is commenced and each step of the way is associated with review policies, an evaluation of impact and a continuing assessment of capacity thresholds. In the light of this process, decisions are made as to terminate projects, revise controls, reset partial limits or continue as planned. Within this process 'thresholds must be seen as part of a dynamic process aimed at overcoming barriers where possible, but one in which it is also possible to exert controls (such as limits) when necessary to satisfy objectives'.

Problems however exist with such approaches, logical and reasonable though they seem. From a strictly conservationist viewpoint it implies that modifications to ecological systems are possible. It is perhaps the salami slice argument. The excuse that 'only 10 acres of land are being developed out of 100, so it will be all right', then to be followed by '10 acres are developed, so another 5 will not matter'. Many environmentalists will argue that change, any change, will so distort drainage patterns, breeding habits, life support systems etc., that the change, once commenced, will generate unlooked for consequences. Secondly, it supposes that tourist developments can happen in an incremental manner. But such is the nature of many modern tourist enterprises that large scale is an inherent requirement. Theme parks require significant land areas to develop the rides, the car parking space and the ambience that is an inherent part of their attraction. Countries such as Mexico have sought to develop 'instant tourist complexes', such as Cancun and Huatulco, due to economic factors of distance from the major American market and the need to develop the infrastructure required to support such resorts. Thirdly, there is an assumption of rationality and regard for legal processes. Tourist resorts in many parts of the world have examples of developments that have been commenced without planning permission, and which have subsequently been permitted to trade. Sometimes this has occurred quite legally because there are no planning controls, in other cases planning controls are simply being ignored. Murphy (1985), Barkham (1973) and many others require that communities play a role in a rational planning process, but this assumes that the community is a homogeneous unit that is capable of making decisions not only in its own self-interest, but for the interest of others. It is perhaps a questionable assumption. In addition, it is perhaps worth noting that both Murphy (1985) and Krippendorf (1987) write from the background of political systems in Canada and Switzerland which permit plebiscites to be held on issues where a comparatively small proportion of the population (in some instances as little as 5 per cent) can sign a petition to the effect that a plebiscite ought to be put before the electorate. This method of community control is lacking in many other countries including the UK and France to name but two.

d) Functional measures

What remains? Possibly what might be achieved is at least some degree of consensus of potential measures of carrying capacity. It might appear this reduces the process to a mechanistic one rather than the dynamic process required by Getz, but at least it serves as a starting point and might serve the required process. The WTO (1982) notes a number of measures when it considered the problem in its report 'Risks of saturation, or tourist carrying capacity overload in holiday destinations'. (It is perhaps a sobering comment that in spite of reminders the WTO obtained only 12 replies, and some States said they had no problems!)

One of the problems facing tourism destinations is the seasonality of the business, and hence measures of the temporal dispersion of business may be of use. Measures relating to the question of peakedness of demand can include:

a) A measure of the maximum numbers of people that can be carried at any one time. The WTO recommends a measure of two-thirds of the maximum number of recorded visits (1983).
b) Weekly/daily maxima can then be calculated on the basis of the peak capacity measured by the time period concerned. In the case of annual figures, the figure will be based on the number of days the attraction

remains open.

c) A measure of the level of crowding can be simply assessed by taking the number of arrivals in a given time and dividing by the total number of arrivals over a longer time period.

d) A better statistic which measures the peakedness of the distribution of visitors is the kurtosis. This is calculated according to the formula:

$$K = \sum_{i=1}^{n} \frac{(Xi - X)^4}{n(SD)^4}$$

where K = the value of kurtosis
      Xi = the number of users at the time i
      X = the arithmetic mean of all Xi
      n = the number of time periods
      SD = the standard deviation of Xi

If K has a value of 1 then the curve has a normal distribution. If it has a value of less than 3, then it is relatively flat in shape and is said to be platykurtic. If it has a value of greater than 3 then it is said to be leptokurtic, and is relatively peaked. In such a case it might be said that the tourist area is heavily congested for at least some small period of the total time.

The level of crowdedness can also be calculated with reference to space. It might, for example, be said that the number of people should not exceed a given number per hectare of space. Perhaps a beach should not have more than 1,000 people per hectare. However, it has to be noted that such a measure of crowdedness fails to take into account the psychological components of the concept of a crowd. For popular beaches part of the fun of the situation, and a generator of the beach atmosphere, is indeed the fact that it is crowded. People go to see people. In other situations, ten people on a beach may be a crowd if what is being sought is peace and quiet.

Carrying capacity is sometimes related to the expected numbers of people. This occurs in such cases as the calculation of car park spaces, the number of restaurants, and the number of shops that are required. Thus, one might say that 1 restaurant place per 2,000 tourists, or 0.2 square metres of shop floor space is required per tourist, or 1.2 car parking space per available bed-space, or 250 car parking spaces per hectare.

Another approach is to assess thresholds. If a factor such as water supply is limited, then the number of tourists that can be catered for may be estimated along the lines of available water supply divided by the consumption per tourist per day. If car parking space is limited, then the number of visitors that may be catered for is the number of car parking spaces divided by the average length of stay per tourist per time period, multiplied by the average number of tourists per car. For example, if 100 car parking places exist, and each tourist stays approximately 30 minutes, then within 10 hours, 2,000 tourists can be catered for if each tourist arrives separately by car. If each car carries 3 tourists, then the limit is 6,000 tourists. If it costs a given amount to develop a tourist attraction, say an interpretation centre, then the number of tourists required to cover the costs, the break-even point, is the total cost of the development divided by the expected average expenditure per visitor.

A popular measure is the host-visitor ratio, and Defert's tourist function is one such measure. This states that:

$$Df = \frac{number\ of\ bed\text{-}spaces\ in\ a\ region}{population\ of\ the\ region} \times 100$$

With specific reference to ecology and rural activities, the number of visitors depends upon the definition of the area. For a forest park, the daily allowable visitor rate may be from 0 to 15 per hectare, whereas for a surburban natural park it may be 15 to 70 people per hectare, and for a recreation sports facility, 80 to 200 per hectare. Camp sites standards vary around the world, again dependent on the nature of the zone within which the site is to be found. In France, many sites operate at 300 persons per hectare, whereas in the USA in wildlife zones, it may only be 2.5 people per hectare (WTO 1983).

e) Types of zones and permitted usages

So complex is the measurement of carrying capacity that an alternative approach might be adopted. This is to undertake an impact study, although it might be said that from many perspectives such studies are complementary to, and not alternative to, the concept of carrying capacity. The idea behind impact studies is to examine development projects with the purpose of identifying the potential environmental impact. Having identified such impacts, the initial proposals may then be modified to minimise the negative impacts. Often associated with the concept of permitted impact is an identification of levels of allowable development. In short, zones of different usage patterns are identified by the planners. In practice, from the viewpoint of tourism, many of these zones relate to rural areas, but of course such zoning also occurs within urban areas. Thus, some urban areas will permit solely low density residential development, whilst other zones may have higher density housing and some retail development, whilst yet others may be characterised by industrial activities. One aspect of urban zoning that relates to tourism is the protection of historical heritage and buildings of historical value within a town. Such buildings may have preservation orders, and in addition any adjacent development that is permitted will have to be of a nature that is sympathetic to the

Table 6.3   Parks Canada land use classification

Special Preservation Areas:
Based on specific and sometimes small areas which possess unique, rare or endangered species. Public access is permitted via the use of licences or permits.

Wilderness Areas:
Areas with specific natural history themes and environments. There is provision for outdoor recreation for hiking and primitive camping facilities, with widely dispersed camping so as to be consistent with a primary preservation role.

Natural Environment:
In these areas intermediate levels of outdoor recreation that are compatible with a natural setting are permitted. Motorised access is permitted, but on a limited scale to the periphery of the region. Thus entry is by pre-determined points. Trails and simple campsites are possible within the natural constraints of the environment.

Recreation Areas:
Within these areas general outdoor recreation facilities are possible, and this includes campgrounds with full facilities, boat ramps, ski hills and permission to use power boats. More motorised access is possible. A common feature is the existence of interpretative centres to explain the local eco-system.

Park Service:
These are highly developed areas with centralised visitor support services. Nonetheless preservation is maintained with buildings etc. consistent with the landscape as far as is possible. Such parks are often found near urban centres.

original ambience of the area.

One of the best examples of a hierarchical classification of rural landscapes indicating levels of potential development is that of Parks Canada. Parks Canada has adopted a five-fold classification as indicated in Table 6.3. It is illustrative of one of the common techniques of tourism management in terms of indicating permitted levels of recreational use with the type of usage being determined by the nature of the ecology to be found in the area. It also highlights the importance of the role of accessibility as a means of protecting the natural environment. Numbers of tourists expand once access is made available. Supply of an area would appear to create its own demand, and with a growth of demand there would appear to be a process of improving access. Distance is now not the barrier that it once was, and even the furthest flung parts of the globe are susceptible to the visit of the tourist. In 1989, for example, approximately 3,000 tourists visited Antartica. The creation of roads generates traffic that may far exceed the calculations of the road planner. This phenomenon is not restricted to tourist areas alone. The M25 orbital motorway around London is such an example. Within but a year of its opening it became evident that the traffic flows far exceeded forecast demand, and schemes to widen the six-lane motorway to eight lanes were announced in 1989. Equally, the very existence of the motorway has helped to generate submissions by property developers for new retail/leisure centres around London's perimeter. So, too, with tourist destinations. One such example would be the Greek island of Lefkas. In the early 1980s Lefkas had some tourism based in Lefkas Town and the village of Nidri. To a large degree this was local Greek tourism, partly attracted to the island not only because of its natural beauty, but also because of its proximity to Scorpios, an island made glamorous by its connections with the Onassis family. By the mid-1980s Nidri was being used by a few, small, specialist holiday companies, whilst at the same time the village of Vassiliki in the south of the island was becoming known amongst the windsurfing fraternity for its strong winds during the afternoons of summer days. However, until 1987 the village of Vassiliki was accessible from Nidri only by a rough road. In that year, however, the road was made permanent with a tarmac surface. Consequently, the larger holiday companies that had followed the smaller, specialist companies to Nidri began to offer Vassiliki within their brochures for 1988, partly because the travel time to Vassiliki had become shorter due to improved communications. Other factors were also important. A similar aspect of accessibility was the increased frequency of flights to the airport of Prevaza which serviced the island of Lefkas. In consequence, the villages of Nidri and Vassiliki have in the last five years begun to change their character in the way described by Young. Thus, accessibility becomes a determinant of change which initiates not only a change of land use from a strictly environmental viewpoint, but also a determinant of social change.

It must also be noted that classifications of areas are an important step towards zoning, and hence care must be taken over the categorisation of land, for such categorisations determine the level of development that will be permitted. For example, within the USA the Wilderness Act defines wilderness in the following terms:

> A wilderness, in contrast to those areas where man and his own works dominate the landscape, is hereby recognised as an area where the earth and its community of life are untrammelled by man, where man himself is a visitor who does not remain.

Searle (1989) argues that if this definition is applied to areas such as Banff National Park, then the true wilderness of Banff is reduced to only about 60 per cent of the park. This partially arises due to Canada Parks Service categories of wilderness, one of which, 'semi-primitive wilderness' permits commercial lodges, large group camps and site hardening. Within the United Kingdom, National Parks policy has always had to recognise that much of the land is in private ownership, and much of it is being worked by farmers. Indeed, the US definition of 'wilderness' would practically not apply within most of England and Wales, although some parts of Scotland might comply with the concept. In consequence, the English authorities have had to set up systems of permitted land use, which contain within them the potential for conflict between the right of individuals to develop their own land as they see fit, and the right of a wider society to open spaces.

If the type of tourism that exists is indeed a reflection of the needs and aspirations of a society, then the relationship between tourism and the physical environment mirrors the values of that society. Arguably, the literature of holidays, with its promises of an unspoilt destination, contains two implicit premises. The first is the recognition of the desire for escape into a 'paradise', a romantic notion of nature as a means of renewing the spirit, an attitude that arguably may be seen as both unnecessarily romantic and mistaken (Walter 1982). Secondly, the brochure implies that the 'unspoilt destination' is a tourist resource for mankind; and it is perhaps with this premise that environmental pressure groups would most argue. Dearden (1989; Dearden and Rollins 1990) has argued, within a Canadian context, that, historically, the environment has been viewed as a storehouse of raw materials, and that the wilderness has value or worth only in relation to its usefulness to humans. In consequence, National Parks, beautiful scenery and the unspoilt areas, only have value if perceived as being a resource for tourism and economic benefit. Such a viewpoint, Dearden argues, fails to recognise the integrity of the areas for their own sake, and instead places on them a value that has nothing to do with economic rates of return. And therein lies the crux of the matter. On the one hand there exists a valid longing for escape, for the pleasure to be found in skiing down the slopes, or sailing in blue seas, to commune with nature within isolated areas, or simply to share beauty with family and friends and so reinforce the feelings of togetherness of any given social group, whilst on the other hand, such desires, when translated into the wishes of thousands if not millions wishing to share the same experiences, become a threat not only to the sought after experience, but also to the flora and fauna, and, as waters become poisoned, and air polluted, to the host communities themselves. Nor, as will be discussed in the next chapter, are the changes posed by tourism limited to the physical environment alone.

MANAGEMENT TECHNIQUES

The above discussion begins to indicate ways in which the planning authorities can start to minimise the negative impacts of tourism, whilst simultaneously, at least under certain conditions, perhaps even enhance the degree of visitor satisfaction. A number of policies might be identified. Essentially, these techniques can be divided into two broad groupings. The first, macro-techniques, relate to planning sites within a zone, and the relationship between them, whilst the second, micro-techniques, relate to the management of flows of people within the zone itself. Both are orientated towards maintaining sustainable levels of usage.

a) Macro-techniques

a) The setting up of 'honeypots'

This involves the development, or the permission for development, of popular resort areas in an attempt to relieve the pressure on more sensitive areas elsewhere. One example of such a policy would be the development of recreational parkland near centres of population in the hope that such areas would attract users, so protecting the more distant fragile zones. Another example would be to permit the development of major tourist resorts. It might be expected that such resorts would help protect their hinterland in two ways. The very gaudiness of the resort would deter visits by the allocentric, explorer type of tourist, whilst the psychocentric, mass-organised tourists would remain content within their touristic bubble experiencing its fun-packed delights. But such a policy may well not work. As any visitor to the Costa del Sol would testify, the hinterland of Andalucia is indeed visited by tourists. In areas such as Ojen, foreign ownership of property is not uncommon, whilst the town of Ronda boasts souvenir and antique shops that it did not possess a decade ago. Incidentally, both developments have in part been encouraged by the improvement of roads that lead from the coast through the mountains, and so again the importance of accessibility is illustrated. The policy might not work because the types of tourists described are in part a caricature of reality. As indicated in Chapter one the modern tourist is capable of playing more than one role, seeking one type of holiday on one occasion and another at yet other times. Yet even within the one holiday, whilst adopting predominantly one mode of behaviour, alternative patterns will be taken up at other times. So the mass-organised tourist will take some days out to explore the hinterland, and thus visit the less popular area. The honeypot thus becomes a nodal point for a series of day-trip activities. Equally, the honeypot tourist area may well be capable of meeting the needs of more than one type of tourist simultaneously, or at least temporally. The types of tourists that visit a popular area in the off-peak season may differ from those who visit during the main season. Thus again, in the off-peak season, visits to the hinterland may not decline proportionately to the decline in visitor numbers to the 'honeypot'. This implies that the policy of adopting 'honeypots' requires careful planning in relation to their location to the more fragile environments. Certainly such fragile areas must be more than a day-trip's distance away. Yet, what is a day-trip's distance away? There is no such set distance, either in terms of miles or hours spent in travel time. The question of accessibility is important. The policy of the 'honeypot' must go hand in hand with other policies, such as zoning and route planning.

b) The policy of dispersion

The problem of the 'honeypot' is that the natural and man-made resources within the area may become stressed. Even if this is not the case, and the policy is successful, then it means, by implication, that the economic benefits that accrue with tourism are being denied to other areas. In consequence, to help maintain a higher quality of natural environment within the main tourist resort area, a policy of tourist dispersion may be adopted. The objective of this policy is to avoid overloading capacity at the main resort and to spread the benefits of tourism. Again, it may also help to enhance the level of visitor satisfaction. Such a policy may be illustrated with reference to South Wales and the Gower Peninsula. The Gower, with its beautiful sandy beaches and coves, has long been a tourist area for the centres of population of the South Wales' valleys, and with the completion of motorways and railway links, has succeeded in attracting tourists from a much wider area. During the 1970s, however, problems became apparent. With increased car ownership, and the improvements in roads as part of the industrial reinvestment in South Wales, a fine summer's day meant that the bays became packed with people, and the car parks were full to overflowing. The installation of a noticeboard on the Gower road leading out of Swansea which gave information on the car parks, and thus warned motorists that there was no parking available, seemed to have little effect. Arguably, therefore, there was reason to develop other tourist destinations that could help to relieve the stress. Equally, it could be argued that, as a tourist area, the Gower was over-dependent on its beaches. When the weather was poor, there was little alternative activity that tourists could turn to, and thus a potential existed for disappointment.

The period since the late 1970s and throughout the 1980s has thus seen the development of a series of alternative tourist attractions in the Vale of Glamorgan and in the area north of Swansea, and more recently in the 1980s, within Swansea itself. Tourists may now visit Aberdulais Basin where redevelopment of the old canal basin has taken place. Margam Park has opened, mining museums exist within an easy car journey from Swansea and other developments have occurred.

Has this policy been successful? On fine summer days the tourist still prefers to be by the beach, and the car parks are still full to capacity. The entrance to Caswell Valley has long since become a tarmac area and only older people can remember its original beauty. The village of Mumbles still suffers from a surfeit of cars, and the sand dunes of Oxwich and Port Eynon are protected only by areas being fenced off and access to the beach being controlled by other forms of resort management. To some extent, the problems arise not only from tourism, but also from increased building in the area over the last two decades as the South Wales area recovers from recession based on its past over-dependence on coal mining and agriculture. Its very success in diversifying its economy has led to some of the strains briefly described. Yet as a case study it illustrates some of the problems with diversification policies. The alternatives may not be powerful enough to divert people from the major activities that cause the initial stress. If the alternatives are strong enough to attract visitors away from the original magnet of tourists during peak periods of activity, then the new combination of tourist assets will probably engender more visitors in total. In consequence, the policy succeeds in attracting more visitors and in potentially generating pressures of land use over a greater area.

c) Zoning

Zoning involves the identification of areas of land, the uses that will be permitted and those uses that will not be permitted. Within Britain the major example of zoning is the categorisation of land near cities as Green Belt, where neither residential or industrial development is permitted. Essentially, these controls were implemented by the Town and Country Planning Act of 1971, but in the period since 1980 a series of orders and circulars have been issued which together have made land development by property developers that much easier. For example, the Department of the Environment circular 22/80, 'Development Control Policy and Practice', states that when there is a decision to be made there must be a 'presumption in favour of development'; in other words, permission will be granted unless there is a strong counterargument. Circular 2/87, 'Awards of Costs and Planning Procedures', indicates that costs could be awarded against planning authorities for 'unreasonable' delay in granting planning permission. The consequences are that in urban locations, where listed buildings might be found within conservation areas, there now actually exist significant pressures upon planning authorities and a potential danger that out-of-character development might be permitted.

One of the common problems associated with tourism development is that in order to protect the important or fragile area, tourism development may be restricted at the location itself. Nonetheless, visitors will continue to come, and hence there needs to be a tourist complex of hotels, swimming pools, restaurants, camp sites and souvenir shops at some distance away from the tourist attraction. The problem that emerges is that of accessibility from the support tourist complex to the attraction. An excellent example of this type of problem is the case of Ayres Rock in Australia. In 1987 it was proposed that a monorail should link the tourist facilities at the Olgas to Ayres Rock — the proposal coming from the director of the National Parks and Wildlife Service, Professor Derek Ovington. The proposal was an attempt to ease tourists' passage in and out of sensitive areas without leaving evidence of them having been there. The combination of modern technology and the ancient site of the aborigines may seem either strange or exciting, depending on one's viewpoint, but the problem is that, whilst it may seem more in keeping with the site that tourists should approach it as did the original inhabitants in order to gain the sense of mystery and awe, the very volume of traffic would destroy such an illusion and would create problems of soil erosion. Equally, to deny entry to the site is to deny any opportunity of seeing and sensing one of nature's wonders.

Zoning need not be on the grand scale. It is in common use when considering the use of water facilities. For example, powered craft do not co-exist successfully with sailing dinghies or windsurfing, and even less with rowing craft. Arguably, for example, the very philosophical premise that lies behind the use of, say a jet-ski, where power is used to overcome the forces of wind and waves, is contrary to that of the windsurfer who attempts to harmonise with the natural forces in order to obtain a sense of freedom and speed. The result is that all over the world water is zoned either spatially or temporally so that different users can enjoy the water that is available. Figure 6.2 is an example of this result.

d) The encouragement of 'soft tourism'

The purpose behind this policy is that tourist activity is dovetailed into existing facilities, and that tourist developments that are extraneous to the nature of the area are forbidden. As previously indicated, it proposes a form of tourism that is consistent with rural and agricultural pursuits. It is argued that tourism serves a purpose of supplementing the major economic activities that exist rather than supplanting them. Attractive as this idea is, and consistent as it may appear with increasing environmental concerns and the changing patterns of tourism demand discussed in Chapter one, this policy is also not without its difficulties. Logically, it would only permit large-scale tourist development, such as theme parks, in only one of two types of areas, namely the already developed area, or the area of derelict or desolate waste land which has little economic or ecological value. In the case of already developed areas, such proposals would perhaps create the problems of stress that are associated with the 'honeypot' policy. It also denies to those living in rural areas the chance of significant economic investments that may serve as a catalyst of change. The objective is one of slow evolution of change rather than revolution, and the problem is that host communities may not accept these restrictions. Much depends on how the host community values the quality and form of the landscape which external bodies feel has value and is deserving of protection. The

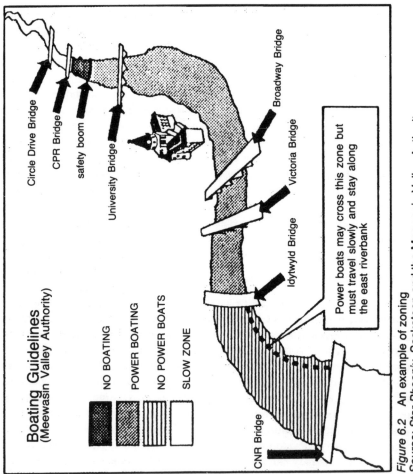

Boating Guidelines
(Meewasin Valley Authority)

NO BOATING

POWER BOATING

NO POWER BOATS

SLOW ZONE

Circle Drive Bridge

CPR Bridge

safety boom

University Bridge

Broadway Bridge

Victoria Bridge

Idytwyld Bridge

CNR Bridge

Power boats may cross this zone but must travel slowly and stay along the east riverbank

Figure 6.2   An example of zoning
Source: Star Phoenix, Saskatoon and the Meewasin Valley Authority.

proponents of 'soft tourism' argue that only in this form of tourism can any form of practical solution be offered to the economic needs of the community and the requirements of conservation.

e) The encouragement of 'green policies'

The encouragement of 'soft tourism' is closely related to the establishment of 'green policies' which seek not simply to protect the environment but to help restore the environment and to offset problems generated by acid rain and other threats, even whilst improving recreational resources. The proposals of the Countryside Commission to develop urban forests is such an example. The plan calls for the commencement of tree planting in the Black Country and Tyneside in 1989, with, within five years, further planting in the London Green Belt, and on the perimeters of Manchester and Sheffield. A second phase would subsequently take place around Nottingham, Leeds, Cardiff, Swansea and Middlesbrough. In Scotland, the Scottish Office announced a 50 million woodland planting programme for Glasgow and Edinburgh. The Commission proposes that the woodland should consist of a 50:50 mix between broadleaf and conifer trees, thereby achieving objectives of a quick growing green landscape which possesses economic value whilst also permitting a re-establishment of oak, beech and other broadleaf trees which provide animal shelter. At the same time, the policy would help restore the loss of such broadleaf trees – the Nature Conservancy Council having estimated that 40 per cent of ancient woodlands have disappeared in Britain since 1945. Antecedents of this type of initiative are not unknown in Europe, and the Countryside Commission quotes as examples the Bos Park near Amsterdam with 2,200 acres of recreational forest, and the Stadtwälder (town forests) of Germany. Granger (1990) describes ways in which parks in Ontario are being 'naturalised' as part of a process of the 'greening of cities',whilst Berg (1990) indicates ways in which the 'greening' of US cities such as San Francisco generates not simply a more ecological awareness but supports a 'profound shift in the fundamental premises and activities of city living'.

From a touristic and recreational viewpoint the urban forest presents an opportunity for becoming a setting for art galleries, concert venues, dry ski slopes, cycle trails and science parks. At the same time their very existence might help to relieve tourist pressures on existing woodland.

Other aspects of green policies might have implications for tourism. The growing demand for organic foodstuffs means that farmers are reducing their use of herbicides and pesticides, and thus in the longer term the quality of water may improve. Currently there are examples where recreational use of water has been stopped because of fears of water pollution from these and other sources. For example, in the late summer of 1989 the use of Rutland Water, a 3,000 acre lake in Leicestershire, by windsurfers and others was stopped because of health fears.

However, it is not to be thought that 'green policies' provide instant solutions to environmental problems created by recreation and tourism. They will often take time in their development, and long-term horizons need to be considered. Long-term commitments are required. Two Canadian examples give ample evidence of this. The Weyerhaeuser 20-year Forest Management Plan is primarily concerned with the creation of forests that can sustain timber processing, but the plan also considers, based on forest simulation models, other activities including recreational use of forest areas. Indeed, it can even project forest growth over a 220-year period to evaluate the impact of various forest management systems and usage patterns. In 1979 the Meewasin Valley Authority began a 100-year plan to consider the use of the valley for both tourist and recreational use within a context of environmental conservation. This plan is subjected to a review process, and in 1989 an updating and modification process was undertaken, yet at the heart of the plan its overall objectives and philosophies continue to be adhered to.

f) The provision of tourist/recreation facilities near urban centres

The idea of the urban forest is but one example of creating a recreational resource near the home location of the tourist. If tourism does indeed pose a potential threat to ecologically fragile areas, and if indeed people's working patterns are changing to permit an increased demand for leisure near to the home location, then the implication is that tourist authorities can respond to the increased demand for day-trip activity near to the home by establishing a number of recreational facilities. Such facilities include not simply urban forests, but also urban farms, the use of water splash parks, the greater use of rivers and riversides within towns and the use of canals. Weekly, as well as occasional, events can be organised within urban settings that attract tourists and local people, and can enhance the local economy. For example, Portland, Oregon, like many North American cities, features special Saturday markets. The resultant economic impact is a form of import saving in the sense that the home area retains spending that would otherwise have taken place elsewhere. At the same time, pressures on other areas are diminished, whilst costs of travel are likewise reduced. It might also be argued that the escape motivations for holidays are equally mitigated in some form or other, and indeed perhaps the very need for holidays is diminished. If it is thought in the final analysis the potential harm that tourism can cause can only be met by reducing the demand for travel, then such policies at least go part of the way in that they lessen the distance travelled.

g) Create environmental awareness holidays and tourists

A further policy that might be adopted is to ensure that tourists are aware of the stresses that large numbers of tourists can cause, so that they might mitigate the pressures by behavioural change. For example, the Centre for Development Education in Stuttgart has worked with tour operator representatives and charter flight companies to provide literature for their clients making them aware of cultural differences and scarcity of natural resources. Other programmes exist on a modest scale. In 1976 in Lower Casamance in Senegal, a programme commenced whereby tourists stay not in large complexes of hotels, but in huts and as part of the village community. Whilst it may be questioned as to the degree of authenticity this actually creates for the tourist in terms of the social experience, it does have the benefit of helping to reduce the ecological impacts of tourism because, in this instance, the tourists are not taking the baggage of their home environment with them.

All of the above policies might be said to be planning policies on a 'macro' scale, i.e. concerned with allocating tourists between destination areas. What about the means of mitigating the tourist impact on the environment when they actually arrive at the destination. At the 'micro' level there again exist a number of policies that managers might use.

b) Micro-techniques

a) Restrictive entry

The first is to control numbers by simply permitting only a few to enter. The levels of control can vary from exhortation, as was illustrated by the car-parking signs in the Gower Peninsula mentioned previously, to the maintenance of quotas by restricting entry to only those with permits, to, at the final extreme, permitting no entry at all. In the tourism of the wilderness areas of North America, impacts of hunting are controlled by the issue of licences, and by anti-poaching campaigns. Entry may also be permitted to national parks at certain points only, and in this respect the location of roads is important. Parks may only have a limited number of roads that enter the park at a specific point, and beyond any given point no wheeled traffic may be permitted. In consequence, distance from the access point becomes a means of reducing usage rates, as tourists may only gain access to them by foot. In addition, restrictions might be imposed on the type of camping that is permitted. Equally, the actual number of camping points becomes a means of control. The Himalayan country of Bhutan maintains a policy of restricting numbers of tourists, and such tourists are only permitted to travel in groups with a qualified guide. The purpose of the restriction is two-fold. Firstly, it reduces the social as well as the economic impacts of tourism to levels that the country can easily absorb, whilst secondly, it permits a greater direction of the economic flows that tourism creates, without causing negative economic impacts such as too high an inflation rate in certain geographical areas, or the sucking in of imports at too high a level.

b) Use of the price mechanism

One simple way of reducing numbers of tourists is to simply charge high prices and create 'exclusivity'. This sense of 'exclusiveness' in turn helps to justify the high price. Obviously, therefore, the higher the price the fewer the number of people who are able to take advantage of the area. However, this conflicts with policies of open access in some spheres of activity. National parks may be part of the tourist package that is offered to visitors, but equally the concept of a national park is that it is open to its own nationals and is to provide educational as well as recreational purposes. Restrictions on access are thus not always constitutionally possible, and nor is the use of pricing mechanisms. The problem becomes more apparent when national parks are designated, but include within them private property, as is common in Britain. Thus, water authorities and other private landowners can indeed charge admission, and will often use such admission charges to raise revenue to maintain the quality of the recreational provision.

c) Site management signposting

One aspect of site management is to use wardens who have various duties including conservation work and the provision of information to visitors. Working from interpretation centres the concept is to inform the visitor so as to make them appreciate the natural environment and so modify their behaviour. One means of behaviour modification is to create signposted walks. The visitor will tend to keep to the 'approved' trail, and this behaviour is reinforced by the provision of information points along the route. Given a leaflet, the visitor is drawn from one point to another, and attention is directed to various features. Not only, therefore, is the visitor taught how to observe and appreciate nature, but the visitor is also kept to those areas that can sustain high pedestrian flow, and so is kept away from the more fragile areas, so permitting flora and fauna to sustain themselves. Underlying this policy is also a belief that elitist attitudes towards nature are eventually self-defeating. Minorities may serve to act as catalysts within societies, but only if the majority are at least sympathetic to the minority viewpoint can desired policies be put into practice. Thus, whilst studies may illustrate that few visitors will move far from their cars, and the cliched picture of the family sitting in the layby viewing the countryside from their car is not without truth, arguably people will not be moved to protect areas or appreciate the need for protection unless they have more knowledge. It has been found that behaviour is changed by the provision of information. If, on arriving at a park, people are told that a number of walks exist, that they are of a certain distance and duration, that the terrain is easy or otherwise, then the distance travelled from the car park tends to increase. People hence enjoy the visit and obtain more from it. Equally, just as the provision of information influences behaviour, so too does the withholding of data. Nonetheless, the desired result is a greater use of areas, the acquisition of knowledge and an appreciation by the public of the importance of things natural, and in the end, hopefully, an increased readiness to support policies of conservation.

d) Protecting footpaths

Such policies are not without associated costs. The paradox is that increased usage is desired, but the routes used must retain a state of 'naturalness'. The selected routes must thus be capable of supporting high levels of pedestrian flow. Care must therefore be shown in the planning of the paths. Where possible it is preferable that use is made of natural rocks and hard surfaces that can sustain higher traffic than grass or soil. Cork and tree chips may be used for the paths within woodland settings. Boardwalks may be used near streams and rivers to protect the banks. Car parks may indeed be parks, but there is a need to protect grass from the wear produced by tyres. One solution is to use small hollow concrete squares. The soil sits within the square and is seeded. The grass grows, but the concrete protects the roots of the grass, and thus it is not worn away by the tyres. Aesthetically, the area retains its greenness and freshness. Other advantages also accrue. The soil is not beaten down and denuded so as to become a hardened area off which water flows. The drainage patterns are less adversely affected, the rainwater can still percolate through the soil, and hence trees continue to be nourished.

On open areas of moorland there may be a need to use even more expensive techniques. Whilst paths may be created from tarmac to overcome the problem of path erosion, and the widening of paths due to trampling effects, there is a resistance to the concept of wild open areas being criss-crossed by black tarmac paths which stand out against the natural terrain. They are man-made and man-imposed upon an area that is supposedly being protected as far as is possible against encroachment by man. Rebuilding footpaths with natural material might appear to be an answer, but the problem is that the very transport of rocks and stones might make the problem worse. Indeed, in Snowdonia, helicopters have been used to transport stone material to help restore footpaths with natural rock. On moorland a number of 'high-tech' solutions are being used to create footpaths that can sustain high pedestrian flow whilst at the same time blending into the natural terrain. The Peak District in 1989 was experimenting with a footpath comprised of three levels. At the base is laid a nylon membrane that allows water to drain through it, but which stops mud from coming up when pressure is laid on the path by the walker. Over this is placed a synthetic net which helps to distribute the impact of the walker over a greater area, thus lessening the pressure on any given surface. Finally, over this is laid a combination of basalt and gritstone which is consistent with the terrain of the Peak District. In other areas grass is sown on top of various layers such as fibretex so as to be consistent with the terrain, and indeed in some cases grass and other plants are being 'forced' by the use of carefully planned fertiliser applications. Opinions about the use of fertilisers are divided, but the reasons that prompt their use are easily understood. In some areas users may be asked to voluntarily adhere to certain practices, for example, to walk in small groups and in single file. Across sand-dunes walkers may have to keep to boardwalks which are placed to avoid the wear on the grasses that help maintain the sand-dune's formation. As the boards become bleached and are covered by drifting sand, they do not appear to be out of place, but there is a continuing need for maintenance.

In setting up paths there is also a need to assess the likely routes that people will take. The temptation to take a short cut seems to be too much for many people to resist. Observation of any park in an urban area, or any open piece of grass will often show that whilst paths may be provided, worn areas of grass show where people take short cuts. This does provide a problem for parks departments. The same sort of path erosion problems that might be found in the open areas of the country can be found in a city's local parks. For example, in the deer park at Woollaton, Nottingham, the circumference of the park now has worn paths created by joggers who use the park for training. Cars had worn away the grass to such an extent that it was replaced by a shale-type surface and car parking is now restricted to specific areas in order to protect other parts of the park.

e) Control of access points

Whilst there may be a reluctance to impose direct controls of access to what are deemed to be national areas of heritage or wilderness areas that belong to the nation, or to areas featured in tourism promotion programmes, indirect means are often being used. Controls over the number of access points are possible as has already been noted. Thus, within park areas, the location and size of car parks, and the spatial relationship of roads to zones of activity within the park are important. For example, in 1988 the car park at Dove Dale in the Peak District was made smaller so as to reduce the numbers who parked there and then walked through the dale. This was to ease the pedestrian flow through the dale so as to permit recovery of paths and to begin work to offset trampling effects. Alternative means of access may be made possible. Again within the Peak District, schemes that reduce car traffic and offer instead a bus service or cycle hire have proven successful. This was done at the Goyt Valley, and one interesting side effect was that the social composition of the visitor changed with higher socio-economic groupings becoming a larger proportion of visitors (Murphy 1985). In the Snowdon National Park the Mountain Goat bus service was established to relieve stress on car parks around Snowdon where walkers parked before taking one of the routes up the mountain. Naturally, there is something of a reluctance by people to forgo the use of their car, but the bus service offered real benefits to walkers in that they could now take two routes in the same trip. There was no longer a need to go up and return by the same route, when they could take a different path down and be picked up by the bus. In addition, a marginal dispersal effect is created.

An important aspect of accessibility is the location of accommodation facilities. They have to be sufficiently near to permit time for visits into the vulnerable areas, but far enough away to protect the area in terms of the support infrastructure that is required by accommodation not intruding upon the protected zone. Sometimes the trip into the protected zone becomes part of the visit experience. Thus, within the Maldive Islands tourists may visit but not stay on certain islands. The boat trip under blue skies upon blue waters is obviously an inherent part of the whole experience and generates visitor satisfaction. Management of zones must therefore look into means of replicating this type of satisfaction under less promising circumstances.

f) Changing usage patterns

One of the great problems in tourism site management is the protection of sites where tourists have already established behaviour patterns that may be inimical to the long-term integrity of the area. Through custom and usage, interests have been generated that some would wish to protect. This perhaps represents one of the major challenges to planning authorities, and one of the most difficult to cope with. The degree of difficulty that is associated with this is illustrated by Waiser (1989) who describes the difficulties the Park authorities had in reversing the development of summer homes erected by local residents within the Prince Albert National Park in the 1960s. Based upon the town of Waskesiu, development had spread into the park, and after the Second World War visitor numbers increased from 50,000 in 1949 to 136,529 in 1958. By the summer of 1950 there were 412 'shack tents' (wooden shacks) in the Waskesiu campsite, and an association was formed that petitioned for them to be recognised and kept for the duration of the whole year rather than being dismantled at the end of every season. However, in 1959 a planning report commented that:

> The present spectacle which confronts the visitor is not a pleasant one, where the key areas in the developed portion of the park are dominated by semi-permanent occupancies. It can be expected as the proportion of touring recreationists grows so will the indignation against the present type of development grow. For it is most obvious this is a misuse of a national park.
>
> (Planning considerations – Prince Albert National Park Report No. 7
> 2–3 1959)

Equally, by the mid-1960s new demands were emerging, and in 1966 the park appointed its first warden for the development of park interpretative services. The result was that in 1967 a plan was announced that only existing shack tenters could apply for permits for a lot in a relocated area. However, faced with opposition, a series of 'temporary' arrangements were made so that by the early 1970s the shack tents had become all around the year structures plugged into the electricity mains supply. In 1971, after further review of the role of National Parks, Prince Albert was designated as a 'national wildland park'. The public hearings revealed the conflicts of perception and use, between those who perceived the role of National Parks as a means of preserving wilderness areas and the flora and fauna they contain, and within Prince Albert, the majority who saw the park as an area of recreation, as a family park, and the whole attempt as a means by which distant central government ignored local custom and sought to impose its will upon those who had developed the park. The conflict is described by Waiser as one where 'the townsite serves the park, not vice-versa, and that the natural heritage values of the park should govern Waskesiu management and development', whereas local townspeople argue that the town constitutes but a small part of the total area, and from the viewpoint of visitors, the park serves local people primarily.

g) Encouraging natural processes

By seeking to meet recreational purposes, many of the natural processes of a wilderness area are interfered with. For example, dams may be built, or woodland fires fought. The Yellowstone National Park provides an example of conflict between permitting areas to be a 'true' wilderness area, and a site meeting preconceived notions of beauty. In 1972 the park authorities decided to permit predators to re-establish themselves within the parklands. Then in the 1980s, the authorities decided that they would reverse their earlier policies on firefighting. It was argued that forest fires should be left to burn out, for in doing so they create opportunities for shrubs and grasses to flourish where they would normally be suppressed by the shade of the trees. The policy generated many new findings. For example, it was found that 80 per cent of fires burnt themselves out quite quickly, particularly if started by natural causes such as lightning strikes. Secondly, it was found that elk, deer and bison manage better with recently-burnt ground. However, in the summer of 1988 the park authorities permitted, as had become normal practice, the fires to rage in June in the expectation of rain in July. But the rain failed to materialise, and the American media showed pictures of fires apparently destroying the park. It did not matter that the park authorities spent $120 million in fire-fighting; the 'impression [was conveyed] that crazed environmentalists were letting the park burn down' (McKenzie 1989). The problem was one where 'although park managers have moved on to sophisticated theories about biosphere management and ecological preserves, people tend to want the same things from parks that they have always sought' (McKenzie 1989). A year after the fire, as North (1989) commented, the park was a 'wilderness enriched by fire', as it bloomed yet again.

SUMMARY

Both the controversy over the Prince Albert National Park and the Yellowstone National Park indicate that park management, and, in a wider sense, the management of tourist and recreational areas, is not simply the technical one of assessing visitor numbers, planning footpaths, calculating the number of car park spaces, ensuring the quality of water supply, and all the other above mentioned aspects. The tourist areas carry with them a heritage and a received perception of roles and functions. It is this aspect of the tourist resort life cycle that perhaps needs examination. Butler (1980), Young (1983) and others generally relate the cycle to built-up tourist zones, but there is also a need to establish a life cycle of perceptions of use of 'wild' and natural areas. Many tourists, as Walter (1982) argues, derive their notions of the countryside from the romantic literature of the late nineteenth century, and thus have perceptions of countryside as both unspoilt and serving purposes of renewal of the human spirit. These notions are projected onto the national parks of many nations, and thus sets of expectations and perceptions are fostered. The case of Prince Albert also shows the conflict that arises between local users of a park and the viewpoint of distant government that sees a park as part of a national asset that plays a role on a larger stage. The management of tourist zones is thus no mere matter of mechanics, but rather a complex balancing act between past heritage and changing perceptions of future needs of many participants – not only human, but also drawn from the natural world of animals, fish and plant life, as is indicated in Figure 6.3. The techniques of tourist zone management require a recognition of problems, and a willingness to accept and impose constraints upon use – a willingness easy to preach in the

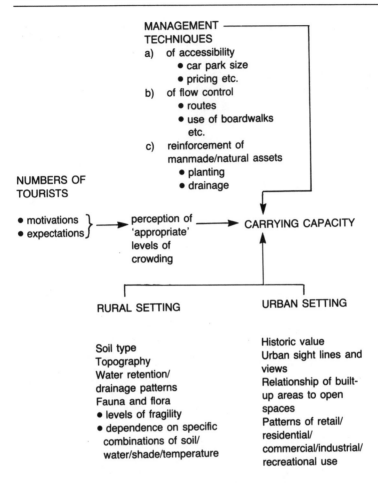

MANAGEMENT
TECHNIQUES

a) of accessibility
  - car park size
  - pricing etc.

b) of flow control
  - routes
  - use of boardwalks
    etc.

c) reinforcement of
  manmade/natural assets
  - planting
  - drainage

NUMBERS OF
TOURISTS

- motivations
- expectations

perception of
'appropriate'
levels of
crowding

CARRYING CAPACITY

RURAL SETTING

URBAN SETTING

Soil type
Topography
Water retention/
drainage patterns
Fauna and flora
- levels of fragility
- dependence on specific
  combinations of soil/
  water/shade/temperature

Historic value
Urban sight lines and
views
Relationship of built-
up areas to open
spaces
Patterns of retail/
residential/
commercial/industrial/
recreational use

Figure 6.3 Factors determining the ecological impacts of tourism

abstract but difficult to practice in the reality of any given situation. Whilst difficulty is no reason for aborting the effort to develop tourism that is consistent with the needs of ecological systems, such developments possibly require different motivations for tourism than those which have characterised much of tourism's growth in the last three decades. So, whilst, as argued in Chapter four, tourist zones become statements about the hosts as well as the tourists, so too, the tourist zone becomes a commentary about the wider issue of man's relationship with nature.

Chapter 7

The social and cultural impact of tourism

THE NATURE OF THE PROBLEM

In 1989 the author and naturalist Gerald Durrell wrote in relation to his beloved Corfu:

> Tourism is a curious modern disease. It attacks the shoeless man, the man of meagre wealth and the bloated man of affluence, whereupon it becomes an epidemic like the Black Death that stalked through Europe in the Middle Ages. It now ranges all over the world. The people of Corfu were blessed with a magnificent, magical inheritance, an island of staggering beauty, probably one of the most beautiful islands in the whole of the Mediterranean. What they have done with it is vandalism beyond belief.

Two years earlier the travel writer Jan Morris wrote with great intensity about what she felt tourism had done to her home area of the Llyn Peninsula in North Wales. She stated that:

> For years I have tried to defend it [tourism] as a valuable asset to a poor region. . . . I stood up for the vast caravan parks which disfigure so much of our coast on the grounds that the caravan was the poor man's holiday cottage. . . . No longer, something has cracked in me. I have come to detest all aspects of mass tourism. . . . It has gone too far, has got out of control – not just in Llyn outside my window, but wherever in the world affluence, big business and officialdom have made it possible. . . too many of the entrepreneurs who are developing tourism in our part of Wales are not local people at all. They are English people who have come to Wales to develop tourism! Their oblivion to the local history and culture is generally absolute – few of them have the courtesy to put up their shop signs in Welsh – and their contribution to the national well-being, vociferously though they claim to represent Welsh progress at planning enquiries or in Letters to the Editor, is virtually nil.

The complaint of both Durrell and Morris is not simply one of tourism damaging the landscape, but of more insidious damage to a way of life, to a culture and to sets of values. Pfafflin (1988) quotes one Hawaiian delegate at the 1986 Third World People and Tourism Conference as stating, 'We don't want tourism. We don't want you. We don't want to be degraded as servants and dancers. That is cultural prostitution. . . . There are no innocent tourists.' MacNaught (1982) lists the negative themes that are stated about the cultural impacts of tourism as being six in total. These are:

a) tourists do nothing to promote international understanding;
b) the strains of hospitality eventually become intolerable;
c) employment in the tourist industry is often dehumanising;
d) tourists have undesirable 'demonstration effects' on residents;
e) tourism debases local forms of cultural expression;
f) the tourist industry adversely affects community life.

Nor should it be thought that tourism brings these ills in situations where the tourist is a foreigner in a foreign land. Ragan (1989) reported on the tourist influx into the Yorkshire village of Malham in these terms:

> Malham is finding it increasingly difficult to cope with the ever-growing numbers. More leisure time and and easier access have made a day out in the Dales a popular outing. But although residents are growing disillusioned with the situation, they accept there is no easy solution.
>
> The numbers taking to the hills and walkways are taking their toll on the landscape. Footpaths are being eroded, dry stone walls damaged and meadows ruined.
>
> While locals say they do not want to deny people the right to enjoy the countryside, they say unless something can be done to preserve it, the village will no longer be worth visiting.

Why is it then that tourism, which brings so much enjoyment to people, and which contains the potential to indeed broaden the mind and enable people not only to relax, but to marvel at the world they occupy, and possibly reinforce concerns over environmental issues – why is it that tourism attracts these criticisms? In Chapter three it was noted that the tourist area is neither fixed spatially or temporally. The change that was described in Young's model of spatial change (1983) obviously has implicit within it a process of social change as the former fishing/farming village becomes an international tourist centre complete with marina and casino. This process of social change has long been recognised, and various authors allocate to the resort life cycle different social implications at each of the stages concerned. This chapter will describe some of the changes with reference to the work of Butler (1980) but then will seek to amplify specific aspects of the relationships between tourists and guests which have emerged as being of importance in the latter part of the 1980s.

THE CHANGING ATTITUDES OF THE HOST COMMUNITY

Butler identifies a six-stage cycle in the evolution of a tourism area, and as such it relates to the product life cycle of marketing theory.

The exploration stage

The first stage he characterises as the exploration stage in which there are a small number of visitors. They may be identified as akin to Plog's allocentrics or Cohen's explorers in that they make their own travel arrangements and seek to merge with the local host community. Often they will speak the language of the hosts and identify with their culture. The hosts themselves will welcome their 'guests', for they bring novelty and open a window to the outside world. They may not realise that these tourists are part of what Turner and Ash (1975) called the 'pleasure periphery'. That is to say, these are the tourists seeking new destinations away from those areas that were once 'unspoilt' but which now have grown in popularity and thus are of no further interest to the 'explorer'. As such these tourists may be precursors of what is to come.

Within the exploration stage the social impact is small. Any commercial activity that occurs is small scale, is individualistically or family based, and there is effectively no adoption of marketing strategies.

The involvement stage

Should the numbers of tourists increase, the second stage is entered. This is the involvement stage. The host community now begins to respond to the increasing numbers of visitors by providing some facilities. In the early part of this stage, such entrepreneurial activities still tend to be family based. Some members of the host community might set aside part of their home and take in visitors. Levels of tourist/host contact remain high, and the marketing of the area remains subdued. Owners of accommodation may simply display signs indicating rooms to let, and possibly a few might later print some leaflets to give to their guests, who will subsequently pass them on to friends. At this stage the relationship between host and tourist is still harmonious, and the tourists still possess high levels of interest and sympathy with the local way of life.

In the later stages of the involvement stage some of the host community might recognise that tourism will continue to grow, and that in order to earn more from it they will have to expand the facilities being provided. Accordingly, they may have recourse to borrowed funding, and may involve not simply family members but also refer to commercial sources of finance. At some stage if there has not previously been a branch of a bank in the village, one will become established as hosts seek safety for their money, a means of earning interest, and of course a source of borrowing. At the same time these 'entrepreneurs' within the village will become more professional in their marketing efforts. Unable to reach directly into the tourist-generating areas they have recourse to those organisations that can. In many instances the first such body is the country's own tourist organisation, which is of course keen to promote its area. Either directly, or through the tourist board, members of the village might also approach other intermediaries, for example incoming tour organisers.

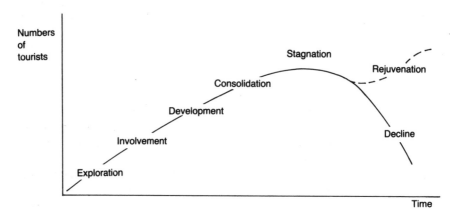

Figure 7.1   The tourist product life cycle (After Butler 1980)

The development stage

Butler then assumes that the process continues, and the numbers of tourists coming now begin to grow quite significantly as illustrated in Figure 7.1. The third stage, that of development is now reached. Butler describes this stage as being the one where the community now becomes a tourist resort. Plog's 'mid-centrics' or Cohen's 'institutionalised tourists' now appear. In the period of late involvement and early development stages the community begins to attract the interest of outside bodies. New retail businesses appear, some of which may be owned by local people, some by nationals drawn from the centres of population and who have retail or catering experience. In the early stages of development the first of the package holidaymakers appear, albeit holidaymakers who are using the services of 'niche' companies who serve that part of the market, who have much in common with the attitude of 'allocentrics,' but who are not 'full-time' travellers and who are operating within constrained time periods. As the development stage progresses the spatial dimensions of the village begin to change rapidly, as described by Young, and following the 'niche' tour operators come the larger tour operators dealing with a mass market within the tourist-generating regions. In terms of the total activity that is now being generated the locally owned businesses are becoming marginalised. The main marketing efforts have now been delegated by the hosts to organisations which are not only outside of their area, but are also, perhaps, outside of their country. The relationships between tourist and host have changed, and tourism is now a business, and no longer enjoys the novelty and excitement that it once possessed. Indeed, in the well-developed tourist enclave, the host community may increasingly have less contact with tourists as the tourist area attracts migrant workers into the hotels and restaurants. In time the growth of the industry slows down. The 'pleasure periphery' has long moved on, the niche tour operators have either left the area, or now market the destination in another way, or have had their operations taken over by the larger, mainstream companies.

The consolidation and stagnation stages

The consolidation phase begins. As the expansion ceases, attention is paid to the control of costs as hoteliers and tour operators find that this is the only possible way of increasing profits. Revenue earned per tourist tends to fall, as the resort loses its 'exclusivity'. 'Resort loyalty' is low, as it has come to resemble many other locations. Take-overs and mergers occur within the industry as the transport − leisure − accommodation company buyouts occur. The tourists now being attracted are the 'organised mass market' and the 'psychocentrics'. Company strategies turn to maintaining the visitor numbers, and hence the stagnation phase is reached. The resort has reached full capacity, perhaps even exceeded it at certain times of the year. The resort has an image abroad of its own − it is distinguishable from the surrounding hinterland. Unfortunately it is not a 'fashionable' area. In order to sustain visitor numbers the tour operators may have to resort to low prices to attract the volume of tourists that they consider necessary to sustain their investment. Falling profit margins lead to maintenance programmes being put off; the resort begins to look dowdy. The attendant environmental, social and economic problems associated with areas past their prime begin to emerge. The host community is faced with a resort where tourist companies are a minority in their own home area. The process of decline thus commences. But associated with the decline there is the withdrawal of foreign-owned businesses. The host community is left to 'pick up the pieces'. It can never regain its original standing as a fishing/ farming village, but it might be able to regain its status as a place in which local people can have pride. The local authorities, mindful of the economic implications of decline, might seek to develop a process of renewal with those organisations that remain in the area, and rejuvenation might then become possible. Thus, new forms of tourism might be sought. Alternatively, the facilities are switched into other uses. The hotels become nursing homes, and the once-thriving seaside resort becomes noted for its numbers of retired people. Failure to either rejuvenate or find alternative uses for tourism assets means that the area will continue to decline, to become characterised by brief bursts of activity in the height of the season, but with a continuing erosion of its assets so that the resort becomes characterised by peeling paint, rusting rails, and memories of days when the place had glamour and excitement.

THE SOCIAL IMPACT OF THE LIFE CYCLE

That the process does exist can be evidenced by various studies, including that by Wilson (1989) which relates to the British seaside resorts. Doxey (1975), in considering the social impact of the life cycle, concludes that specific changes in attitude exist within the host community towards tourism as the cycle unfolds. As indicated above, initially there is what he terms, euphoria. The host community is pleased to see the tourist for reasons relating, at the very least, to hospitality, and if that community is economically poor, then the economic promise of tourism is welcomed as a source of income that, at least in the initial stages, supplements the region's low wages. As the cycle moves into its involvement stage, Doxey observes that it is generally a minority of the host community that is involved. As the numbers grow the tourist is no longer a rare sight. A process of habituation occurs. The later arrivals may not speak the language of the host community, and are perhaps less interested in the daily life of that community. Apathy sets in, and the second stage of Doxey's model commences. By the time development is well under way, the tourist:host ratio has so changed that the host community is becoming marginalised in its own home area. The host community faces queues in the shops. Many shops change their role, and souvenir shops are of little use to the local person. The roads are full of traffic, and it becomes difficult for local people to park in areas that are convenient to them. They may well feel that they live in a car park, for whilst each individual tourist is present for but a short time, the local person lives in the area for all of the tourist season. Apathy turns to annoyance. In turn, faced with the problems of over capacity that can occur at the stagnation phase of the life cycle, annoyance turns into antagonism, as was perhaps demonstrated by the quotations at the start of this chapter. As a highly visible industry characterised by the fact that the consumer comes to the provider of the service, tourism is blamed for changes that have taken place in an area. Nor is the antipathy reserved for the tourists alone. Milligan (1989) parallels Doxey's earlier work in her study of Portuguese workers in Guernsey. As indicated in Table 7.1, Milligan argues that just as the local people become annoyed with the tourists because of the problems of crowding that they cause, so, too, that anger is directed at those who serve the tourists, particularly if they too are 'outsiders'. Milligan's study was within a somewhat different context than that usually associated with applications of Doxey's Irridex in that Guernsey is not a developing area, but enjoys all the advantages of being a tax haven with all that that implies for employment in the financial sector. Nonetheless, tourism has for many years been a significant part of Guernsey's economy; but with local people having full employment, they were not dependent on jobs in the hotel and associated sectors.

Table 7.1   Doxey's Irridex and Milligan's Modification

Doxey's Irridex		Milligan's 'modified version'	
Euphoria	– visitors are welcome and there is little planning.	Curiosity	– that people should accept jobs that the hosts consider beneath them in status, pay and career prospects.
↓		↓	
Apathy	– visitors are taken for granted and contact becomes more formal.	Acceptance	– of immigrants on the island, tourism is no longer a concern of the local people.
↓		↓	
Annoyance	– saturation is approached and the local people have misgivings. Planners attempt to control via increasing infrastructure rather than limiting growth.	Annoyance	– coupled with an annoyance with tourists is an antipathy towards immigrant workers who are seen as contributing to deteriorating standards.
↓		↓	
Antagonism	– open expression of irritation and planning is remedial yet promotion is increased to offset the deteriorating reputation of the resort.	Antagonism	– both sides are aware of resentment, and the situation amongst young people is volatile. Immigrant workers are blamed for all that tourists cannot be held directly responsible for.

TOURISM AND CULTURAL ACTIVITIES

Tourists often buy souvenirs. It has been argued previously that the economic benefits from tourism are increased if the purchases that are made are of locally manufactured items. Ritchie and Zins (1978) indicated various areas of culture with which tourism may interact and these are discussed below.

Handicrafts

These are often the first things that local communities may be able to produce as souvenirs. Tourism may therefore lead to a resurgence in local art forms. However, if the tourist is not aware of the past traditions of the culture, there is little awareness of what constitutes either 'good art' or 'authentic art'. The tourists use the norms with which they are familiar, and these are of course derived from their own cultural background. The artist, in order to sell, might then introduce changes that are not consistent with past traditions. It is difficult to assess whether this is good or bad – exposure to new ideas that might stimulate the imagination may not be a bad thing. In part, it might depend upon the significance of the art that is being produced. Art that is associated with religious symbolism may lose its meaning if it begins to meet totally different sets of criteria that may be imposed by what the tourist wants, or is perceived to want. However, in many respects such an artist is perhaps in no different a situation from their counterparts in the tourist-generating countries, or from those in the past, in the sense that artists have a tradition of having to produce work to meet client wants and artist's own creative impulses. Only rarely have these separate needs coincided.

Languages

Language has an important role in that it is not simply a means of communication but also a means of shaping the perception of the world. It reflects what is seen as being important by the users and creators of the language. The Inuit have many different words to describe differences of snow; modern English has generated a host of words relating to technology, topography, relationships, climate, science, religion – all these issues colour, and are coloured by, language. It is perhaps no accident that within the English language economists talk of the buying and selling of 'goods'; a word that is associated with positive virtues, rather than the buying and selling of 'bads'. So, language is a means by which the host society can maintain its distinctiveness from the tourist, or indeed any 'outsider'. The erosion of language thus has significant implications for the host society, for it implies a supplanting of its norms and values by an outside culture in the very matter of everyday communication.

Traditions

Tourism creates employment opportunities, but in a form that may be inconsistent with past work patterns. Rural economies may be based on seasonal patterns of work, like tourism, but with a different daily pattern, and a different pace. Tourism replaces the agricultural timetable with work that is based on buildings and not fields, with work based on service to those engaged in leisure and not seeking food as a necessity, and with work that continues into the late hours rather than that based on the rising and setting of the sun. It thus affects people's ability to maintain past patterns of life, but this would be true of any work based on western technology. In addition, the tourist indulges in different behaviour patterns that the host society may find shocking.

On the other hand, it has been argued that tourism can regenerate traditions, and there are many such examples. To take but one, the Maine Windjammers Association is able to maintain its fleet of sailing vessels which recreate the past by catering to the tourist trade, and as such this is but one example of 'heritage tourism'.

Gastronomy

In discussing economic impacts of tourism, it was mentioned that some studies indicate that tourist developments end with the importing of food that meets a perceived tourist need for an 'international cuisine' rather than providing the dishes that are eaten by local people. This, too, reflects differences in culture, and implies that the local food is not 'good enough' for the 'guest' or 'tourist'. However, as tourists are increasingly prepared to try new things, so the need for importing food begins to decline, and the host community takes pride in its own style of food preparation (Belisle 1984, Henshall-Momsen 1986).

Art and music

The type and numbers of tourists are again important, for the influx of large numbers of tourists into the Mediterranean has brought the sound of the disco to replace the guitar. The popular 'Viva Espana' and the 'Birdy Song' is played in many bars throughout Spain, and every year songwriters and composers seek a catchy tune that will appeal to the northern Europeans so as to obtain sales of records not only at the holiday resort, but also in the tourist-generating countries, on the basis that the tune is a means of evoking holiday memories. Yet, again, tourism is not the sole mechanism by which pop music reaches any culture. Interestingly enough, there are increasing signs of cultural change and diversification that is appearing in the musical life of tourist-receiving countries that represents a positive response to the pop idioms of the USA and Northern Europe. The first is the development of hybrid musical styles as pop artists, like many other types of artists before them, incorporate that which they find appealing within their own musical idioms. A form of 'rock flamenco' has developed, albeit without much success outside of Spain, whilst African rhythms from many different parts of that continent have had an impact on the popular music of Europe. An example would be Andy Kershaw's work involving Mali rhythms and sounds in 1988 and 1989. As tourists become increasingly curious about host societies, so the host society rediscovers the values of its own music, or, it takes solace in its own music as a means of re-asserting its cultural distinctiveness. In either case musical life becomes enriched.

Architecture

It is a cliche of holiday travel that many resort complexes may be interchangeable. Indeed, for the business traveller, a number of hotel chains take pride in the fact that their hotels are the same the world over, for in this manner the tired business travellers are presented with no strange customs or manners, but rather are within a familiar milieu whereupon it is easier for them to relax. However, the establishment of a conformity of architectural style is not restricted to the hotel and its pool surrounded by gardens and sun loungers that are familiar to many travellers. With the renewal of waterfront and urban areas that are, to at least some extent, utilising tourism as a means of such rejuvenation, there is arguably some danger of an architectural uniformity emerging. Nor is it simply a fact that many examples of waterfront developments (at least in the UK) contain a marine museum, and a waterside restaurant with a nautical theme! In March 1988 the Royal Town Planning Institute addressed the issue of contemporary urban design in its journal, *The Planner*. One result was a series of varying opinions, and it was noted (North 1988), that in the case of waterfront development a similar architecture was being developed in many of the sites throughout Britain. In comparing photographs of, say, the developments of Liverpool, with those of Swansea, or London, a similarity of red brick, false colonnades, bands of orange colour, painted wooden circles or diamonds set in the walls, abound. Indeed, this type of architecture is to be found away from the waterfront, for example in new housing near Beverley Minster. It is thus difficult to tell the places apart. The reasons for the similarity of architecture are partly a question of cost and the current methods of building, which North (1988) compared to the use of Legoland bricks. Increasingly buildings are assembled from parts manufactured elsewhere. There is a concept of the waterfront development which is typified by a complex of villas painted white with bougainvillea, the dash-board houses of New England, the white-washed houses of the Mediterranean, and thus the architects meet the preconceptions of the holidaying tourist throughout the world. It can be contended that Boorstin's pseudo-event or Papson's notion of 'spurious reality' is not confined to the enactment of folklore events, but also to the maintenance of the 'set'.

This is not of course new, nor is it without some value. One of the loved eccentricities of North Wales is Portmeirion, the Italianate village set in beautiful surroundings and started in 1926. One difference between a location such as Portmeirion and the various marinas that exist lies in the motivation behind the buildings. Sir Clough Williams-Ellis, the architect for whom Portmeirion was the fulfilment of a life's dream, sought specifically to design an area that consisted of attractive buildings that harmonised with, and enhanced, the surroundings. Sight lines from the cottages, and views from the wooded valley towards the village were thus carefully designed. In Florida a similar development is the town of Seaside, a town constructed to a code which controls the shape, height, colour and materials to be used, and which dictates the amount of open space, and where this is to be located. Unlike Portmeirion, Seaside is occupied by permanent inhabitants, but its popularity has brought with it increasing land values which means that only the most affluent can buy properties. Whilst undoubtedly popular, Seaside has its critics. Guest (1988) refers to it as being primarily a 'rich man's holiday resort', pointing out that only 15 per cent approximately of the 100 homes or so are completely occupied all the year round, the rest being rented out for holiday use, and concluding that 'Seaside is perilously close to being a model village, a pastel coloured pastiche of classical, Victorian and Georgian versions of the old sharecropper and dogtrot houses. It either looks too good to eat or good enough to scrawl graffiti on – depending on your point of view.' Behind the modern marina developments lie other motivations. Enhancement of the area undeniably does exist, but within a context of what is deemed to be marketable, commercial and cost effective. Taylor (1987), in discussing inner city renewal issues, commented that many such developments are fitted with such labour-saving devices as being able to bring in the milk off the doorstep without getting out of bed, so small were some of the flats being built!

Any discussion of the relationship between architecture and tourism must recognise that it can only exist within a much wider context of the relationship between man and his surroundings; but if the advocates of the 'community architecture movement' such as HRH, The Prince of Wales, and Rod Hackney, RIBA President, are correct in their assumptions that architecture must relate to the needs of people as both individuals and as communities, then within the framework of holidays, such assumptions must be even more valid. The tower-like, 400-or-more-bedroom hotels with their poor sound-proofing may be rejected by tourists who are increasingly showing their preference for self-catering chalets and similar forms of accommodation. Yet, ironically, the search for greater individual freedom by the tourist generates greater costs. High rise is high density housing, but low rise and low density tourist complexes are more space demanding, with all that implies for the environment.

One social feature of tourism is that the architectural style that in the past has characterised many tourist complexes has been one that may make only a token gesture towards the society within which the resort is located, and then only within the confines of meeting the stereotypes of the holidaymakers. Consequently, some societies have sought to control the design and shape of the housing, and in this respect Lanzarote, inspired by the painter and architect, Caesar Manrique, has required all developments to conform to certain traditional features of its architecture.

The demonstration effects of tourist upon host, and host upon tourist, are not restricted to modes of behaviour. Architecture has long been the expression of aspirations of a society; and indeed that is one reason why tourists flock to cathedrals and palaces, and to the homes of both the mighty and the humble of the past (the Welsh National Museum of St Fagans is an example of the latter). In this respect therefore, the type of architecture that is adopted for tourist complexes is again a reflection of priorities that are deemed to be important. Arguably, the tower-block hotel reflects priorities of cost, of seeking to achieve high rates of return upon investment in the short and intermediate term. Other styles of architecture may reflect the norms of the host society, or the preconceptions of the incoming tourist. If tourism is an agent of social change, then the architecture and buildings of the tourist industry are the expressions of that process and the type of tourist activity that the host society has sought to attract.

Religion

Tourists wander through the great cathedrals of Europe with varying degrees of awe. The churches become museums; the shell of a Middle Ages' culture stripped of the sense of worship that motivated their very construction all those centuries ago. Himalayan trekkers strip outside of the holy places of Buddhism in order to wash after a day's climb. The bare-breasted sun worshippers regard the mullah's cry as a nuisance that breaks their reverie. Whilst there are many differences between the tourist and the host, the differing attitude towards religion may be amongst the most marked, especially when the tourist originates from an increasingly agnostic if not atheistic western culture and the host is from the developing world where religious belief may still be strong. Like all generalisations, neither the tourist nor host can be so easily categorised, and the individual tourist may indeed be more religious than the individual host. However, the impact of tourism upon religion is difficult to assess. That western societies permit tourists to throng through the cathedrals is a reflection not simply of the impact and importance afforded to tourism, but also of the importance attached to its Christianity.

It may be argued that the income from tourism is important to the maintenance of cathedrals, and indeed this is the case; but the recognition of this fact implies an acceptance that the average person is more prepared to pay to see the cathedral than to worship within it. But even this type of statement withers before the data collected by the Commons Select Committee on the Environment (1987), when it was found that York Minster attracted 2.5 million visitors in 1986, and raised £359,000, (an average of 14p per visitor), to help offset annual maintenance charges of £600,000. Problems may emerge when the same attitude is shown in locations where the tourist fails to appreciate the importance of religious shrines to the host, who views them not as curios from the past, but as an essential part of everyday life. But, as in many other aspects of the debate about tourism making an impact upon components of culture, the ability of the host society to withstand the cultural changes potentially inherent in tourism is dependent upon the strength of that culture.

Dress and leisure activities

Tourists may cause shock amongst hosts by their dress, or lack of it. Cohen (1982) in his paper on 'marginal paradises', the beaches of Thailand, observes how nudity gave offence to the indigenous people; and this type of observation has been made many times. Equally, hosts may view certain types of dress as inappropriate. Thus, for example, in Spain in the 1960s, female tourists had to be properly attired before entering a church, and a bare head and a mini-skirt were definitely not appropriate. Males would have had to wear shirts with sleeves, and long trousers. Today, in the tourist areas, the bare-headed female or the short-sleeved male may enter the church without fear of generating disapproving stares. However, to argue that this is due solely to tourism, would be to under-estimate the other changes within Spanish society in the last 20 years, changes which have transformed Spain from a dictatorship to a Parliamentary democracy within the European Community.

Tourism has affected dress in the sense of helping to create an interest in traditional dress. Whether it is Morris dancers in England, Highland dancers, grass-skirted 'hula' girls, North American Indian costumes and dancers – throughout the world the tourist shows help to maintain the existence of traditional dress as a means of retaining distinctive elements of a culture, and as expressive statements of a tradition and past which are an explanation of the present. However, just as Ropponen (1976) refers to the faking of antiques for the tourist trade, so, too, it might be queried whether the occasion for the wearing of traditional dress is not also faked for the tourist.

Just as it is for dress, so too with some of the traditional times of rejoicing within societies. Greenwood (1977) charts the commercialisation of the Alarde, a festival held in Fuenterrabia, Spain. Originally commemorating a victory over the French in 1638, it was a community festival, but promoted by the tourist authorities it began to lose its spontaneity, and over time became but a shadow of its former self. Equally, the large processions of Semana Santa in the major Spanish cities have become a tourist sight. Staged Indian weddings, staged African dances – throughout the world, culture is being offered as a tourist resource, a commodity to be sold to the coach parties. Initially motivated by a pride in their dance and dress, the sheer repetition means the community event becomes a professional show performed by paid actors. As a show, the performance becomes packaged in one-hour time slots to fit the timetable of the tourist without any reference to the original purpose or duration of the event. Yet, in a changing world which moves at a different pace from that of the past, the evolving modern societies might arguably have no place for these past traditional performances were it not for tourism maintaining at least a bank of skills in dance and dress, so that the host society can call upon the traditions when it sees fit.

FACTORS THAT PROTECT AND ERODE HOST COMMUNITIES' CULTURE

As with all these types of arguments there are at least two questions that come to mind. The first is, what are the causes of the process that is envisaged, and secondly, is the process inevitable? Certainly there is much to indicate that annoyance with tourists is not restricted to situations where the host country is a developing country and where large gaps in cultural and social norms exist.

Murphy (1985) notes that there are three determinants of community attitudes towards tourists. The first is the type of contact that is made with the tourist. Krippendorf (1987) makes the point that there is a specific truth about the tourist/host relationship. The one is on holiday and seeking relaxation, the other is at work. He describes the relationship thus:

> Tourist and native are in diametrically opposite positions. The one is at leisure, the other at work. Natives distinguish between tourist and guests, and tourists are merchandise. Spontaneity is difficult for the umpteenth group of tourists. Meetings are meaningful when there is common ground, but there is little of that. The tourists are visiting a phantom of a place – an illusion of cliches – they are drawn by the unusual – not the minutiae of everyday reality - the very thing they seek escape from. Natives also view tourists through stereotypes – they are rich, they come from cold countries. Neither knows the world of the other.

De Kadt (1979) notes that there are three contact situations. The first is when the tourist buys a good or service. The second, when tourist and host find themselves side by side at an attraction that both are using, for example, a beach, golf course or nightclub. Finally, the third situation is when the two come together for an exchange of information and ideas. As the first two situations are by far the most common, the great majority of tourist/host relationships are marked by a transitory nature. In addition, it might be argued that the third type of situation may have differing degrees of informality. If, therefore, the nature of the relationship tends to be so fleeting, how is it that tourists present the challenge that they do to the social and ethical norms of the host society?

The answer to this question, Murphy (1985) believes, lies in two other domains; the relative importance of the tourist industry to the individual and the community, and whether or not a host group can handle the amount of traffic that tourism is generating. Tolerance of the tourist is thus a function of the returns and compensations that tourism creates, and the amount of 'nuisance' that it brings. It can, therefore, be easily envisaged that if tourists are large in numbers but bring little economic or other benefits, and intrude upon the local patterns of activity, then the stage is indeed set for Doxey's annoyance and possibly antagonistic stages. However, there are a number of issues that influence this process, for clearly most communities are at some point between the continuum of welcoming or hating tourists, and other factors pertain. Also, there is no simple model of linear or sequential sets of relationships that can determine the degree of social change that tourism creates. It is also difficult to relate social change to tourism alone. Whilst tourism may bring economic wealth, the way in which that wealth is spent is determined by the recipients of the income, and it is not inevitable that they spend it in ways that simply ape the life styles of the foreigner. Local communities are not passive sponges that soak up foreign ideas, and any resultant social change is a reflection not only of tourists, but also the underlying strength of the host culture. Furthermore, it might be argued that in well-established tourist areas, what emerges is not a culture that reflects fully either the culture of visitor or native, but some hybrid reflecting the non-permanent relationships that occur within tourism. In short, a 'tourist culture' emerges, which is recognisable to all participants as being something outside of the norm. The characteristics of such a culture might be said to include the following:

a) large numbers of visitors staying for a short duration;
b) large numbers of seasonal workers;
c) transient relationships between visitor and visitor, and visitor and temporary worker;
d) tourists are freed from the constraints of their normal life style;
e) leisure is the main motivation;
f) spending is comparatively unrestrained;
g) neither worker nor tourist fully conforms to the habits or norms of their

usual peer groups, i.e. the groups from which they come, but are selective as to those norms they wish to adopt;

h) usual patterns of daily activity are different, even to the normal patterns of sleeping and waking times;

i) businesses reflect the importance of tourism, e.g., retail outlets have a different merchandise mix compared to shopping centres in non-tourist areas;

j) the cultural expressive symbols are based on stereotypes and caricature;

k) superior/inferior relationships exist in varying degrees between guest and host;

l) lack of long-term commitment to the area by tourists and possibly many of the workers;

m) communication may be through intermediaries and partly-spoken languages. If it is argued that language is the medium of conveying complex ideas full of nuances and subtleties, the fact that the parties concerned may have an incomplete knowledge of each other's language means that communication lacks those facets that are of importance in conveying culture. The communications within the tourist area may thus be dominated by 'crude' concepts related to only a few (leisure) aspects of human behaviour.

Yet, the channels of cultural change are also many, diverse and complex. In the emergence of the 'global village', where American 'soaps' are beamed by satellite into villages with a communal television set, it is difficult to disentangle the separate processes of change mechanisms. Tourism may be a catalyst of change, but the direction of change is uncertain. Nor must it be thought that the participants within the process are tourist and host alone. Some tourists come to stay, whilst immigrant workers are attracted to the jobs that tourism brings. Thus, the social changes that tourism brings are not restricted to the tourist zone itself, but are felt in the hinterland from which the workers come. Nor must it be thought that the quality of change is always 'bad'. Travis (1982) noted at that time just how 'grossly inadequate has been the consideration given to the disbenefits of tourism' in the mainstream writings of authors such as Burkhart and Medlik (1974), and even today similar criticisms can still be made (Middleton 1988). However, there is equally a danger that all tourist activity is being perceived as negative, and in his review of the literature Travis (1982) indicates that studies considering socio-cultural and political impacts of tourism are overwhelmingly of the opinion that tourism generates negative impacts by nearly a ratio of 3.8:1 (an admittedly crude calculation it must be emphasised).

What then are the processes and issues that need to be examined? The process of social change induced by tourism is illustrated in Figure 7.2. Within the tourist zone the nature of the interaction between host and

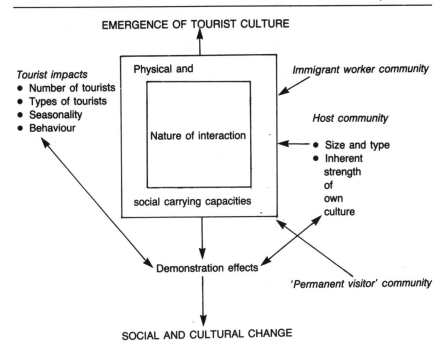

Figure 7.2   The process of social change

tourist is determined by the nature of the tourists, the belief and cultural systems of the host and the physical carrying capacities of the area that determine the degree of stress that is being generated. However, physical carrying capacity also has psychological aspects. Not only is it a question of the perception of, and tolerance of, physical crowding by the tourist, but also by the host — a set of perceptions and expectations that are shaped by their own culture. Within this process of interaction, sets of behaviour have demonstration effects. Again, this can be on both tourist and host. Generally, the literature relates the demonstration effects upon the host community, particularly upon the young within that community (Cohei. 1982, Loukissas 1982, Jafari 1981, 1982, Krippendorf 1987), but theoretically, and especially when the tourist:host ratio is small, hosts can influence the behaviour of tourists, at least within the setting of the host community. Thus, the tourist complies with the norms of the host. Such demonstration effects feed back into the nature of interaction. However, in the more developed tourist area, the host community also has two other groups to cope with, those who are drawn to the area seeking work, and those visitors who come to stay. Both groups also have their norms. Indeed, those visitors who come to stay in the area might be the very people who exhibit most alarm over physical changes in the zone.

The impact that tourism will thus have on a society is the result of an interaction between the nature of the change agent and the inherent strength and ability of the host culture to withstand, and absorb, the change generators whilst retaining its own integrity. From the viewpoint of the host culture there may therefore be mechanisms of protection such as withdrawal from tourist activity, or the confinement of tourism, and the 'pseudo-event' and the 'tourist bubble' become protective mechanisms in that they limit touristic impacts; and there are 'erosion' factors, such as the type of tourists, the number and background of immigrant workers, and the 'permanent visitor'. An important component of the protective mechanism of the host culture is the role and views of 'opinion leaders' within their own community.

Communities are not necessarily homogeneous, and the Doxey Irridex can be criticised for implying both a process of inevitability and a homogeneity of opinion. Bjorklund and Philbrick (1972) present a matrix whereby the hosts may be active or passive in terms of their behaviour towards tourism, and negative or positive in terms of their attitude. This gives rise to a four-cell matrix as indicated in Figure 7.3. The difference between this and Doxey's framework is that the matrix recognises that a variety of opinions may be found within the host community, and that opinions can indeed change in any one of the four directions. It may be that Doxey's Irridex represents the general tone of opinion, whilst the Bjorklund and Philbrick model represents the attitude disaggregated into its various components. Each of the various sectors within the host society, the entrepreneurs, public planning authorities, general public, conservation groups will each have their own paradigms of behaviour and attitude. Murphy (1983), in a survey of residents, the business sector and local government, found that the entrepreneurs generally had the most positive attitudes towards tourism. If they and the local authorities are the change agents and opinion leaders amongst their own communities, then tourist development is more likely to occur.

However, it should not be thought that residents have a simplistic attitude towards tourism, for it has been shown that they are more than capable of distinguishing between different impacts. Liu, Sheldon and Var (1986), in a comparison of Wales, Turkey and Hawaii, found that whilst the economic benefits of tourism are recognised, residents tend to rate as more important to them, particularly in the more developed tourist areas, the intangible disbenefits of tourism.

For both Hawaii and North Wales, notions such as environmental protection ranked more importantly than certain expected costs and benefits. The rank order was as follows:

Environmental > economic > social > cultural
protection   benefits   costs   benefits

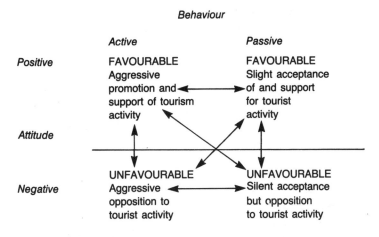

Figure 7.3   Host attitudinal/behavioural responses to tourist activity
Source: Bjorklund and Philbrick (1972) quoted in Mathieson and Wall (1982).

However, there were differences between aspects of the different dimensions. For example, residents of Hawaii were concerned with the ability of tourists to create higher standards of living, whilst 'Residents of North Wales appeared to be more altruistic and willing to undergo personal sacrifice for environmental protection'. Similarly, Milman and Pizam (1988) interviewed residents of Florida and found that whilst residents recognised the economic benefits of tourism, tourism was perceived as a factor that would contribute to worsening traffic conditions and crime. Ryan (1989) used the same questions as Milman and Pizam for the town of Nottingham, England, and found that the results were comparable, in that the economic benefits were recognised but, if anything, there was greater doubt about the social implications. Similar studies by the BTA of Londoners' attitudes towards tourists show concern with traffic conditions, aspects of courtesy and other similar considerations.

The relationship between attitudes and behavioural change is not a simple one. Attitudes may be said to comprise of three components:

a) the cognitive component – what is, or is thought to be, true about a situation. A process of belief as much as perceived objective truth;
b) the affective component – the emotional aspect of attitude;
c) the conative component – the predisposition to act upon the cognitive and affective components.

In the case of tourism, the cognitive component may be based on a series of, at best, partial truths – the stereotype of the image of the place on the part of the tourist, whilst the host perceives the tourist as a rich, leisured person, without any concept of the work that person usually undertakes. (Thus the learning processes available to the tourist are important.) From these perceptions arises a series of emotional (affective) feelings; and the predisposition to behave in a particular manner consistent with the feelings of being a tourist emerges. However, given any set of cognitive, affective and conative aspects, the link between attitude and behaviour is still complex because a series of inhibiting, external factors may dampen the behaviour consistent with any given attitude. Thus, the tourists who are unhappy about aspects of their holiday may be reluctant to express an opinion if their peers are seen as 'having a good time'. In this respect, as Fishbein (1967) observes, it is not only the content of belief, but the importance attached to that belief that is important. The reluctant tourists may, inspite of inhibiting pressures, act in accordance with their beliefs if it is deemed important enough. Equally, in Fishbein's extended model, they may take into account the perceived outcomes of their action. In such a case, whilst attitude may motivate change, equally, the expected outcome can also determine behaviour. Thus, the attitude of, and to, tourists is dependent on a complex pattern of not simply belief, but the importance of norms and the values attached to potential outcomes of behaviour. Host societies may not like some aspects of tourist behaviour, but tolerate it on the basis of expected economic benefits. What might be said is that the attitude of hosts towards tourists is not always revealed by the behaviour of hosts to tourists – their behaviour is simply the result of a series of compromises between conflicts of objectives of varying importance to them.

TOURISM AND DEVELOPING AREAS

It can be envisaged that the greatest impacts will be made where there is a greater gap between the culture and income of both host and tourist. It is a cliche of the literature that the American tourist in Canada will have little impact, but the same American tourist in a developing country will have a far greater influence. Adapting the arguments of Heron (1990) it may be argued that cultures are characterised by differential use of three types of time dimension. These are:

a) Sacred time – time used for communal participation not simply for worship, but in any type of rite which establishes the relationship of that community with its environment. Its characteristic is that it is a time shared with others where common beliefs are expressed and reinforced.
b) Profane time – is functional and mechanistic in nature. It is time that is measured; it is the time where appointments and meetings are made; where timetables are established by man and are adhered to.
c) Personal time – is that time used for personal reflection and re-creation in the sense of determining the individual's relationship with environment, community, family and self.

Heron argues that developed nations tend to emphasise 'profane time', whilst a characteristic of developing nations is the more central importance of 'sacred time'. Hence, the impact of the industry of tourism (with its time schedules of events, arrivals and departures) contains a fundamental cultural change whereby the host community shifts from using 'sacred' to 'profane' time.

Nor will the impact of tourism be restricted to the immediate tourist zone. In her study of Spanish immigrant workers in Lloret de Mar, Lever (1987) traced, over a five-year period, the effect of working in the tourism industry upon young people from the village of San Santiago, a village in the hinterland of the Costa Brava. The majority of such workers were females and from the poorer sections of village society. The demonstration effects of tourist behaviour as well as the changes of life as a chambermaid or worker in a bar created a number of social impacts. The young women were freed from the conservative life styles of male-dominated homes, and could go to discos and have relaxed friendships with males. They lived in flats with their peers with no parental presence. They became important sources of family income, perhaps earning more than their fathers did from the soil. They might have played a role in the burgeoning trade union action of the immediate post-Franco period. In short, the conservative life styles with clearly defined roles were being changed. Further, the changes were recognised by the village, if only because a person who was financially independent and who contributed to the family income had to be treated very differently from someone who effectively worked in a role as a subordinate upon the family farm. Overall, because tourism created a new role for women, it might be said to have been beneficial. Further, the income that tourism generated helped to sustain the farms for without such an income the area might have followed what had long been a traditional pattern of Spain, and that was the emigration from the land to the city.

The relationship between tourist city and rural area is a complex one. In some areas of the Mediterranean, for example in Cyprus, it has been the males who have tended to go into the tourist zones, such as Ayia Nappa, in order to start up tourist-related businesses such as snack bars and restaurants; and while the younger women work in the hotels, it is the older women who may take over some of the work on the farms such as picking fruit and vegetables. Thus, the women are being displaced from a purely domestic role into more of an income earning role, but it is still a subsidiary function. The development of tourism in developing, peripheral economies undoubtedly changes female roles, and potentially male/female relationships within the host society. Of importance are the monies that tourism can create. For rural societies that are little mechanised, the burdens of hard work are well ingrained. The work in hotels and bars, whilst hard and exhausting, might be seen as easier in comparison with agricultural work, particularly if the tourist season is well defined and restricted to approximately the four or five months of the spring until the autumn. If locally owned businesses are able to flourish, then the tourist area will attract workers from other industries. It will also perhaps attract, into supervisory management roles, the better qualified and educated from the host society away from other jobs which might be more needed by the host society but which are also low paid. Such alternative jobs might include teaching, nursing, social work of various forms and local authority administration. For the balance to be rectified, it becomes important as to how much of the economic benefits generated by tourism are retained by the host community, and the means by which these benefits are distributed.

Reference has been made to tourism influencing not only the host community, but having a wider impact on immigrant workers. In Lever's example there was a homogeneity in the culture of the immigrant and the host, but that is not always present. In his study of the islands of southern Thailand, Cohen (1982) traces the development of two beach resorts. In the second resort, that on the island of Phuket, he observed that much of the property ownership was not in the hands of the Thais, but in Chinese ownership, and Cohen comments that 'The marked difference in the ownership structure of the tourist facilities on the two beaches is of crucial importance for their differential developmental dynamics'. In the case of Phuket the beach sites were evolved with little outside interference. On the other hand, on Sawadee, the islanders had no comprehension of the motives that brought the tourists, and there were diametrically opposed sets of values as to the value of sunshine. The tourists perceived the beach as an island paradise, and swam naked in the blue seas. For the natives, naked bathing was indecent and sunshine was damaging to the skin. In Phuket, the landowners were in negotiation with multi-national hotels. Cohen's study of the 'marginal paradise' raises a whole range of issues about tourist/host interactions, but it is also of interest in terms of the role of the outsider as landowner and intermediary between tourist and host.

If host communities are to retain the integrity of their own culture, they have to develop means by which they can restrict the influence of the tourist. Paradoxically, the 'tourist bubble' and the 'pseudo-event' that is so much criticised by Boorstin is such a means. If tourists stay within the walls of the holiday village, then it is true that their appreciation of the host culture is small. But equally, it is true that the demonstration effects of topless bathing, of affluence, of drinking alcohol and other practices that might give offence are not on display for the mainstream of life within the host community. The 'pseudo-event' satisfies the tourist wish to see the culture of the area, and it does so in a package which is of meaning to the tourist. It avoids the situation whereby the host community finds that its own events become a 'theatre experience' for the tourist. The host community is able to retain the meanings of its own events. MacNaught (1982) argues that host societies are quite able to distinguish between the tourist show and the real event, and thus to argue that tourism undermines the integrity of the host culture is simplistic. The danger, however, is that the host community is unable to maintain its own social events without them becoming a 'sight' for the tourists, and thus the very presence of the tourist begins to change the ambience, and in time, the meaning of the event for the host community. Equally, it must be recognised that social events are not fixed in format. Increasing affluence generates change. People reach gatherings by car and not by foot; food is cooked in ovens and not over fires; the externals of the social meeting are changed. The question is whether or not tourism changes the internal meanings of the event for the host community. Certainly there is evidence that tourism creates stress. Smith (1977) relates how the Eskimo women of Kotzebue, Alaska, had to build fences and barricades to stop tourists photographing and viewing the process of butchering carcasses. Finally, they had to take the carcasses into the privacy of their own home, and thus the social aspects of the process were being destroyed. To complain that tourism changes a society in terms of the female/male roles, that it leads to the emigration of young workers from the rural areas to tourist complexes, that it changes traditional patterns of extended family networks, that it even changes the frequency of use of minority languages (White 1974) is in many cases no more than to state that the areas that are so changed were areas that were economically vulnerable to change. But the argument can be taken further. The charge against tourism may not be that it has induced change but that the nature of the tourism permitted has generated a change that is potentially inimical to the culture of the host society, and not one that is supportive. Tourism developments do not have to take the form of a wide dispersal of large numbers of people that create a tourist:host ratio where the hosts are unable to escape from the tourist. As previously indicated, soft tourism policies are possible. Yet the case against tourism is far from proven. It may be argued that in the case illustrated by Lever (1989), the position of young females was improved, that the conventional male-orientated society of rural Spain needed to be changed. It can be argued that no culture is either 'sacrosanct', to be preserved from change, or indeed necessarily contains within its norms and values, ethics that are beyond challenge. In the final analysis, it may be that those cultures that have modes of life that have meaning for their citizens will prove to have the tenacity to meet any challenge that tourism poses.

TOURISM AND HERITAGE

But, there are yet further paradoxes in the relationship between tourism and culture. Some critics argue that the challenge that tourism poses is not simply one whereby tourism creates change, but in fact the opposite. Tourism might calcify a culture into a 'frozen' picture of the past.

McCannell (1976) argues that what takes place is a process of 'sight sacralisation'. This is characterised by a number of stages:

a) The naming stage   a process of authentication whereby the site, sight, or event is differentiated from its other similar events.

b) The framing and elevation   the putting on display and enhancement of the place.

c) Enshrinement   the framing material is in place, and the first stage of the sacralisation process begins.

d) Mechanical   the creation of the copy, so that the tourist becomes aware of that reproduction, and seeks the 'real' thing.

e) Social reproduction   the original is a model after which others name themselves.

Whilst McCannell's examples include the Mona Lisa, and what might be termed the expressive artefacts of a culture, arguably the process occurs to the very processes of culture. Nowhere perhaps is this seen more clearly than in Heritage tourism. Hewison (1989) highlights a process whereby myths of a past are created – the past is seen in the way in which we would like to see it, and not in the way that it was. Barrett (1988) comments that:

> The Rhondda Heritage Park is the latest in a series of large scale heritage parks like Ironbridge in Shropshire, the Black Country Museum in the West Midlands and Beamish in the north-east that have a 'cast' of characters in period costume. For the most part these are people recruited at Government expense from job creation schemes: the unemployed of the Eighties paid to pretend to be the employed of the Twenties. For these 'museums' the temptation is to 'sanitise' the past: trim out the nasty bits, omit the poverty, the hunger and the strikes – to see life as a newsreel film of the Thirties and Forties, where the working classes are always irrepressibly cheerful.

A 'culture' is named, and stereotyped. The visitor seeks to see the characteristics of the image of the culture, and the host society provides the expected 'treat'. Boorstin's 'pseudo-event' is born. But the danger is that the myths are incorporated into the culture; succeeding generations do not know anything but the enactment of a past that may not have existed, and come to accept it. However, once again it depends upon the ability of the culture to distinguish between the contrived and the real. The processes are complex and subtle, and whilst the host community may wish to use tourism as a means of change that is in keeping with its own perceived integrity, not only are there visiting tourists who wish to maintain the status quo, but there is also the 'permanent visitor'.

In analysing the impacts of tourism upon developing countries, an interesting concept that may help to describe the processes is suggested by Wallace (1956). According to Wallace, societies can be subjected to a revitalisation process which consists of five stages, although there is no guarantee that any society will exhibit all five stages, or indeed experience them in the order he suggests. The stages are:

a) The steady state

Social and cultural forces exist in a dynamic equilibrium, whereby change does take place, but does so within the internal dynamics of the society, which thus retains its integrity and is able to handle processes that may cause stress.

b) The period of increased individual stress

The society has been pushed out of equilibrium due to some external event. From our viewpoint, such an event can be the development of tourism. The previous existing cultural system can no longer satisfy the needs of all of its members. The opportunities and demonstration effects of tourism may create a process of conflict within individuals as they seek to reconcile the developing changes with a framework of values that relates to a previous social and cultural setting.

c) The period of cultural distortion

This period is characterised by piecemeal attempts to restore equilibrium and so reduce stress, and the conflict between community members that is now being expressed. Special interest groups emerge, either seeking a restoration of previous ways, an establishment of a new consensus, or some other form of adaptation. Generally however, such effects are initially ineffective.

d) The period of revitalisation

This takes place with the realisation that the community's culture is maladaptive but for the society to be successful a number of changes must occur. From the processes of cultural distortion, there must arise a 'blueprint' for a 'better' society, i.e. one which reduces stress. This new 'blueprint' acquires followers who both defend and enforce the new code. The movement must also be routinised so that the new culture can establish its own methods for handling change.

e) The new steady state

This occurs when social disorganisation and personal stress return to tolerable levels and a new dynamic equilibrium is evolved.

Wallace's model relates to homogeneous native societies, but the process can be observed in relation to tourism, where host communities develop 'coping strategies' to maintain their business adjacent to the tourist activity that takes place within their community. There is, however, nothing within the model which indicates the nature of the new steady state. For some societies, it may be a resurgence of old values within a new context, in that it is the traditional values that define the distinction between the hosts and the guests. From another context, that of the native peoples of North America, or the Basques of Spain, it is these traditional aspects that define their being separate from the majority. Some societies may even seek to use tourism as a means of reinforcing their uniqueness to both themselves and to the tourist. Examples of this can be found in the Amish societies of Lancaster County, Pennsylvania, and the Mennonite communities of Southern Ontario. At St Jacobs, Ontario, the Mennonite community has established a small interpretative centre which portrays the history of the movement from its European Anabaptist origins. Visited by tourists, the centre fulfils many roles. It interprets the community's culture for the tourist in a manner that the Mennonites wish to portray. It seeks to establish an empathy on the part of the tourist for the community; to generate the understanding of different practices which O'Grady (1981) sees as an essential component of 'responsible tourism'. In challenging the tourist to respect the differences between the tourist's everyday life and that of the Mennonite, it also serves to reinforce the uniqueness of the Mennonite culture. In short, tourism might require sophisticated social skills from host communities if their differences are not to be submerged in some form of 'international' culture. It requires that the hosts can maintain their own homogeneity, even whilst they move from one world to another, as, for example, they move from work in the hotel back to their home. In practice, the best from both worlds will often be selected. In a sense therefore the hosts practise the same skills that immigrant societies practise, albeit on a different scale and within a different context.

THE IMPACT OF HOLIDAY HOMES

Of the tourists that come, some may seek to stay. They may initially be considering a holiday home, or it might be that they are about to retire and wish an escape from the winter of their home area. One of the differences between developed economic regions and the peripheral areas is not simply in the income earnt during a working life, but also access to accumulating wealth. Amongst the professional groups of Northern America and Europe – areas characterised by demographic trends whereby the old are becoming a larger part of the population – part of that access to wealth lies through the possession of pension plans that offer inflation proofed income in retirement. In addition, such social groups may also inherit wealth due to their parents having owned houses, whilst they too own their homes. Data drawn from HM Inland Revenue shows that in 1983/4 there were nearly 300,000 inheritances in England and Wales with an average value of approximately £31,000, whilst the total number of properties passing at death were 149,000. This age group thus possesses the means to buy holiday homes and do not have to be the 'yuppies' of popular fancy to own such holiday apartments, flats and houses. By their nature, the rural, scenic tourist areas tend to be areas of low income and low housing costs. A number of mechanisms are set into action. One is the increasing costs of homes in the tourist area. Nowhere has this been better documented and recorded for over a decade than in North Wales (Coppock 1977). Many communities of the Welsh-speaking areas of Wales have found that English holidaymakers are drawn to the country because of its beauty. Many find that the properties are relatively cheap compared to the urban zones of the south-east of England, and thus will buy a holiday home. This tourist demand drives up the price of houses and indeed between 1987 to 1989 the prices of many detached properties in the Snowdonia National Park area more than doubled. In consequence, many newly marrieds in the area find it increasingly difficult to find the means of buying their own home. Some local councils have sought to respond to the problem by building properties that can only be let and purchased by local people. The same problems have occurred in Whistler, British Columbia, (Brent Ritchie 1988) where a community of approximately 3,500 have, as a result of the development of ski runs, seen tourist numbers rise to nearly a million per year in a short period, with the resultant acceleration of property prices by over 40 per cent in just over a year in the period 1988/9. Searle (1989) gives examples of property development in Banff, Alberta, where 'prime residential' lots climbed to C$160,000 within a few years. Fagan (1989) reports how the resort of Phuket, Thailand, changed from being a haven for students and hippies in the early 1970s to a tourist-developed area where, from 1982 to 1989, seaside land increased in price from $3,500 to $350,000 per acre. It is easy to find such examples throughout the world. On the other hand, it must be recognised that property prices within communities can rise due to any influx of outside demand, and not simply due to tourism. For example, the building of the Honda Accord plant in the 1980s at Marysville, Ohio, led to increases in house prices in what formally was a rural area. Thus, once again in Sessa's (1988) terminology, what may be seen as a tourism impact is in fact a facet of the process of establishing urban poles.

The second aspect is that the nature of the community changes. Some villages may be characterised by an absent population; the village is 'full' only during the season. Younger local people leave to find areas where they can buy cheaper houses. The withdrawal of such people leaves an older population. Local schools may have a falling number of pupils, and are thus forced to close. Other village services are also threatened including general stores, post-offices, medical services and the like. Slowly, the support structures of rural life can be undermined, and the businesses that may arrive cater for the tourist and not the local people. On the other hand, the purchase of holiday homes in certain areas may help to stop declining property prices which slowly undermine the wealth of families, and hence inhibit their capacity to move to other areas that do offer employment in other than a declining agricultural industry. If the homes that are being purchased become permanently occupied, then the retreat of population from the rural areas is, if not totally reversed, at least slowed. It may indeed become possible to keep schools open on the basis of existing populations and potential future child births. However, the 'newcomers' may have several different social impacts. They may not know the language, and hence much depends upon their willingness to learn it, and the tolerance of the host community towards such efforts. Secondly, the newcomers have been drawn to the area because of its special qualities of peace and quiet; theirs is a retreat from the urban pattern of life. They might become a force for the retention of the status quo, now that they have found their niche within it. Thus, they become a force which seeks to protect the environment and possibly the culture which they have entered into, but in doing so they seek possibly to hinder the evolution of a society.

In the assessment of the culture and society of developing areas, there needs to be an awareness of what Walter (1982) would characterise as a romantic ideal. Whilst it may seem to the urban citizen of an 'advanced' economy that the peasant of a developing region does in fact possess riches of a spiritual sort, in that, for example, their way of life is more 'natural', such a viewpoint overlooks the harshness of that way of life. Thus the motivation of the subsistence farmer turned hotel keeper, catering for the tourist who comes to enjoy the sunshine, is easily understood and difficult to criticise, for to criticise such an action is to deny the aspirations for advancement of not only the farmer himself, but of his family and children.

TOURISM AND CRIME

One aspect of tourism that has attracted attention is the hypothesis that tourism generates crime. Mathieson and Wall (1982) surveyed existing literature on the relationship between crime and tourism, and noted that 'The literature on crime as an externality of tourist development is not large, but most is empirically based'. McPheters and Stronge (1974) and Pizam (1978) indicate a positive correlation between tourism and crime in studies of Florida. Certainly many residents perceive a link between tourism and crime for it seems to them that as tourism increases so too does crime (Rothman 1978, Milman and Pizam 1988). In their study of Miami, McPheters and Stronge (1978) note the relationship between increases in crime and the tourist season. Pizam and Pokela (1985) indicate that residents were highly aware of linkages between the 'sexualisation' of their community and drugs and organised crime due to a legalisation of their community and drugs and organised crime due to a legalisation of gambling in an attempt to attract tourists. Certainly, in terms of Mediterranean reports, there is almost a folklore about young men on scooters stealing handbags from the shoulders of tourists, whilst in Paris the pickpockets flourish during the tourist season. Mathieson and Wall comment:

> In summary, it appears that tourism contributes to an increase in crime, especially on a seasonal basis. It does this through the generation of friction between the host population and tourists which may be manifest in criminal activities. In addition, the target for criminals is expanded and situations are created where gains from crime may be high and the likelihood of detection small.

However, what has developed as a possible new theme in the intervening years since Mathieson and Wall undertook their study, is that the victim is not always the tourist. Within the trade and daily press of Europe, there has been the reporting of tourists as the aggressors, and not the victims. The *Independent* newspaper reported that:

> The British package holiday subtly dominated the news at the weekend. There were fresh scenes of congestion at airports. . . and from Majorca came reports of five Britons remanded in custody after the death of a taxi driver.
>
> (*Independent*, 4 July 1989)

Throughout 1988 and 1989 drunken behaviour by holidaymakers on aircraft and at Spanish destinations led to officials of the Association of British Travel Agents (ABTA) meeting with representatives of the Spanish government to discuss means of handling the issue. In the summer of 1988, a British Minister, Tim Eggar, flew to Spain to discuss the problem further, but seemingly with little effect in that the same stories of violence were to be heard the following year. In 1989 the Spanish authorities reinforced the police force at the main resorts to protect not the tourists from the Spanish so much as to protect the tourists against their own drunkenness, and to avert if possible, worse cases of violence. It would appear that the variables that are significant in these situations are:

a) tourists whose cultural norms include:

     (i) peer group cohesiveness,
    (ii) intolerance of those outside their group,
  (iii) values which justify behaviour patterns that include excessive
       drinking, indulgence in violence and casual sex where possible;
b) perceived freedom from normal constraints;
c) expectation of a 'good time' that conforms with their norms. Such
   expectations are shaped by:
     (i) perceived images of holiday destinations and companies shaped by
       stories, media activity and past experience – e.g. publications such
       as *Beach Party – the Last Resort*, Benny Dorm (pseudonym), 1988,
       which confirms derogatory stereotyping, and activities such as
       'happy hours' where drinks are sold half-price, and pub crawls
       organised by couriers,
    (ii) belief that they can impose their own values on the host community
       and other tourists;
d) holiday destinations that are not 'foreign' – i.e. the general milieu is in
   fact a familiar one to this type of tourist, and is primarily one of pubs,
   clubs and discos.

Studies relating to football hooliganism may be pertinent to such behaviour, and if this is the case the stereotypes of young, low income and uneducated groups of men would not be totally valid as a description or explanation of this phenomenon (Chittenden 1989). Reference has to be made to sets of norms, values and ethics which generate a predisposition to violent action if this type of crime is to be understood.

Tourist crime may take many different forms. Hamilton (1988) reports the case where customs officers at Bristol Airport detained a holidaymaker returning from Ibiza with a suitcase of 500 Ibiza wall lizards. An endangered species, each lizard was valued at £30 each. Arguably, this is not tourism crime *per se* in that the motivation had presumably little to do with holidays, but it nonetheless indicates the opportunities that easier travel related to tourism brings.

There is one other aspect of crime which has received little attention from researchers and that is exploitation undertaken by corporations. Indeed, within Doxey's Irridex, it might be argued that one factor that generates antagonistic attitudes towards tourism is the feeling of exploitation that members of the host society might feel. Hoosie (1990) reports that a government history of the building of Cancun, the Mexican tourist resort, relates how a Mexican lawyer disguised himself as a local landowner with a casual interest in buying land in Cancun, thereby the tourist agencies were able to buy the land at extremely cheap prices. In 1984, at Huatulco, 50 acres of land were being purchased for approximately US$3,000 and by 1989 the value of the same land was estimated as being about US$3.5 to US$4 million. Today Cancun attracts more than a million visitors a year and in 1988 earned about US$0.6 billion from tourism. The original landowners received little of this money. However, Hoosie (1990) reports that the lessons have been learnt, and Fonatur, the Mexican tourist agency has been taken to court by the former residents of Huatulco seeking compensation for low land prices. In short, there are examples of where the wish to develop tourism for the jobs and foreign currency that it promises has led corporations and governments to show the 'unacceptable face of capitalism', and to do so in situations where the host community is not necessarily opposed to tourism, but is being denied a part to play in its development.

TOURISM AND PROSTITUTION

Amongst the attractions of European cities such as Hamburg and Amsterdam are the brothels, and the streets are often thronged by curious tourists who wish to see the girls. More recently, attention has been drawn by Christian groups to the nature of sex tourism in areas such as the Philippines and Thailand in a series of conferences at Penang (1974), Manila (1980), Chiang Mai (1984) and at Bad Boll (1988) and again in London in 1989. Whilst tour operators and agents in the tourist-generating countries have varying degrees of openness about the nature of some of the bars in places such as Patpong, within the hotels of Bangkok literature is easily available for any interested tourist (Wyer *et al.* 1986). Christian groups such as the Asian Women United, a Protestant group, have researched tourism in South East Asia, and have arrived at high estimates of the number of women working in prostitution and related activities such as masseuses and bar hostesses. Breen (1988) reports a finding that the number of prostitutes in South Korea may be between 600,000 and 1,000,000 in a country of 41 million; whilst one report estimated that there were in 1985 approximately 500,000 prostitutes in Thailand. It is also thought that there may be as many as 100,000 'hospitality' girls in Manila. Most of these estimates date from the early 1980s, and would now need to be tempered by the impact of AIDS, but even so it would appear that sex tourism is still of significance in the tourist economies of some of the Far East countries.

The Centre for the Protection of Children's Rights, Bangkok, has over the years collated a catalogue of examples of young children being purchased from farmers not only for prostitution but also for labour in work places under insanitary conditions. In the worse cases children may be chained to the places of work. It has also been estimated by Church groups that perhaps 50 per cent of the prostitutes may be children under the age of 13 (Ecumenical Coalition on Third World Tourism ECTWT 1986).

The reasons for such business in terms of the supply of prostitutes are easily explained in part by the heritage of the wars of South East Asia, the poverty of the area, and attitudes towards women by the host communities. It would appear that prostitution had always existed on a larger scale in places such as Thailand compared with western European countries, and indeed, the concept of the courtesan, as evidenced by the original tradition of the kisaeng and geisha, as cultured young ladies who provided musical entertainment allocated to such girls a respected place in their societies. However, the impetus of the wars in Korea and Vietnam in the 1950s and 1960s with first French and then American involvement reinvigorated the tradition through the provision of R & R (Rest and Recreation) facilities for the armed forces away from the battle field. The difference in the wealth of the foreigner, and the poverty of the girls, also generated a series of misconceptions and hopes amongst the prostitutes. Cohen (1982b) reports the motivations of the girls as including the hope of meeting a foreigner, getting married, and then emigrating to an affluent western society. However, the essential reasons for the girls entering into prostitution are in many ways no different in type, although possibly different in degree, from that of their European and American counterparts. The main reason is poverty, particularly the poverty of the rural areas from which many of the girls come. In addition, there is the need for women to maintain their children after desertion by their husbands. In this respect there is a cultural difference, in that such women, and indeed widows, are seen as no longer being eligible for marriage (Jones 1986). With no social welfare benefit system, and if they possess no marketable skills for use in commerce and industry, prostitution may well seem to be the only means of supporting their families. In addition, the demonstration effect, whereby only those girls who are working in the bars appear to have money, will also reduce their opposition to such activities. Indeed, as Cohen (1982b) comments, the peer group of fellow prostitutes becomes possibly the only support group that the girl possesses.

Whilst there is a growing literature on the relationship between tourism and prostitution in South East Asia, some of which is speculative, there has been little research into the subject in countries such as Britain. However, based on studies such as those by Kinnell (1989), it can be tentatively suggested that the relationship between tourism and prostitution is weak. Kinnell states:

> It is evident that prostitution in Birmingham is not a service industry to visitors from outside the region who seek commercial sex because they are away from home, or as a form of tourist entertainment. Approximately 60% of clients in both data sets lived in the City of Birmingham, and 83%–95% within the West Midlands Regional Health Authority boundaries.

A review of the evidence leads to a conclusion that tourism is not necessarily a cause of the practice of prostitution or of the fact that such young children are involved. The practices are seated in the culture and norms of the host society. The case against tourism is rather one that it helps to perpetuate the practice. Indeed, as Cohen (1982b) comments, under the circumstance where a few girls do in fact marry foreigners, the presence of the tourist creates the situation whereby the 'lucky' girls act as role models for the majority, and so sustain their hopes. Cohen concludes that prostitution is but a short-term solution to most of the problems the women experience, but when considering the alternatives open to them, the prostitutes are better off financially than their counterparts, even though they undergo more social and psychological stress and damage. It would also seem that the only other impact of tourists and American military is some change in sexual practices, for example a greater use of kissing and oral sex than previously was the case. Jones (1986) in a study of Balinese prostitution notes that whilst foreplay elicited a positive response from prostitutes, they were not in favour of mouth to mouth kissing.

The 'predatory tourist' seeking sexual pleasures is not always male. Yamba (1988) claims that the largest group of Africans in Sweden consists of 1,500 Gambian boys 'imported' into Sweden by mature Swedish women who befriended them on holiday. As the Gambian culture tends to disapprove of sexual relations between males and older women, the boys tend to tire of their older girlfriends and seek relationships with girls of their own age. Yamba argues that the result is that often they are then thrown out onto the streets.

In other parts of the world prostitution can be found in tourist areas. Amsterdam's red light district is itself a tourist sight, whilst the legalised brothels of Nevada are widely advertised in tourist areas such as Las Vegas. Mathieson and Wall (1982) conclude that the proposed relationship is akin to that of the relationship between tourism and crime, namely, the processes of 'tourism have created locations and environments which attract prostitutes and their clients', whilst in addition the hedonistic nature of the holiday might also have a role to play. However, the examples they considered are primarily drawn from the American continent, and it would appear that in the case of South East Asia, the existence of prostitution is due to much more serious social causes.

It must also be noted that sex has for long been the fourth 's' – the others being 'sun, sea and sand' – and sex from a romantic viewpoint has often been utilised in the selling of the holiday product. Equally, the promise, or potential, of sex in a more explicit manner has not been unknown in the promotion of holiday products. Nor has it always been the tourist who has been the seeker of sexual pleasure. Another of the stereotypes of the Mediterranean has been that of the 'Latin lover'. Cohen (1971) and Bowman (1988) recount how young Palestinian shopkeepers in East Jerusalem gossip about bargaining with wealthy European and American women for sexual favours, and then, in order to establish the required male supremacy after receiving payment, will abuse them. Within Athens, professional playboys, the 'kamakia' (or harpoons) earn money from commissions paid by owners of discos, bars, restaurants and tourist shops for taking female tourists to these outlets. On Rhodes, in 1989, the 'kamakia' formed an association whereby their members carry a card showing a negative AIDS test result; this card also entitles the holder to discounts at local cafes, bars, restaurants and discos.

From the research that has been undertaken it would appear that the practice of prostitution does differ in different areas with reference to such factors as a) whether it is locals, or people coming from outside the tourist zone who provide the service and b) whether it is a service being provided for the indigenous population within a tourist zone with some tourist participation, or whether it is primarily aimed at tourists. Equally, not all prostitutes are drawn from poor backgrounds. In the case of the 'cool mimos' of Nairobi it appears that several are drawn from women with university backgrounds, although a motivation is to obtain money to help finance their studies. If, therefore, there is no consistent impact related to tourism upon such practices, it might be argued that there is nothing inherent in tourism *per se* to cause the problem, but rather that tourism might simply confirm some patterns that already exist. Equally, the very flows of tourism to areas have helped to draw attention to the problem, and may cause counter-measures to be taken against prostitution, or, as in the German and Dutch cases, cause it to be regulated.

SUMMARY

In looking at the potential impacts of tourism it would appear that a number of variables are of importance. Amongst these might be included:

a) the numbers of tourists
b) the types of tourists
c) the stage of tourist development
d) the differential in economic development between tourist-generating and tourist-receiving zones
e) the difference in cultural norms between tourist-generating and tourist-receiving zones
f) the physical size of the area which affects the densities of tourist population
g) the extent to which tourism is serviced by an immigrant worker population
h) the degree to which incoming tourists purchase properties
i) the degree to which local people retain ownership of properties and tourist facilities
j) the attitudes of governmental bodies

k) the beliefs of host communities, and the strength of those beliefs
l) the role of intermediaries, and the degree to which those intermediaries identify with tourists or hosts
m) the degree of exposure to other forces of technological, social and economic change
n) the policies adopted with regard to tourist dispersal
o) the marketing of the tourist destination and the images that are created of that destination
p) the homogeneity of the host society
q) the accessibility to the tourist destination
r) the original strength of artistic and folkloric practices, and the nature of those traditions.

It is possible for societies to retain patterns of life that are different to those of visitors, and in this respect the Amish and traditional Mennonite communities of the USA and Canada are examples where communities, bound by a strong sense of commonality and purpose, are able to sustain their life styles in the very midst of what might be termed 'main-stream North American cultures'. Equally, the Navajo Indians have been able to reassert their life styles to the degree that they wish, albeit the discovery of raw materials on their reservations has helped the establishment of economic stability (even though the long-term questions have yet to be answered).

Cultures change because the environment within which the culture exists changes – an environment which is both physical and social. Many of the cultures studied exhibit processes of change independent of those thought to be associated with tourism, and tourism is but one means by which acculturation (the borrowing from one culture by another) occurs. However, where it might differ from other sources such as exposure to ideas, images portrayed by mass media and business practices is in the fact that the source of change is there, physically, in the heart of the host society. It is this factor that has attracted attention, along with the transitory nature of many individual relationships. What may be concluded is that whilst tourism can be a catalyst for change, the nature of the change is not always predictable should host societies be aware of the potential that tourism has for such change, particularly if, at an early stage, they seek to make decisions upon the volume and type of tourism they want. If, however, the host community leaves the development of tourism to outside bodies, in many cases the models of large resort complexes will emerge with the now all-too-familiar refrain of societies reacting to changes that are imposed from without. It is perhaps this factor more than many others that accounts for the differences in tourism development between such areas as, say, the Costa del Sol, with its ready access for tourists, and the Maldive Islands, where tourist flows are restricted to certain islands, or between

Nepal, with its fairly open access to tourists, and Bhutan, where only limited numbers of tourists are permitted, and then only in groups. If it is said that the freedoms enjoyed by societies have the price of perpetual vigilance, this is also true in the case of tourism.

Chapter 8

Marketing issues in tourism

THE PLANNING PROCESS IN TOURISM – DIFFICULTIES AND PROBLEMS

The previous chapters have highlighted a number of problems that relate to the impacts of numbers and types of tourists upon locations, and also with regard to problems related to seasonality and other issues. A number of authors including Baud-Bovey and Lawson (1977), Mathieson and Wall (1982), Murphy (1985), and Krippendorf (1987), to mention but a few, have called for more responsible planning of tourism destinations. Yet there are a series of paradoxes involved in tourism, which means that plans must attempt to reconcile what may be irreconcilable variables. Some of these variables are discussed below.

Host communities wish to generate revenues that help perpetuate desired patterns of life. Often, in the case of rural, or marginal economies, the desired life style is the status quo, with a reversal of the factors that lead to depopulation with the youngest people leaving the community. In short, additional income is sought to make the continued existence of the community a viable operation. Yet, increased visitor numbers and the demands of visitors generate changes within the community so that the status quo is not viable, not from an economic viewpoint, but from a social one.

Host communities may wish to use natural assets as tourism resources, but the development of 'nature' means that an urban tourism industry style of infrastructure of hotels and roads is imposed on 'nature' and hence the existing landscape and eco-system are changed. Therefore the original resources become less of an asset. To retain an asset base which is attractive to the tourism industry, other assets are constructed, and so the host community becomes dependent on man-made and not natural resources.

Small-scale developments may be perceived as a potential solution to the above problems, in that there is little threat to the patterns of life within host communities, and such developments can be sited on wasteland, or low grade land, so that the development may even enhance 'nature' and not detract from an area's beauty. However, to restrict developments to a small scale means that host communities need to accept restrictions on income that might otherwise be generated, whilst property developers have to accept higher costs per bed-space developed in that the cost of laying roads, water supplies, sewage treatment and other utilities are shared by fewer units of accommodation, and thus the development may not reach a size where it generates the desired rates of return. Therefore, there are economic pressures towards large-scale tourism developments.

If, within any given region, there is a denial of developments in some areas and the granting of tourist centres in others, a problem of income allocation is created. The host community which permits no tourist development obtains no income for the protection of ecologically fragile areas, nor for the contribution that wild areas make to an eco-system in terms of contributing to clean air, clean water, and plant, animal and insect species. In addition, the neighbouring area that permits tourist development gains, arguably, an enhanced revenue due to a lack of competition for tourist expenditure. That area which restricts tourist development therefore arguably contributes income to that zone where tourism does occur, but receives no revenue in recognition of that contribution.

The development of tourism resources within urban areas might overcome environmental problems in that such developments may enhance urban settings, and if located within inner city areas, might generate jobs and income where previously unemployment and little or no income existed. However, such a policy reinforces towns as centres of economic life, and denies tourist expenditure to rural communities who may need the economic support such expenditure can bring.

Tourist development within inner city areas might enhance the city, but not necessarily the life of those living in the inner city areas. Such populations might not possess the skills required by the tourist or other incoming industries. In addition, or, if they do find employment, they may not earn sufficient income to continue living in their home area, which is threatened by inflated land prices, and clearance and higher costs of living resulting from the incoming industry, retail developments, office blocks and tourism/leisure-orientated activities.

It may be stated that the very act of planning is a process that seeks to overcome such problems, but if the system contains irreconcilable variables, then the process can only generate a series of compromises or second best solutions. Further, if the planning processes are initiated by elected political bodies, the eventual outcomes might be no more than a reflection of political groupings showing existing power bases that originate in a past that it is increasingly inadequate to deal with future problems. Within democracies, planning bodies have often limited powers with processes of appeal against decisions taken. Equally, it must be noted that planners and their political masters do not generally possess the means to control factors outside of the zones for which they are responsible. The English Tourist Board (1978) has argued that any adverse social impact in a local area needs to be viewed against the considerable national benefit accruing as a result of the individual's enjoyment of his or her holiday experience. Noting this, Duffield (1982) in some ways poses an opposing viewpoint when he writes:

> Care must be taken to avoid the instrumental use of marginal areas for the interests of the economic core areas and economic criteria must be subject to social constraints if the economic benefits are to be secured without socio-cultural dislocation. Thus an increase in wealth per se, is insufficient unless those benefits accrue at all levels of society.

TOURISM GROWTH AS AN OBJECTIVE

Yet, inspite of the difficulties, there has emerged a significant literature on planning in tourism, and increasingly governments are producing strategic plans, (for example, Tourism Canada's Discussion Paper on a National Tourism Strategy of August 1989). Equally, the role of the environment within those plans is being recognised, and the United Nations concept of tourism attractions as sustainable resources is slowly being accepted. Indeed, the Globe '90 conference at Vancouver in March 1990 specifically included tourism in its considerations of environmental impacts. This represents a significant change, at least in principle if not yet in action, in terms of tourism planning, which in the past has often been characterised by tourism *promotion* as distinct from tourism planning in the wider context discussed in the previous pages. Yet, old habits die hard, as any review of the trade press will reveal. Size and growth are still often perceived as worthy objectives, and thus publications such as 'Tourism in Action' prefer to lead with headlines such as 'Records tumble, overseas visitor spending boom' (September 1988), or the BTA's 'Strategy for Growth', as described in 'British Travel Brief' (April 1989), indicates targets in terms of both increased volume and spending without reference to environmental issues. Equally, the impression gained from the tour operators is one of concern with market share and the need to achieve yet further increases in sales. In February 1989 the Travel Trade Gazette had a headline, 'Goodman bids to rule the skies' next to a comment column in which it referred to the travel trade's attitude towards the British consumer 'as [being] one big malleable mass' – whereas, it is, in fact, one which is 'waking up' and needing to be treated a little better (16 February 1989, page 6).

It may be that as the tourist industry enters the 1990s the question will increasingly become not one of achieving growth, but one of achieving quality that is consistent with sustaining the physical and social environments. Such arguments are sustained by the changing attitudes towards the work:leisure ratio described by Emery (1981) and Papson (1979), and by the increasing desire of tourists for independence. If this is the case, a number of implications follow, including:

a) a need to enhance visitor satisfaction; this may involve a recognition that sometimes the social carrying capacity may be less than the physical carrying capacity (Lamb 1989).
b) a need to accept that a growth in visitor numbers may be inconsistent with objectives of maintaining environments and tourist satisfaction.
c) a need to more carefully market an attraction, not simply in terms of promoting a tourist attraction as such, but rather more carefully engaging in matching tourist zone with type of tourist, and the particular needs of the tourist. The marketing of the tourist zone must therefore be incorporated into the planning process.

THE ROLE OF MARKETING

The role of marketing within the planning process can be shown to be important for a number of reasons. Such reasons include:

a) the creation of awareness of the nature of the tourist resource.
b) the creation of the image of the tourist zone.

It has been argued previously that the perception and image of a zone becomes part of the perceptual process of the tourist which leads to the formation of sets of expectations, and that in turn these expectations help to shape behaviour whilst at the resort. If the tourist perceives a zone as possessing degrees of fragility, and thus requiring responsible behaviour on the part of the tourist, then, whilst there is no automatic link between attitude and behaviour, at least certain conative predispositions are set in motion.

c) the targeting of appropriate groups of tourists. Arguably satisfaction will be generated where expectations coincide not only with perception, but also interest and aptitude. Use of geo-demographics and pyschographics by tourist promoters may help to match destinations to tourist types.
d) market research techniques might help to identify attitudes towards the resort area, and tourist perception of the quality of experience, and the components of that perceived quality.
e) the marketing process thus becomes a part of the planning process. Marketing is not so much as simply a means of promoting a tourist zone to attract more people regardless of the quality of experience that the

tourists then receive, but also, if need be, is the means by which messages may be sent to deter people, by indicating that perhaps the resort may not be for them.

If this is thought to be a perverse approach for marketing, it needs to be recognised that, increasingly, in areas outside of tourism, marketing personnel are beginning to recognise that a 'societal' concept of marketing can succeed, and is indeed consistent with other aspects of organisational change that is emerging in the last years of the twentieth century. Somers *et al.* (1989) maintain that the marketing concept can be compatible with a societal perspective with a refined broadening marketing concept characterised by:

A philosophy whereby a company strives:
– to develop an integrated marketing program
– that generates long-run profitable sales volume
– by satisfying the long-run wants of:
– the customers of its products and services
– the other parts of society affected by the firm's activities.

To the traditional concepts of marketing, two new components are being added, an extended time dimension, and a broader viewpoint. Both are quite consistent with consumers' current and future demands. The role of long-term profits over short-term maximisation policies has been well established in economic studies, whilst the increasing concern with environmental issues has already led to companies beginning to undertake research into the wider implications of their products, as evidenced by the emergence of 'green' products on supermarket shelves.

FUTURE TOURISM POLICIES

a) The controlled environment

Is there any evidence of such viewpoints beginning to emerge within the area of tourism? The answer is in the affirmative. Middleton (1988) notes that:

One may discern two diametrically opposed management philosophies at work in travel and tourism in the 1980s concerning the nature of destination products, both of which appear likely to intensify and become more divergent by the year 2000. These are the philosophy, which aims to deliver marketing designed products within purpose-built, enclosed, and closely controlled environments; and its opposite, in which products are delivered with the minimum of control by the supplier over the visitor's experience at the destination.

Middleton gives as examples of the managed tourist resort Disneyland and the Languedoc-Roussillon area of France, and this is of interest in that both are in fact extremely well established and approximately two decades in age. In short, the trend discerned by Middleton has long antecedents. Perhaps what is newer, at least within a European context, is the increased willingness to recreate climates artificially, as has been done by Sports Huis, whilst the closer relationship between retail and recreational environments has led to 'themed' shopping areas. One such area is the Roman Forum within the Metro Centre, North East England, which was developed by John Hall, and which was partly inspired by Edmonton Mall complete with its sub-aqua rides. In the shopping malls, the interactive museums and historical experience centres, such as Fort Walsh or Colonial Williamsburg (complete with their staff dressed in period costume), and the theme parks, as illustrated by the American Adventure, Ilkeston, or Disneyland near Paris, the environment is managed to such an extent that pedestrian flows are carefully calculated, queueing theory is applied, and attention to details is perceived as the basis for success. From the marketing viewpoint, the controlled environment is seen as further development of the tourism product to a standard where 'consumption' of the product will generate tourist satisfaction. Equally, however, the same techniques can be applied to outside environments. The control of pedestrian flow is practised in many cases within environmentally fragile environments. For example, in the case of Beaver Creek, administered by the Meewasin Valley Authority, Canada, the creek is now able to sustain over 30,000 visits per year whereas before the Authority took it over, visitor numbers of approximately 2,000 were creating damage and despoiling the area (Lamb 1989). Within urban settings, pedestrian flow is increasingly being considered with reference to the location not simply of sites for viewing, but also of retail opportunities for the host community. The Freedom Trail in Boston is an example of the means by which tourism traffic is directed through a city context in a way which potentially means that the visitor can not only easily find the historic sites, but also is led through open areas complete with appealing retail outlets. Waterfront developments are planned so as to support a retail mix in the same manner as a shopping mall. Inasmuch as marketing is concerned with the product, price, promotion and distribution of goods and services, these examples are indications of the type of product evolution that tourism permits. In short, it appears that many of the techniques referred to by Middleton (1988) are, to some extent at least, applicable in a wider framework than simply the enclosed environment.

b) The uncontrolled environment

Middleton (1988) postulates that the opposite type of tourist experience is the 'uncontrolled' environment, where the tourist seeks an authentic destination and experience. Middleton believes that such environments will only appeal to a minority, but if this is the case it is a large and growing market segment. The size and growth of this sector was revealed in the growing sales of the Association of Independent Tour Operators and the emergence of holiday 'brokers' such as Greco-File, which exists to provide information on holiday types and destinations to tourists who are seeking other than the typical 'package holiday' offered by the large British tour operators. That the demand existed was further recognised by the publication of the *Guide to Real Holidays Abroad* (Barrett 1989). In the North American continent the demand is indicated by the growing success of the 'outfitters' in attracting business to the northern regions of Canada, where holidaymakers, far removed from city environments, canoe, camp in the open and have no contact with any building, much less a hotel. The search for the authentic is opening opportunities for ethnic minorities, where, for example, tourists will stay with North American Indian or Eskimo bands. Sometimes, the search for a new experience incorporates the element of fantasy, as is the case where Japanese tourists in Alberta partake in a cattle drive across the prairie. (Since, however, the trip is taken at grazing speed, the degree of authenticity may be questioned – but the saddle sore tourist certainly feels that the experience is indeed authentic!) Yet, even in this context, the purchasing opportunities exist whereby the host community can obtain revenue from the tourist, even though the package price may have been paid in Tokyo. Additional items of cowboy dress can be purchased, alcoholic drinks are available from the 'chuck wagon' and there is the video featuring the tourists themselves as a souvenir of the occasion.

THE WIDER MARKETING CONTEXT

What these examples indicate is that the wider marketing concept of Somers *et al.* is not only being practised, but is also being successful. The examples reflect the wider marketing context for they involve:

a) Developing a marketing concept where the tourist product is being carefully planned as an integrated whole, rather than simply being a collection of parts brought together by a tour operator, who often will disclaim responsibility for the quality of any one part of the holiday provision, as is easily seen by scrutiny of the small print in most holiday brochures. (In this respect the proposals of the European Community to ensure that tour operators are liable for performance after 1992 may indeed lead to a better holiday product.)
b) Satisfying the wants of tourists for different types of holiday experiences to that offered in the past, and for reassurance about quality and other

factors perceived by them to be important. For example, market research on behalf of Center Parcs (Sports Huis) revealed that one of the factors accounting for the success of their developments in Britain was the reassurance parents felt in that their children could have a good time in open spaces without any serious risks. This reassurance was offered by Center Parcs not only in terms of the supervision of activities, but also the presence of security personnel at gates, where only paying guests or those having business with the management were permitted to enter the park.

c) Consideration of the wider impacts of the tourist development upon the environment. The theme park, the holiday village and similar developments today involve a planning of their landscape. If such developments are permitted in damaged land, for example, former waste tips, or areas where barren land is the norm, then the landscaping only enhances the environment. Many waterfront developments, for example, those at Salford, England, took place on derelict land inhabited by rusting machinery and rats. Equally, the creation of the 'tourist bubble' means that demonstration effects are reduced to some degree. Tourism can generate economic benefits, given responsible planning.

If the discussion in the 1960s, 1970s and early 1980s was of the need to recognise the environmental impacts of tourism and to incorporate such features into plans, the discussion of the 1990s will increasingly be one of how to implement the plans that do contain environment impact assessments. Responsible planning that incorporates the wider societal marketing concept should not lead to the example quoted by Geshekter (1978) where similar wording was used by two different tour operators to describe two totally different parts of Africa, the Gambia and Kenya.

THE ROLE OF ADVERTISING IN SHAPING PERCEPTIONS OF PLACE

If marketing within tourism is to become part of the tourism planning process that seeks to match tourist types to appropriate destinations, a number of issues emerge, including:

a) What is the impact of the advertising content on the formation of attitudes to holiday destinations?
b) How might attitudes towards destinations be measured?
c) How can appropriate advertising be created?
d) Who does the advertising address?

There is a small but growing literature on the role that pictorial content of advertisements plays in the formation of perceptions about tourist destinations. Weaver and McCleary (1984) found, for example, that within the USA the use of single male models in the pictorial matter tended to mean that the company was less reputable as far as an older market segment was concerned. Marsh (1986) discusses the impact upon Japanese tourists of seeing pictures of Japanese people engaged in touristic activities in Canada, and the impressions that these create. Olsen *et al.* (1986) undertook factor analysis of respondents' replies to 'matching' photographs of Utah and the People's Republic of China, and concluded that responses fell into nine patterns. Destinations were regarded as being stimulating or frightening, as offering a relaxing vacation, possessing human qualities, offering a beautiful location, offering opportunities for inner reflection, or the scenery was of an untamed land, an isolated land, or a land for romance. Each of these categories represents a potential continuum of response sets; for example, a land may be stimulating, or may be perceived as 'boring'. The researchers also applied each of the factor groupings to three different types of pictorial content, people, landmarks and scenery. They conclude that:

> Analysis of the data yielded three significant interaction effects between familiarity with the destination and type of pictorial theme. Familiar landmarks were seen as indicating a less stimulating destination. People may already be so familiar with the landmarks, that they are considered another aspect of everyday life. The accomplishments of mankind may be more appreciated when they are strange or foreign. A second interaction effect was found between scenery and familiar destination. People seem to show a greater appreciation for scenery which is familiar to them. Unlike landmarks, people do not seem to lose their appreciation for nature's gifts. Familiar scenery was also seen as more romantic. Perhaps the familiar location evokes memories of past vacations with successful romantic pursuits.

They go on to write that 'the theme of the pictorial element used in tourism advertisements can influence potential vacationists' evaluations of the vacation experience provided by a destination'.

The tourist viewing the brochure does so from a set of references compiled from past knowledge and experiences, and thus the advertising is interpreted in the light of this reference set. Clues are sought in the advertising to dispel worries, and, as the stereotype is familiar and stereotyping itself is a means of interpreting incomplete information, the advertisement may help to either create or confirm required stereotypes that overcome a lack of knowledge about the destination. However, whilst recognising that advertising is an influence, it is not the only influence. Indeed, in the case of car-borne tourism, serendipity, the knack of making happy discoveries, cannot be under-estimated. Tourists will see a road sign, and on the whim of a moment, follow the sign to see what there is to be seen. Such behaviour might easily account for over 10 per cent of visitors to certain types of attractions. Groves, Moore and Ryan (1987) found that 8.6 per cent of summer visitors to Staunton Harold Hall simply visited because they had seen it signposted, and had no prior knowledge of the Hall or its grounds. For many 'secondary' tourist attractions which are dependent on traffic flows generated by much larger and more heavily promoted tourist zones, visitor numbers may be more influenced by good signposting rather than any other form of promotion.

Within a wider context advertising has many other purposes. In general terms, it might be said that advertising seeks to increase sales, i.e. shift the demand curve to the right, whilst simultaneously it may be said to be an attempt to create a more inelastic demand for any given product, and even to attempt to shift the product or service into the 'Giffen Good' category, whereby more is demanded when the price increases. The concept of brand loyalty is important in this context, because the brand loyal consumer will be retained if the price of a given commodity is slightly higher than a similar commodity offered by a competitor; and in this way profitability is potentially increased, whilst also denying market share to the competition. Equally, advertising might be used to help confirm the higher price, in that it is the advertising perhaps more than the actual product that justifies the quality that is associated with a high price. In short, it is the advertising that seeks to confer the 'added value'. However, in the case of tourist destinations, the same considerations are applicable only to a limited degree. In the case of fast-moving consumer goods, profits are often reaped from high levels of repeat purchasers once penetration of the market has been achieved. In the case of resort zones, the same concept of destination loyalty may be weaker than is the case with products. A number of factors may account for this.

a) Firstly, there is no consistency of experience or use. As has been noted, resort zones are subject to spatial change, whilst the group of peers that made the holiday so enjoyable the first time may not be present on the second occasion.

b) Secondly, for example, much of the advertising within the British package holiday context is not destination orientated, but seeks to engender loyalty to a specific tour operator rather than to a given destination. Thus, the guarantor of quality is the name of the tour operator, not the inherent attributes of the destination itself, other than at one step removed, in that tour operators can only retain the desired image if the resort is compatible with the market segment they serve. From this viewpoint therefore, the image of a specific tourist destination may be in part generated from the images of the tour operators that promote holidays in that area.

c) Thirdly, the very concept of tourism involves travel, and hence the moving on to other destinations in the future.

THE MEASUREMENT OF ATTITUDES – A FUNCTIONAL APPROACH

Personal construct theory

Arguably the first step in the measurement of attitudes towards a holiday destination area is to determine the criteria that people utilise in forming an attitude. Allport (1961) argued that individuals possessed central dispositions, which were highly characteristic of an individual, but which were surprisingly few in number. Similarly, Kelly (1955) claimed that just as few traits are needed to explain most components of personality, so too only a few dispositions are needed to explain the construction of an attitude. He developed a process whereby respondents are presented with a list of, say, holiday destinations, that they divide into three separate piles; those they might like to visit, those they would not wish to visit, and those they are unsure of. From each of the like and dislike piles, four destinations are drawn, to which is added one unsure destination. The destinations are then numbered from one to nine in the sequence where one is a liked destination, two, a dislike, three, a like, four, a dislike, five, a like, six, a dislike, seven, a dislike, eight a like and, nine the unsure destination. The respondent is then presented by the researcher with groups of three, in the combinations of 123, 456, 789, 147, 258, 369, 159, 357 and 258. Other groupings may be presented. The respondent is asked to select the 'odd' item, and to explain how it differs from the other two. In practice, what tends to happen is that the respondents, after approximately seven or eight responses, begin to repeat themselves, albeit perhaps using different words to describe the same characteristics. Equally, it has been found (Harrison and Saare 1975) that comparatively small sample sizes can produce valid constructs, often perhaps with as few as 20 respondents, because the number of constructs being used by members of any given group tends to be repeated. In the responses made respondents are being asked why the selected item differs from the remaining two, and in consequence a dichotomy is being set up. For example, one destination may be seen as too hot, and hence others are too cold, one is too crowded, another is perceived as being free from crowds. Bi-polar constructs are thus elicited, and as such can be used in the construction of semantic differential questionnaires or Likert scales. From such scores, factor analysis may be used to arrive at, or confirm, the number of constructs that are used in the formation of an attitude.

Such approaches have been used to assess attitudes towards a variety of holiday destinations and recreational facilities. Bowler and Warburton (1986) found that constructs varied between different groups based on sex, age, social class and degree of usage of water facilities, but characteristics such as beauty, character, attractiveness and usage rates were of importance to the respondents. In the case of hotels, Saleh and Ryan (1990) concluded on the basis of a factor analysis of responses that tangibles, conviviality of service and reassurance were of importance in the formation of attitudes towards the quality of service received. Gyte (1988), Gyte and Phelps (1989) and Denis (1989) in studies of attitudes towards holiday destinations found constructs such as the price of the holiday, the beach, friendliness of hosts, attractive scenery, history and culture were amongst the determinants used in selecting holiday destinations. Riley and Palmer (1975) used these techniques to assess seaside resorts and concluded that resorts could be grouped on the basis of six components; these components included the following factors:

a) expensive, exclusive, warm with good scenery;
b) good hotels, foreign, more sunshine, different food;
c) quiet, less commercialised, mountains;
d) family resorts;
e) for young people;
f) good for touring.

Multi-attribute theory

The use of personal construct theory has a number of advantages, of which one is that it permits the construction of semantic differential or Likert scales that utilise variables that are not simply thought to be important by the researcher, but which reflect the attributes considered important by the actual or potential users of a resort or tourist zone. Indeed, a research project can be set up which, by incorporating Kelly triads, multi-attribute models and factor analysis, can include checks upon findings as to the importance of the perceived attributes of a resort area in generating its image, and the tourist perception of that resort. Fishbein (1967) initially argued that there were two important components of attitude, the evaluative component, and secondly the importance of that belief. In the formation of an attitude, a number of beliefs might be involved. Accordingly this can be written as:

$$A_o = \sum_{i=1}^{n} B_i\, a_i$$

where A_o = attitude towards destination o
    B_i = strength of belief i about destination o
    a_i = evaluative aspect of belief
    n = number of beliefs

On this basis it becomes possible to devise a two-part questionnaire. The first would consist of a number of questions asking respondents to indicate the degree of importance they attached to specific variables (as revealed by the use of Kelly triads) when selecting a holiday destination. A five-point Likert Scale ranging from 'very important' to 'of no importance' could, for example, be used. The second part of the questionnaire could relate to a specific destination, the respondents being asked to indicate the degree to which a destination possessed a specific attribute, and again a five-point scale might be used. This technique has been widely used, e.g. Scott *et al.* (1978) with reference to New England States, by Tourism Canada (1988) and Tiechk and Ryan (1990). In the Tourism Canada study the results were presented in a manner which reflected the methodology. This disaggregation of the total score implied in the Fishbein formula overcomes a number of objections, at least in part, namely:

a) Can it be said that within the attitude the relationship between the component parts is a multiplicative one?
b) To what extent is the process of summing together factors to produce an univariate (and possibly uni-dimension score) valid?
c) Does the approach fully document the processes of compensation that occur between the various components that create the attitude?

Thus, in the example of Hong Kong personnel perceptions of Canada as a tourist destination (as shown in Figure 8.1), resort areas and budget accommodation are viewed as being of equal importance, but whereas Canada is perceived as offering good resort areas, the question arises, does this offset, to any degree, the perceived lack of budget accommodation? To some extent the answer is given by the total score arrived at for Canada compared with scores achieved for competing destination areas.

Each of the cells shown could be said to represent four different positions as shown in Figure 8.2. What marketing might seek to do is to change the perception of certain attributes so that, say, attributes of a given destination which are currently regarded as unimportant will come to be regarded as important, and vice versa. Alternatively, if a destination lacks something thought to be important, then, in terms of product development, that factor might be added.

Fishbein extended his theory to discuss the concept that attitude is a precursor of behaviour in that a person does not simply construct an attitude, but also considers the expected results of pursuing a course of action. This can be expressed in the formula:

$$A\text{-act} = \sum_{i=1}^{n} b_i\, e_i$$

where $A\text{-act}$ = the individual's attitude towards performance of the action
$\quad\quad b_i$ = the belief that action will lead to consequence i

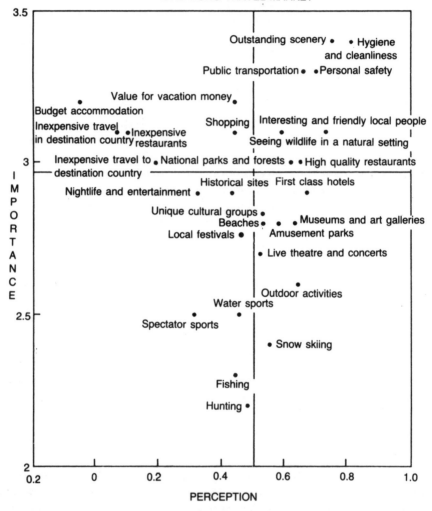

Figure 8.1   Attribute importance vs. perception – Canada
Reproduced with kind permission of Tourism Canada, *Pleasure Travel Markets to North America*, (1989)

Degree of importance of the component	High	Important attributes perceived not to be present in the destination	Important attributes perceived to be present in the destination
	Low	Unimportant attributes perceived not to be present in the destination	Unimportant attributes perceived to be present in the destination
		Low	High
			Perception of existence of attributes

Figure 8.2   The four cells of the Fishbein measurement of attitude

e_i = the evaluation of consequence i

n   = the number of salient consequences.

It becomes possible to hypothesise a summation of the two aspects of the attitude as therefore being:

$$\text{Strength of conviction} = \sum_{i=1}^{n} B_i \, a_i + \sum_{i=1}^{n} b_i \, e_i$$

In terms of holiday destination the consequences of going to one destination are at least two-fold. The first is that the simple fact of going on holiday means expenditure on vacations is not available for expenditure on alternative pursuits. Secondly, the selection of one destination means the forgoing of another, or at the least, a delaying of the opportunity to visit the competing location. Assuming that holidaymakers allocate within their budgets a sum for going on holiday, it does raise the question as to whether or not individuals form attitudes towards a holiday destination independent of their beliefs about the attributes of other resort areas. It has already been noted that the scores for Canada have meaning only if the scores for competing destinations are known. Taking the initial Fishbein formulation, this implies an extension of the model:

$$BI_{ij} = A_{ij} = \sum_{j=1}^{m} \sum_{k=1}^{n} (B_{ijk} \, V_{ik})$$

where i   = holidaymaker

j   = holiday destination

k = attributes of holiday destination

n = number of attributes

m = number of holiday destinations

BI_{ij} = holidaymaker i's behavioural intention towards destination j

A_{ij} = a unidimensional measure of consumer i's attitude toward brand j

B_{ijk} = the strength of holidaymaker i's belief that attribute k is possessed by destination j

V_{ik} = the degree to which attribute k is desired by holidaymaker i.

However, in considering a range of holiday destinations the holidaymaker does not consider every destination, but only those that are thought to hold some appeal. Thus, the consumers are considering only those of which they are aware, and of these, only those that evoke positive images. In the terminology of Howard and Sheth (1969) the inert and inept sets are not considered, only the evoked set of alternatives. Scott, Schewe and Frederick (1978) postulate that if this is the case, then a 'proportionality of product knowledge' exists, and this can be calculated as:

$$PPK_{ij} = \frac{PK_{ij}}{\dfrac{1}{m} \sum\limits_{j=1}^{m} PK_{ij}}$$

where i = holidaymaker

j = destination

m = number of destinations in the evoked set

PPK_{ij} = proportional knowledge of holidaymaker i of destination j

PK_{ij} = knowledge of holidaymaker i for destination j

Hence, this can be added to the previous formula to give:

$$BI_{ij} = A_{ij} = \sum_{j=1}^{m} \sum_{k=1}^{n} (B_{ijk} V_{ik} PPK_{ij})$$

In practical terms the implications for market research into the attitudes and perceptions of the image of any given holiday destination must involve not only an identification of attributes thought to be important, but also an assessment of the degree to which competing destinations are thought to possess such attributes weighted by degrees of knowledge about such destinations as possibly measured by familiarity with resorts. Familiarity might arise from previous visits to given destinations, or destinations thought to be similar. Questionnaires must thus include questions that elicit responses as to frequency of holiday trips undertaken, and places visited within a given period of time, and cover a number of competing holiday destinations. The inclusion of other destinations also has advantages in overcoming problems involved in analysing responses such as acquiescence sets, or predispositions to score low or high, in that the presence of alternatives will help to cause a distribution of scores and perhaps avoid bunching around the mean.

If it is possible, the researchers may wish to utilise all the phrases elicited in a prior study using Kelly triads, in that the data can then be used to conduct a factor analysis, and so confirm the categories that are being used to describe the attributes of holiday destinations.

Table 8.1 Conjoint measurement of attitudes towards holiday destination choice – initial ranking of preferences

	Prices		
	£350	*£300*	*£250*
Majorca, winter	12	10	6
Majorca, spring	9	4	2
Majorca, summer	8	3	1
Majorca, autumn	11	7	5

Conjoint measurement

One of the problems associated with multi-attribute models is that it is objected that holidaymakers, when making choices, do not in fact separate the individual components of a holiday destination, but rather compare a concept of the total image of a place. Marketing research has devised means of measuring such responses, and one such approach is that of conjoint measurement (Green and Rao 1971, Johnson 1974, Hair *et al.* 1987). The basis behind the approach is that the respondent might be given a number of possible destinations at various prices, and is asked to rank them in order of attraction. In Table 8.1 the respondent is asked to select between, for example, the same destination at different times of the year, and at different prices. The research problem is one of specifying the relationship between the product attributes and the preference rankings, and thus 'utility' values will need to be placed for each attribute level to 'explain' the consumer preference rankings. The normal method for doing this is to use a computer statistics package and apply values derived from a monotonic analysis of variance (MONANOVA), but general linear models have also been shown to work (Cohen 1968, Hair *et al.* 1987). A worked example of this method of measuring components of attitudes is given on page 159. The method produces a table of predicted rankings of choice, and hence the next step is to test whether the differences between the predicted and actual rankings are indeed a good fit. June and Smith (1987), in a study applying conjoint measurement to hotel service, utilised the stress test devised by Kruskal (1964, 1965), that is:

$$\text{Stress} = S = \sqrt{\sum_{i=1}^{n} \frac{(Ri - \hat{R}i)^2}{(Ri - R)^2}}$$

where Ri = the actual monotonic transformation of the rank, i to n versions

$\hat{R}i$ = the initial rank

R = the mean of the estimated rankings

Kruskal (1964) provides a means of interpreting the results and a value of below 5 is seen as good, whilst a value of above 20 represents a poor fit between predicted and actual rankings.

Hierarchical techniques

Even with this approach there are a number of problems. It is requiring the holidaymaker to rank a series of choices, in this example, from 1 to 12, but it is not known how significant are the differences between say, the fourth and fifth ranked choices as against the eighth and ninth. It might be that the respondents had difficulty in deciding which was fourth and which was fifth, whereas the distinction between the eighth and ninth choice was quite clear in their minds. In other words, there is no consistency of interval between the rankings. Saaty (1980) recommends the use of hierarchical techniques which overcomes the problem by requiring the respondent to undertake pairwise rankings and indicate the strength of preference on a 9-point scale. Suppose that a tourism board is wanting to assess the attractiveness of its region or country as against others. Let us assume for the sake of simplicity that it is concerned with only a few countries. It might ask respondents to compare countries on the 9-point scale as shown in Table 8.2.

Suppose that a respondent has to judge Britain compared with France, Germany and Norway. This would produce a matrix of 16 cells, but 16

Table 8.2 Scale of Saaty hierarchical choices

1 = the two countries are of equal attractiveness.
3 = the first country is slightly more attractive than the second.
5 = the first country is strongly favoured over the second.
7 = the first country is demonstrably better than the second and is very strongly favoured.
9 = the first is overwhelmingly better than the second and is of the highest order of affirmation.
2,4,6, and 8 are intermediate values between two adjacent judgements.

responses are not required. In four cases the diagonal across the matrix is a comparison between the same countries, whilst, if rationality is assumed, the half below the diagonal is a mirror image of the top segment, and thus the reciprocal can be entered. The respondent may consider Britain to be slightly more attractive than France, and so may enter a 3 in the matrix, of equal attractiveness to Germany, but Norway is considered strongly more attractive than Britain, and hence the reciprocal of 5 is entered in cell Britain/Norway as shown in Table 8.3. The rest of the matrix is filled in, but it can be seen that only five comparisons are needed, that is, those comparisons above the diagonal. The next step is to calculate a vector of priorities from the given matrix. A number of different methods can be used, but assuming the lack of a computer, the process recommended by Saaty (1980) is to divide the elements of each column by the sum of that column (i.e. normalise the column) and then add the elements in each resulting row, and divide this sum by the number of elements in the row. This means that averaging over the normalised rows takes place. The sums of each column are 7.33, 13, 7.5 and 1.54. Normalising the columns yields the matrix shown in Table 8.4. Each row is now added, so that 0.14 + 0.23 + 0.13 + 0.13 equals 0.63. This is then divided by 4, the number of items in the row, and this produces the vector. The final column in Table 8.4 represents the column vector of priorities. That is to say, in our example, Norway is the most attractive country, accounting for 63.5 per cent of the weighting, Britain the next attractive, accounting for 15.7 per cent of the weighting and so on. What has also been produced is a method of creating attractiveness indices for use in gravitational models that may be used for predicting traffic flows between destinations. A means of further improving the result is quite simple, and this is to raise the

Table 8.3 Pairwise comparisons between countries

	Britain	France	Germany	Norway
Britain	1	3	1	1/5
France	1/3	1	1/2	1/7
Germany	1	2	1	1/5
Norway	5	7	5	1

Table 8.4 Pairwise comparisons between countries (normalised columns)

	Britain	France	Germany	Norway	Row sum	Vector
Britain	0.14	0.23	0.13	0.13	0.63	0.157
France	0.04	0.07	0.07	0.09	0.27	0.067
Germany	0.14	0.15	0.13	0.13	0.55	0.137
Norway	0.68	0.54	0.67	0.65	2.54	0.635

matrix to arbitrary large powers and divide the sum of each row by the sum of the elements of the matrix. Saaty (1980) gives examples of this, and also shows how to calculate a consistency ratio.

What this section has indicated is that a number of quite simple research techniques exist to answer the question of how attractive is a destination, and what are the components of that attractiveness.

THE CREATION OF ADVERTISING COPY FOR TOURIST LOCATIONS

Having identified the per eptions of the place, there may be a need to generate ideas for advertising copy. Whilst the conventional picture may be one of where advertising personnel sit down and have a 'brainstorming' session, the need to meet client needs and time schedules has given rise to a number of aids for 'structuring' the creative process. One of the better known of these is the grid created by Maloney (1961), in which he postulates different types of appeal; the rational, social, sensory and ego satisfaction. Associated with each of these appeals are three factors that relate to the use of the product or service, thereby giving rise to a matrix of twelve cells as indicated in Table 8.5.

Table 8.5 Maloney's grid

Potential rewarding experiences	Types of appeal			
	Rational	*Social*	*Sensory*	*Ego satisfaction*
Results of use experience				
Product in use experience				
Incidental to use experience				

Thus, if an agency is considering the advertising of sailing and windsurfing holidays in Greece, the 'rational' appeal and 'results of use experience' cell might generate messages such as the acquisition of new skills in favourable climatic conditions. The 'social product in use' cell might create ideas about a shared experience amongst like-minded people, the 'sensory/incidental to use' appeal might cause warnings about strong exposure to sun, the 'ego satisfaction/results of use' cell may create the message about feeling good as a result of being able to perform new manoeuvres. In many cases it is quite possible that the cells might simply repeat ideas; for example, the acquisition of a sun-tan could meet all four types of appeal. Duplication of ideas within different cells does not matter, as the practical purpose of the grid is not simply to categorise, but also to act as a generator of ideas.

An even simpler type of grid has been used with great effect by Foote, Cone and Belding Communications Incorporated (1987). Based on the ideas of Howard and Sheth (1969), the grid is formed by two continuums, as indicated in Figure 8.3. The vertical axis measures the degree of involvement required by the purchase decision. Is it one that requires a large outlay of money, or one that is a decision shared with other family members? Generally such decisions relate to infrequent purchases. At the other extreme is the habitual purchase, often involving small sums of money, and little prior discussion. The horizontal axis represents the continuum between the decision that is primarily based on emotion to that based on rationality. Based on interviews of more than 20,000 respondents in 23 countries with reference to 500 products, Foote, Cone and Belding have refined a questionnaire whereby by subjecting the responses to eight questions to mapping techniques, products can be easily located on the grid. It can be objected that the two dimensions are perhaps not entirely independent variables, but again from a practical viewpoint this does not entirely matter, as the agency utilises the grid to help in the generation of ideas for advertising copy. Holidays usually occupy a place in the top right-hand cell (as indicated in Figure 8.3), but located reasonably near to the vertical axis. In a campaign for the State of Alaska, the agency found in its research that Alaska conjured up specific sets of images, and the appeal of the untamed wilderness created a more than average emotional response. The company sought to capitalise on this by building an advertising campaign that located Alaska a little further to the right than was normally the case for holiday purchase decisions. Consequently, the theme of Alaska being a 'state of mind, a dream waiting to be fulfilled' was utilised with the copy headline of 'Once you've gone to Alaska, you never come all the way back'. The campaign also featured portraits of older people against a vista of lakes and mountains as a means of establishing figures to which the target market segments could relate.

Market research techniques are increasingly sophisticated in the generation of ideas for advertising copy. Bayley and Stops (1988) indicated a 'reversed' application of Kelly grid techniques whereby rather than seeking to identify components of an attitude, they sought to establish which of famous personalities, places and things actually exhibited characteristics of a given attribute. Instead of asking respondents to, for example, distinguish between Malta, Majorca and Greece as holiday destinations, and then indicate what the distinguishing feature was, the technique can be reversed by presenting an attribute, say, friendly hosts, and then asking which destination most closely resembles the attribute of having friendly people. Again the objective is the same, to generate ideas for advertising copy which will elicit positive responses from potential holidaymakers.

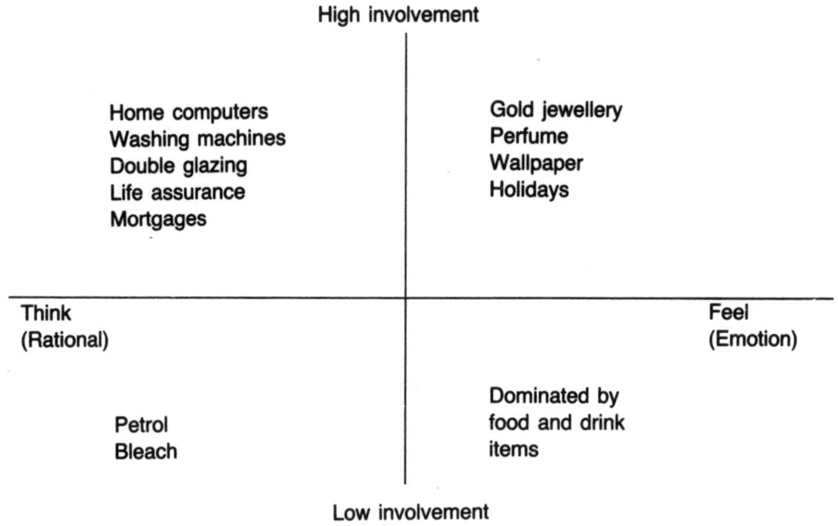

High involvement

Home computers	Gold jewellery
Washing machines	Perfume
Double glazing	Wallpaper
Life assurance	Holidays
Mortgages	

Think   Feel
(Rational)   (Emotion)

	Dominated by
Petrol	food and drink
Bleach	items

Low involvement

Figure 8.3   The FCB grid

TARGETING THE TOURIST MARKETS

General issues

Increasing interest is being shown in market segmentations within tourism. Anderson and Langmeyer (1982), Bryant and Morrison (1980), and Crask (1981) are all examples of literature relating to segmenting tourist markets. The processes of undertaking research into perceptions of places and generating advertising copy cannot take place without reference to the type of clientele the destination might appeal to. Already, various typologies of tourist have been identified using the classifications of 'mass organised tourist', 'allocentric' and other similar groupings. Equally, it is quite easy to identify the type of tourist by the main activity undertaken, and hence statistics based on classifications such as VFR (visiting friends and relatives), conference traveller, business travellers, day-trippers and many similar classifications are used. Equally, many research projects will elicit socio-economic data about tourists who visit a destination, such as their age, level of income and socio-economic grouping. It thus becomes possible to identify locations on the basis of types of tourists attracted, and a profiling of resorts becomes possible. This can be spatially represented as in Figure 8.4. More sophisticated plotting can be undertaken by the use of discriminant analysis, whereby many variables are taken into account.

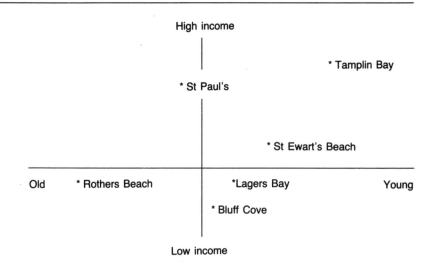

Figure 8.4   Profiling beaches by tourist types

Life style characteristics

Arguably, as recreation and tourism is part of a life style that people may seek to obtain for themselves, a categorisation of tourists by life style may be more effective than utilising the more traditional socio-economic classifications. Generally, the argument is that social class is becoming less of a determinant of consumer behaviour for a number of reasons. One is that the income gaps between a number of skilled and unskilled manual jobs and a number of middle-class professional occupations have in fact closed, so that, for example, teachers may earn less than plumbers. Secondly, a growth of income permits greater spending on leisure and associated activities whereby a greater expression of individual beliefs and values occurs, thus presenting more opportunities for niche marketing to take place. It might also be said that the homogeneity of values within any given social class might also be breaking down. Under these circumstances the predictor variables of consumer behaviour are more likely to be attitudes and values rather than income levels, age, or type of occupation. Thirdly, there are surprisingly high levels of instability in terms of class membership, at least as recorded by market research surveys. O'Brien and Ford (1988) report that during a six-month period 41 per cent of respondents in a survey undertaken for Granada TV had apparently changed social class, and, once errors had been rectified, 10 per cent of the sample had in fact had such a change of circumstance that a change of recorded social class was justified.

Accordingly, various attempts have been made to define tourist markets in a way that reflects these types of concerns, and which perhaps gives more of an insight into the motivation of holidaymakers. Mazanec (1981a) analysed the German market using factor analysis, and concluded that on the basis of responses to 16 statements such as 'I would do without a lot of things, but never without my holiday trip' or 'Travelling is no longer a pleasure, for everything gets more and more expensive everywhere', the German population could be divided into a total of 12 categories, (7 male and 5 female), which, on the basis of attitudes towards leisure and travel, could predict the propensity to travel. Similarly, Young, Ott and Feigin (1978) identify six types of Canadian holidaymaker, these being, briefly:

a) Friends and relatives − non-active visitor (29 per cent of the market). These visit friends and relatives, seek familiar surroundings, and are not inclined to engage in any activity.
b) Friends and relatives − active city visitor (12 per cent) − they seek familiar settings, but will engage in sightseeing, shopping and cultural and other entertainments.
c) Family sightseers (6 per cent) − look for a new place that would be a treat for the children and an enriching experience.
d) Outdoor vacationer (19 per cent) − seek clean air, rest and beautiful scenery. Many are campers, and children are also important.
e) Resort vacationer (19 per cent) − they are interested in beach locations and popular places with a big city atmosphere.
f) Foreign vacationer (26 per cent) − look for places they have not previously visited with a foreign atmosphere and beautiful scenery. Money is not of major concern, but good accommodation and service are.

The use of factor analysis to generate such typologies is undoubtedly useful, but a number of practical and conceptual difficulties exist. The first practical difficulty is that many tourism studies relate to comparatively small samples and for specific purposes. There is little comparative work that is undertaken, and in consequence, from the commercial viewpoint, there is little in the way of any database linking such attitudes to other aspects of consumer life that will enable any form of direct marketing to take place. Increasingly, therefore, reference will be made to those psychographic profiles that do possess these advantages.

Within North America one of the longest established is the VALS (Values, Attitudes and Life styles) index. Now into a second version, VALS 2™, it was originally constructed on the premises underlying Maslow's (1943) hierarchy of needs. This established a series of needs, ranging from

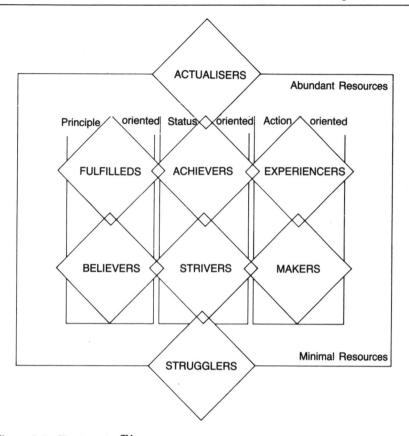

Figure 8.5   The VALS 2™ network

basic needs for shelter and food, to higher order needs culminating in self-actualisation. Figure 8.5 shows the categories of the VALS 2™ network, which is based on 'a conceptual framework that is called self-orientation, and a new definition of resources' (SRI International 1989). The advantage that the VALS 2™ grouping possesses is that it enables tourism planners not only to identify attitudes of various potential market segments, but also to relate them to socio-economic data and potentially other forms of data such as magazine readership.

   Within Britain a similar index that is beginning to attract attention is 'Outlook', which has six categories, the Trendies, Pleasure Seekers, Indifferent, Working Class Puritans, Sociable Spenders and Moralists. This system arises from work done by Baker and Fletcher (1987) utilising the 20,000 responses made to the British Market Research Bureau's Target Group Index. This monthly survey not only includes questions about purchases of products, but also includes responses to over 190 attitudinal/life style questions, and also covers respondents' use of media. Consequently, the correlation of Outlook with use of media presents opportunities not only for identifying types of tourists, but also the newspapers they read and the television programmes they watch.

However, a number of caveats need to be identified. Some stem from the nature of the analysis itself. Most categories arise from the use of cluster or factor analysis, where the objective is to determine as few categories as possible which explain the greatest part of the variance (usually six groups accounting for about 80 per cent of the variance). It seeks to identify underlying themes. If more groups exist, or the groups so identified explain but a small part of the variance, or the factors are unequal in the variance explained, it is usually held that there are no common themes. In short, the researcher is electing to use a technique that is deemed to have produced a 'failed hypothesis' if other than a few categories emerge. It is for the users of the data to decide whether the reduction of complex motivations of large populations into six or seven groups does produce, in the light of their experience, identifiable classifications that have meaning for their purposes. There is, arguably, a significant difference between saying, as Kelly (1955) and Allport (1961) do, that comparatively few constructs are required to identify personality or an attitude, and saying that only a few life style groupings exist amongst the total population of several million within any given country.

Life-stage factors

The test of the proposals, as with competing systems, is the degree to which they help in predicting consumer behaviour and the extent to which they help tourism planners to identify the types of tourists who will feel most at ease with the attraction that is being considered. The use of psychographics in tourism planning is comparatively new, although segmentation policies based on vacation preferences, demographics and personality types were described in detail by Crask (1981), Bryant and Morrison (1980) and Mayo and Jarvis (1981), amongst others, in the early 1980s.

In the wider field of marketing the evidence is mixed as to the effectiveness of such techniques. O'Brien and Ford (1988) found that social class and life-stage had stronger predictive power than life style classifications, whilst Cornish and Denny (1989) argue that social grade often under-performs because 'individuals will often be graded in the field on a shortened and subjective version of the measure'. A combination of socio-educational grade, income and life-stage is, they argue, a powerful predictor of consumer behaviour, whilst they also point out that (based on data drawn from the National Readership Survey) for package holidays disposable net household income is a strong discriminator. Similarly,

Alexander and Valentine (1989) propose that age cohort effects exist, whereby shared lifetime experiences common to a particular age group shape their world view, and that, over time, this becomes more important and possibly absorbs the style clans of the teenage world. They comment, 'at the younger end we are strong on style-clanning and weak on age cohorting; then, as we get older, the polarities reverse – and when we're old we become better age cohorters and less effective style clanners'. On the other hand, Baker and Fletcher (1987) indicate that Outlook was a better predictor than Social Class in areas relating to leisure activities such as pub going and taking package holidays. However, what psychographics does hold out for the planning of tourism is the means by which profiles of tourist types can become much more refined than the crude generalisations that might otherwise exist. One type of consumer categorisation that is being used by package holiday companies is that of geo-demographic systems.

Geo-demographic systems

Geo-demographic systems incorporate socio-economic data into not simply a listing of peoples' addresses, but also a description of the neighbourhood in which they live. The basic data that most geo-demographic databases will hold is drawn from the census of population annually updated in the case of Britain by the electoral register, which permits an identification of areas characterised by stable or rapidly changing populations. Consequently the database is likely to hold records of the names of people at a given address, the size of house in terms of number of rooms, whether the residents own or rent the house, the occupation of the members of the household and their educational level. In addition, the systems will contain descriptions of housing areas, for example, MOSAIC type 25 – smart inner city flats with few children, an area of Victorian high-status housing, or MOSAIC type 31, a high unemployment estate with the worst financial problems occupied by those with low income and a high incidence of inability to pay credit.

MOSAIC is the database of CCN Systems, Nottingham, and contains 60 elements in the construction of 58 classifications of neighbourhoods. In addition to the above data it also contains information on the incidence of use of credit cards and other forms of credit, and the levels of county court judgements on debt. MOSAIC, ACORN, PinPoint and other systems all offer similar types of data, and mapping facilities, but differences do exist reflecting the basis of group determination and additional data sources used. However, as in any other form of direct marketing, once a tourist-related company possesses a list of names and addresses, the list can be subjected to analysis to assess whether or not any significant groupings exist in that company's profile of customers. The most loyal purchasers of a given holiday type can be analysed, and once the patterns have been identified it becomes possible to buy lists of addresses with matching profiles. In this way the company can target potential new customers. Equally, the catchment areas of restaurants, leisure centres and other recreational facilities can be analysed, and new locations with catchment areas matching those of the successful outlets be found. These systems are increasingly being used by holiday companies to help identify the profiles and characteristics of their customers. (With respect to this it should be noted that in Britain, in 1989, under ABTA regulations, a customer who books through a travel agent is the customer of that travel agent, and the tour operator is not permitted to make a direct approach to that customer.)

The full potential of the systems becomes apparent when matching takes place, for example, between ACORN classifications with use of media patterns and past holiday behaviours. The English Tourist Board now offers a database of over 400,000 names and addresses of people interested in British holidays, and combines this with socio-economic classifications, size of family, car ownership, responses on a holiday life style questionnaire, newspaper readership and types of holiday preferred. In 1989 the cost of purchasing a 1,000 names and addresses of any given profile was but £60. Similar, albeit different classifications, are also available for purchase in other western countries.

The practical implications for resort planning are obvious. It becomes possible to identify a target type of clientele, and provide the sort of facilities that will attract any given type of tourist, based not on broad generalisations, but quite detailed patterns of past behaviour and income. It does not matter if the tourist concerned has been inconsistent in the sense that they have undertaken different sorts of holidays, in that such apparent inconsistency is but a reflection of the tourist seeking different experiences from different types of holidays. It is sufficient to know that they have either expressed interest in the type of holiday being offered, that they have undertaken that sort of holiday in the past, or have characteristics that match the profile of existing holidaytakers using any given resort or holiday attraction. It means that in the writing of advertising copy messages appropriate to the target market can be quite specific, and equally those same messages serve to deter those who would feel out of place in any given destination.

Just as it is with advertising copy, so, too, it can be with the design of the tourist attraction. Those resort zones that are, for example, family orientated, seeking to meet the needs of young couples with young children can devise a different type of holiday experience from those facilities that are offering holidays to what might be termed 'empty nesters', that is, people whose children have left the family home. The potential for dissatisfaction caused by a gap between the tourists' perceptions of the nature of the holiday and the actual service provided is, at least theoretically, minimised. Increasingly, as people have the means of meeting different needs at different times, and are undertaking more than one holiday per year, so the need to more carefully demarcate the potential tourist experience becomes important. The mass market is becoming more segmented in areas other than holidaying, and, inasmuch as this is a reflection of social trends, the same can be expected of holidaytaking.

SUMMARY

From the viewpoint of tourism planners and resort developers, access to the above types of data on holidaymakers enables them to be more specific in their planning of the resort destination zone. In planning the resort the planner or developer is thus not simply concerned with the provision of a facility, but rather with the type of facility required by any given group of potential customers. This marketing information also has implications for the planner. If host communities are concerned about the potential impacts of tourist facilities upon their communities, it becomes feasible to identify more carefully the type of holidaymaker they would wish to attract, and seek to develop that type of holiday facility that will attract the required sorts of tourists in the desired numbers. If the key to better planning is information, then the developing databases on consumers and their preferences may be of help.

Calculating coefficients for conjoint measurement

If no access to MONANOVA exists the contribution of each factor can be calculated quite easily in situations where there are few cells by using a simple compositional rule of additive main effects, that is, the choice of holiday is based on destination plus season plus price in our example. The steps are:

a) calculate average score of preference – for n choices this is $1+2+3+4+$
   . . . n divided by n,
   e.g. if 12 choices $(1+2+3+4+5+6+7+8+9+10+11+12)/12$, i.e. 6.5,
b) calculate the average score for each variable,
c) calculate for each variable, the difference between the variable and the overall average (i.e. calculate the deviation),
d) square the deviation,
e) sum the square of the deviations,
f) calculate the contribution,
   i) multiply the deviation squared by the number of variables divided by the sum of the squares of the deviation,
   ii) take the square root of this calculation.

This can be illustrated using the original rankings of preference as shown in Table 8.1 on page 183.

The average score of the preferences is thus $1+2+3+4+5+6+7+8+9+10+11+12$, i.e. 6.5. We can now examine the difference for each ranking from the mean. In the case of preferences for winter holidays, this is $12+10+6 = 28$, divided by the 3 possible occurrences, and this gives an average of 9.3^3. Repeat this process with every variable to arrive at the scores shown in Table 8.6. The deviation between the variable mean and the mean for all the rankings is calculated, as shown in the column headed 'deviation'. The next step is to square the deviations. Now, sum the square of the deviations. In this example there are 8 variables, so the next step is to take each of the deviations, multiply each deviation squared by 8/39.19, and take the square root to arrive at the contribution.

Table 8.6   Calculation of coefficients

Variable contribution	Mean	Deviation	Deviation^2	Contribution
Majorca	6.5	0	0	0
Winter	9.3	+2.8	7.84	+1.26
Spring	5.0	−1.5	2.25	−0.67
Summer	4.0	−2.5	6.25	−1.12
Autumn	7.6	+1.1	1.35	+0.52
£350	10.0	+3.5	12.25	+1.58
£300	6.0	−0.5	0.25	−0.26
£250	3.5	−3.0	9.00	−1.35
			39.19	

The process can be taken further, and interaction differences calculated. In addition, a series of rules exists where many cells exist. For example, a 4 variable model, with each variable operating at 4 levels would create 256 possible interactions. Rules exist to narrow down the process to those where interactions exist. Hair *et al.* (1987) indicate the basic processes and also provide readings and additional references for those wishing to pursue this further.

The more normal situation is where there is a series of locations as well as time and price variations. For example, the following choices and rankings exist, as shown in Table 8.7. The mean ranking is thus 36!/36, i.e. is $1+2+3+4 \ldots +36$ divided by 36 i.e. (18.52). The variable rankings are thus:

For £350 $36+21+17+35+22+28+29+30+33+20+19+34 = 324$
          Mean equals 324/12 = 27

For £300 $31+14+12+32+8+15+16+9+26+13+11+27 = 214$
          Mean equals 214/12 = 17.8

Table 8.7   Ranking of choices

		Prices		
		£350	*£300*	*£250*
Majorca	Winter	36	31	25
	Spring	21	14	5
	Summer	17	12	1
	Autumn	35	32	24
Austria	Winter	22	8	6
	Spring	28	15	4
	Summer	29	16	18
	Autumn	30	9	7
Greece	Winter	33	26	23
	Spring	20	13	3
	Summer	19	11	2
	Autumn	34	27	10

For £250 $25+5+1+24+6+4+18+7+23+3+2+10 = 128$
Mean equals $128/12 = 10.7$

For Winter $36+31+25+22+8+6+33+26+23 = 210$
Mean equals $210/9 = 23.3$

For Spring $21+14+5+28+15+4+20+13+3 = 123$
Mean equals $123/9 = 13.6$

For Summer $17+12+1+29+16+18+19+11+2 = 125$
Mean equals $125/9 = 13.8$

For Autumn $35+32+24+30+9+7+34+27+10 = 208$
Mean equals $208/9 = 23.1$

For Majorca $36+31+25+21+14+5+17+12+1+35+32+24 = 253$
Mean equals $253/12 = 21.1$

For Austria $22+8+6+28+15+4+29+16+18+30+9+7 = 192$
Mean equals $192/12 = 16$

For Greece $33+26+23+20+13+3+19+11+2+34+27+10 = 221$
Mean equals $221/12 = 18.4$

The contribution can now be calculated in the manner indicated previously, which gives rise to Table 8.8.

From this table it can already be seen that within the total perception of each of the choices the strongest factors that seem to be operating are price, in that £350 is seen as expensive, and £250 is attractive to people, whilst there is a preference for summer and spring, and the country itself is less important. In interpreting the results the convention is to reverse the signs,

Table 8.8 Contribution of each factor

	Mean	Dev	Dev^2	Contribution
£350	27.0	8.48	71.91	+1.73
£300	17.8	−0.72	0.51	−0.15
£250	10.7	−7.92	62.73	−1.62
Winter	23.3	4.78	22.84	+0.97
Spring	13.6	−4.92	24.21	−1.01
Summer	13.8	−4.72	22.28	−0.97
Autumn	23.1	4.58	20.97	+0.93
Majorca	21.1	2.58	6.65	+0.52
Austria	16.0	−2.52	6.35	−0.52
Greece	18.4	−0.12	0.01	−0.002

so that the most important items are noted as having positive values. What now remains is to calculate the value of each of the combinations. Thus, a winter holiday in Majorca costing £350 has the weighting of:

$$
\begin{aligned}
\text{Winter} &= +\ 0.97 \\
\text{Majorca} &= +\ 0.52 \\
£350 &= +\ 1.73 \\
\hline
&\ +\ 3.22
\end{aligned}
$$

At this point the sign is reversed, thus confirming that such a selection is not particularly attractive. The same process is undertaken for each combination to give the values that can be used for ranking the alternatives, as is done in Table 8.9.

Visually it can be seen that the fit between expected and actual rankings is poor, and this arises from the highly diverse nature of the resorts in mixing a winter holiday resort area with two summer resort areas. Therefore, whilst winter originally has a low index value of −0.97, (following the convention of sign reversal), it is for Austria a positive factor in the perception of holidays there. Majorca, however, because it is perceived by the sample as being a less attractive country than Austria, is receiving predictions lower than that originally scored. The example serves to illustrate the difficulty of composing a mix of heterogeneous factors that may contain biases towards certain patterns. In practice, this does occur with smaller numbers of variables; in the case of the above example, only 10. With a larger number, and using computer programs, then, as Hair *et al*. (1987) discuss, the matching becomes closer.

Following June and Smith (1987), Kruskal's stress test can be applied to the predicted as against actual rankings to assess the validity of the estimated importance of each of the factors. 'Raw stress' might be said to be no more than the square of the deviation between the predicted ranking and the actual ranking, i.e.:

Table 8.9 Predicted and actual ranking of alternatives

		£	Value	Predicted rank	Actual rank
Majorca	Winter	350	−3.22	36	36
		300	−1.34	30	31
		250	+0.13	18	25
	Spring	350	−1.24	27	21
		300	+0.64	15	14
		250	+2.11	5	5
	Summer	350	−1.28	28	17
		300	+0.60	16	12
		250	+2.07	6	1
	Autumn	350	−3.18	35	35
		300	−1.30	29	32
		250	+0.17	17	24
Austria	Winter	350	−2.01	31	22
		300	−0.30	22	8
		250	+1.17	11	6
	Spring	350	−0.20	19	28
		300	+1.68	7	15
		250	+3.15	1	4
	Summer	350	−0.24	20	29
		300	+1.64	8	16
		250	+3.11	2	18
	Autumn	350	−2.14	32	30
		300	−0.26	21	9
		250	+1.21	10	7
Greece	Winter	350	−2.70	34	33
		300	−0.82	26	26
		250	+0.65	14	23
	Spring	350	−0.72	23	20
		300	+1.51	9	13
		250	+2.63	3	3
	Summer	350	−0.76	24	19
		300	+1.12	12	11
		250	+2.60	4	2
	Autumn	350	−2.66	33	34
		300	−0.78	25	27
		250	+0.69	13	10

Raw Stress $= S = (Ar - Pr)^2$

where Ar = Initial rank

and Pr = predicted (transformed rank).

There are a number of problems related to this, and Kruskal (1964) recommends the introduction of a scaling factor, and hence the Stress might be defined as:

$$\text{Stress} = S = \sqrt{\frac{(R_i - \hat{R}_i)^2}{\sum_{i=1}^{n} (R_i - R)^2}}$$

where R_i = the actual monotonic transformation of the the rank, i to n versions

$\hat{R}_i$ = the initial rank

R = the mean of the estimated rankings

Applying this formula to the rankings shown in the Table 8.9 gives us:

$$\text{Stress} = S = \sqrt{\frac{6}{143}}$$

$$= 0.20$$

Kruskal (1964) provides a means of interpreting the results and a value of below 0.05 is seen as good, whilst a value of above 0.20 represents a poor fit between predicted and actual rankings.

Chapter 9

Final thoughts

The previous chapters have argued that the essential component of the tourist product is the tourist experience of a location and its people. In part, the degree of satisfaction gained from that experience relates to the expectations of the tourist, the degree of reality on which those expectations are based, the ability of the tourist to adapt to perceived realities, and the nature of the critical encounters that shape that reality. In a sense, therefore, the previous chapters have looked at three zones as is illustrated in Figure 9.1. These three zones are discussed below.

The tourist-generating zone

This is only in part a geographical entity. It is geographical in the sense that the tourist comes from a place, but that place is also a network of social and political institutions that shape patterns of thought. In addition, it is a resource bank which determines the ability of the tourist to travel.

The host zone

Again, whilst this is obviously geographical, it, too, consists of a network of social and political institutions, and resources that shape the hosts' attitudes towards the tourists. With reference to its geographical location, it is not simply the tourist destination itself, but the wider framework within which the zone of interaction resides, and upon which it may draw a migrant labour force and peripheral tourist attractions.

The zone of interaction and interpretation

This is the tourist destination zone, but, as previously noted, it changes both temporally and spatially. It is the place of interaction between the tourist and host. It is not simply a geographical entity, but also a psychological and social one that exists within a 'place'.

The tourist-generating zone, as was discussed in Chapter two, is the source of demand, whilst the host zone creates a set of resources and

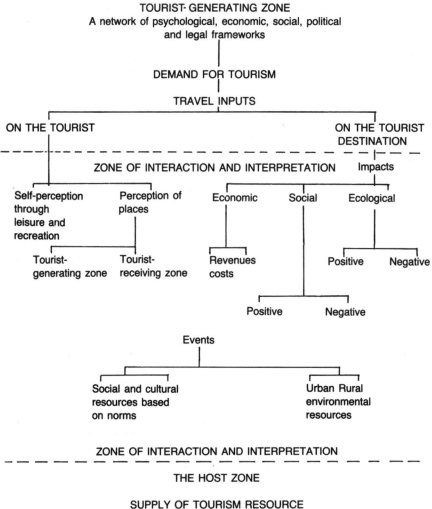

TOURIST- GENERATING ZONE
A network of psychological, economic, social, political
and legal frameworks

DEMAND FOR TOURISM

TRAVEL INPUTS

ON THE TOURIST

ON THE TOURIST
DESTINATION

ZONE OF INTERACTION AND INTERPRETATION   Impacts

Self-perception
through
leisure and
recreation

Perception of
places

Economic

Social

Ecological

Tourist-
generating zone

Tourist-
receiving zone

Revenues
costs

Positive

Negative

Positive

Negative

Events

Social and cultural
resources based
on norms

Urban Rural
environmental
resources

ZONE OF INTERACTION AND INTERPRETATION

THE HOST ZONE

SUPPLY OF TOURISM RESOURCE
A network of psychological, economic, social, political
and legal frameworks

Figure 9.1   The overall view

attitudes on the part of hosts within which the tourist will reside during
the holiday period. These tourist inputs begin to interact with the tourist
prior to the tourist's arrival, because those social and physical resources will
be the basis of an attitude formation process on the part of the tourist
which helps to shape the decision to visit. Obviously, however, the manner
in which those resources reach the tourist, through marketing channels and
other media, and the way the tourist interprets the data received is partially

dependent upon the functioning of the tourist-generating zone.

As it is, Figure 9.1 simplifies the previous discussion in that it is seen from the viewpoint of the tourist. It omits, for example, the shaping of hosts' perceptions of the tourist and the tourist-generating zone. The tourists themselves are transmitters of information about the tourist-generating zone which helps shape hosts' perceptions of that zone in both its geographical and social senses. Nonetheless the figure reinforces the primacy of the zone of interaction and interpretation which is the essence of the tourism 'product'. It also presents the vulnerability of tourism to future mega-trends which may be pessimistic in nature. The deterioration of the globe's natural environment may mean a decrease in our material standard of living, and in reaction to this leisure policies may become guided by responses to environmental, social and economic reforms than be guided simply by a demand for touristic opportunity. Within this framework, the psychological framework may change in terms of the location of recreation and the role of the holiday within leisure. On the other hand, concern with environmental, stress-free living patterns may place leisure and holiday activities within a framework of stress avoidance techniques – that is, the avoidance of both personal and environmental stress.

Schwaninger (1984, 1989) argues that the following trends are both apparent and long term. These trends include the following:

a) further increasing differentiation and pluralisation of demand;
b) emergence of new specialised markets and market segments;
c) a decrease of physically and culturally passive forms of vacation in favour of more active pastimes; and
d) a shift towards maximising individual liberty in recombining elements for custom-made holiday packages (modular product design).

Further, he argues that the need for the non-standardisation of services arises from:

a) the quest for self-determination and 'do-it-yourself';
b) the advanced level of travel experience in the population which leads to a more critical and quality-orientated approach as well as a growing sophistication and rationality of choice;
c) an increasing desire to relate to nature;
d) higher levels of environmental consciousness and sensitivity to the quality of life in general; and
e) the increasing effort to learn, which often manifests itself in serious attempts to get to know foreign cultures.

All of these themes have emerged in the book, and it can be argued that these trends are not solely determined by the presence of economic growth, and thus could resist a downturnin the economic environment. Yet all of these trends point to the growing importance of 'societal marketing' within the tourism industry. Greater segmentation of markets allied with the increasing sophistication of databases must mean that such marketing will play a greater role in the future of tourism.

From a research viewpoint, one of the implications of current trends is not only that researchers must look more carefully at the implications of market segmentations and the process by which individuals transfer from one market segment to another, but also that researchers must pay closer attention to the relationship between tourism on the one hand and recreation and leisure studies on the other. Such a relationship also needs to be explored within a context of usage patterns of natural resources, and from this viewpoint the literature relating to the usage of national parks (e.g. Dearden 1989) is of interest to students and teachers of not only recreation, forestry management techniques, but also of tourism.

Finally, it must be noted that if the nature of the tourism product is an experience of place at a particular time, and with either different groups of people or alone, then any study of tourism is bound within a psychological, geographical and cultural milieu. The role of mood in the shaping of the perception of the tourist experience is important (Pearce 1988, Yardley 1990). The complexity of the tourist experience becomes increasingly apparent to researchers. Whilst Cohen discussed the concept of authenticity in terms of a gap between perceived and 'objective' authenticity, Pearce (1988), in his work, *The Ulysses Factor*, discusses a nine-stage model of authenticity. Just as the tourist destination zone is dynamic, so, too, is the tourist experience. In consequence, the study of, and management of, tourism remains an absorbing and stimulating exercise.

Bibliography

Adams, R. (1973) Uncertainty in nature, cognitive dissonance, and the perceptual distortion on environmental information, *Economic Geography*, vol. 49, pp. 287–297.

Ahmed, S. A. (1986) Understanding resident's reactions to tourism marketing strategies, *Journal of Travel Research*, vol. 25, no. 2, pp. 13–18.

Ajzen, I. (1988) *Attitudes, Personality and Behaviour*, Open University Press, Milton Keynes.

Alexander, M. and Valentine, V. (1989) *Cultural Class – Researching the Parts that Social Class Cannot Reach*, Market Research Society Annual Conference Paper, London.

Allport, G. (1955) *Becoming: Basic Considerations for a Psychology of Personality*, Yale University Press, New Haven.

— (1961) *Pattern and Growth in Personality*, Holt, Rinehart and Winston, New York.

— (1968) *The Person in Psychology; Selected Essays*, Beacon Press, Boston.

Anderson, B. and Langmeyer, L. (1982) Under 50 and over 50 travellers, *Journal of Travel Research*, vol. 20, no. 4, pp. 20–24.

Andronikou, A. (1987) *Development of Tourism in Cyprus – Harmonisation of Tourism with the Environment* Strovolos, Nicosia.

Anon, (1988) Stress and strain of Christmas with the family, *Independent*, 19 December.

Arbel, A. and Pizam, A. (1977) Some determinants of urban hotel location – the tourists' inclination, *Journal of Travel Research*, vol. 15, pp. 18–22.

Archer, B. H. and Owen, C. B. (1971) Towards a tourist regional multiplier, *Regional Studies*, vol. 5, pp. 289–294.

Archer, E. (1984) Estimating the relationship between tourism and economic growth in Barbados, *Journal of Travel Research*, vol. 22, no. 4, pp. 8–12.

Bacon, A. W. (1975) Leisure and the alienated worker: a critical reassessment of three radical theories of work and leisure, *Journal of Leisure Research*, vol. 7, pp. 179–190.

Baines, G. B. K. (1982) *South Pacific Island Tourism, Environmental Costs and Benefits of the Fijian Example*. In *The Impact of Tourism Development*, ed. F. Rajotte, Environmental and Resources Studies Program, Trent University.

Baker, K. and Fletcher, P. (1987) Outlook – TGI's new lifestyle system, *Admap*, March, no. 261, pp. 23–29.

Barkham, R. (1973) Recreational carrying capacity – a problem of perception, *Area*, vol. 5, pp. 218–222.

Barrett, F. (1988a) Have a nice day Boyo!, *Independent*, 2 January.

— (1988b) Profiting from the taste of the British yob, *Independent*, 20 July.

— (1988c) A man not tired of London, but tired of tourists, *Independent*, p. 19, 14 May.

— (1989a) On the Algarve's road to ruin, *Independent*, p. 45, 22 July.

— (1989b) An unhappy birthday for the package holiday industry, *Independent*, 9 August.

— (1989c) *Guide to Real Holidays Abroad – the Complete Directory for the Independent Traveller*, Independent Publishing, London.

Baud-Bovey, M. and Lawson, F. (1977) *Tourism and Recreation Development*, CBI Publishing, Boston, Mass.

Baum, T. (1989) Scope of the tourism industry and its employment impact in Ireland, *Service Industries Journal*, vol. 9, no. 1, pp. 140–151.

Bayley, G. and Stops, L. (1988) *An Adaptation of Personal Construct Theory to Identify the Underlying Significance of Advertising Properties and their Future Applications*, Market Research Society Conference Paper, London.

Belisle, B. (1984) The significance and structure of hotel food supply in Jamaica, *Caribbean Geography*, vol. 1(4), pp. 219–233.

Bello, D. C. and Etzed, M. (1985) The role of novelty in the pleasure travel experience, *Journal of Travel Research*, Vol 24, no. 1, pp. 20–36.

Benny Dorm, (pseudonym), (1988) *Beach Party – the Last Resort*, New English Library, Hodder and Stoughton, London.

Berg, P. (1990) *A Green City Program With a Bioregional Perspective: Developing the San Francisco Green City Plan*. In *Green Cities – Ecologically Sound Approaches to Urban Space*, ed. David Gordon, Black Rose Books, Montreal.

Bird *et al.* (1987) Classifying people, *Admap*, May, pp. 20–53.

Bitner, M. J., Booms, B. H. and Tetreault, M. (1990) The service encounter: diagnosing favourable and unfavourable incidents, *Journal of Marketing*, vol. 54, January, pp. 71–84.

Bjorklund, R. and King, B. (1982) A consumer approach to assist in the design of hotels, *Journal of Travel Research*, vol. 20, no. 4, pp. 45–52.

Bjorklund, R. and Philbrick, A. K. (1972) Spatial configurations of mental process, Quoted by Mathieson, A. and Wall, G. *Tourism – Economic, Physical and Economic Impacts*, (1982) Longmans, Harlow, Essex.

Bland, R. (1987) Low pay in the Cornish tourism industry, Letters Page, *Independent*, 14 July.

Blois, K. (1987) IT and marketing strategies in service firms, *Service Industries Journal*, vol. 7, no. 1, pp. 14–23.

Bodur, M. (1988) Pre-planning orientations, *Tourism Management*, vol. 9, no. 3, September, pp. 245–250.

Boorstin, D. J. (1961) *The Image – a Guide to Pseudo-events in America*, Harper and Row, New York.

Bosselman, F. P. (1978) *In the Wake of the Tourist – Managing Special Places in Eight Countries*, The Conservation Foundation, Washington DC.

Bowler, I. and Warburton, P. (1986) *An Experiment in the Analysis of Cognitive Images of the Environment; the Case of Water Resources in Leicestershire*, Leicester University Geography Department, Occasional Paper no. 14.

Bowman, G. (1988) *Impacts of Tourism*, Paper from the Conference on the Anthropology of Tourism, ed. Tom Selwyn, Froebel College, London.

Boxhill, B. (1982) *Employment generated by tourism in the Caribbean Region*, Caribbean Tourism Research Centre.

Breen, M. (1988) Olympics fuel a dream more potent than fear of AIDS, *Guardian*, 26 July.

Brent-Ritchie, J. R. (1981) *Leisure – Recreation – Tourism – a North American Perspective*, Paper from 31st AIEST Annual Conference, AIEST, Berne, vol. 22, pp. 82–90.

Brent-Ritchie, J. R. (1988) Consensus policy formulation in tourism – measuring resident views via survey research, *Tourism Management*, vol. 9, no. 3, September, pp. 199–212.

Britton, S. G. (1982) The political economy of tourism in the third world, *Annals of Tourism Research*, vol. 9, no. 3, pp. 231–261.

Brownrigg, M. and Greig, M. A. (1976) *Tourism and Regional Development*, Fraser of Allander Institute, Speculative Papers, no. 5.

Bryant, B. E. and Morrison, A. J. (1980) Travel market segmentation and the implementation of market strategies, *Journal of Travel Research*, vol. 18, no. 3, pp. 2–6.

Burkhart, A. and Medlik, S. (1974) *Tourism, Past, Present and Future*, Heinemann, London.

Butler, R. (1980) The concept of a tourism area cycle of evolution, *Canadian Geographer*, vol. 24, pp. 5–12.

Carbyn, L. N. (1974) Wolf population fluctuations in Jasper National Park, Alberta, Canada, *Biological Conservation*, vol. 6, pp. 94–101.

Caribbean Tourism Research Centre (1984) *A Study of Linkages between Tourism and Local Agriculture*, Caribbean Tourism Research Centre, Barbados.

Cater, E. (1987) Tourism in the least developed countries, *Annals of Tourism Research*, vol. 14, pp. 202–226.

Cater, E. (1988) The development of tourism in the least developed countries. In *Marketing in the Tourism Industry*, eds Goodall and Ashworth, Croom Helm, London.

Chadwick, G. (1971) *A Systems View of Planning*, Pergamon Press, London.

Chadwick, R. A. (1981) Some notes on the geography of tourism: a comment, *Canadian Geographer*, vol. 25, pp. 191–197.

Chittenden, M. (1989) Drink, fight, drop – it's summertime in Spain, *Sunday Times*, 30 July.

Christaller, W. (1964) Some considerations of tourism location in Europe; the peripheral regions – underdeveloped countries – recreation areas, *Papers of the Regional Science Association*, vol. 12, pp. 95–105.

Cipollaro, P. (1981) *Tourism as a Function of Free Time*, Paper from 31st AIEST Annual Conference, AIEST, Berne, vol. 22, pp. 168–178.

Clark, P. J. and Evans, F. C. (1955) On some aspects of spatial patterns in biological populations, *Science*, vol. 121, pp. 101–119.

Clough, P. (1988) The state of the Alps, *Independent*, 16 January.

Clousten, E. (1988) Rambles spell cash flow to water companies, *Guardian*, p. 2, 27 December.

Cohen, E. (1971) Arab boys and tourist girls in a mixed Jewish-Arab community, *International Journal of Comparative Sociology*, vol. 12, pp. 217–233.

— (1972) Towards a sociology of international tourism, *Social Research*, vol. 39(1), pp. 164–182.

— (1973) Nomads from affluence; notes on the phenomenon of drifter tourism, *International Journal of Comparative Sociology*, vol. 14, pp. 89–103.

— (1979a) Phenomenology of tourist experiences, *Sociology*, vol. 13, pp. 179–201.

— (1979b) Rethinking the sociology of tourism, *Annals of Tourism Research*, vol. 6, no. 1, pp. 18–35.

— (1979c) (ed.) Sociology of tourism, *Annals of Tourism Research*, vol. 6, pp. 17–194.

— (1982a) Marginal paradises, *Annals of Tourism Research*, vol. 9, pp. 190–227.

— (1982b) Thai girls and Farang men: the edge of ambiguity, *Annals of Tourism Research*, vol. 9, pp. 403–428.

— (1987) The tourist as victim and protege of law enforcing agencies, *Leisure Studies*, vol. 6, May, pp. 181–198.

Cohen, K. (1968) Multiple regression as a general data-analytic system, *Psychological Bulletin*, vol. 70, no. 6, pp. 426–443.

Cohen N. (1989) Pennine Way to put down carpet against erosion, *Sunday Times*, 1 September.

Collinge, M. (1988) *The Size of the Opportunity*, Proceedings of Waterside 2000, An International Congress on the Rejuvenation and Development of Waterfronts, Bristol City Council, Bristol, pp. 10–19.

Cook, S. (1988) British resorts see silver lining to Gatwick gloom, *Guardian*, 19 July.

Cooper, S. P. (1981) Spatial and temporal patterns of tourist behaviour, *Regional Studies*, vol. 15, no. 5, pp. 359–371.

Coppock, J. T. (1977) *Second Homes, Curse or Blessing*, Pergamon Press, Oxford.

Cornish, P. and Denny, M. (1989) Demographics are dead – long live demographics, *Journal of the Market Research Society*, vol. 31, no. 3, pp. 363–374.

Countryside Commission, (1989) *Forests for the Community*, (CCP 270) Countryside Commission Publications, Manchester.

Cowell, D. (1984) *The Marketing of Services*, Heinemann, London.

Crask, M. R. (1981) Segmenting the vacationer market: identifying the vacation preferences, demographics and magazine readership of each group, *Journal of Travel Research*, vol. 20, no. 2, pp. 29–33.

Crompton, J. (1979) Motivations for pleasure vacations, *Annals of Tourism Research*, vol. 6, pp. 408–424.

Csikszentmihalyi, M. and Csikszentmihalyi, I. S. (1988) *Optimal Experiences; Psychological Studies of Flows of Consciousness*, Cambridge University Press, New York.

Cullen, R. (1986) Himalayan mountaineering expedition garbage, *Environmental Conservation*, vol. 13, no. 4, pp.293–297.

D'Amore and Associates (1976) *Tourism in Canada*, Report for Tourism Canada.

Davies, G. H. (1988) Birdland's barrage of discontent, *Independent*, 19 November.

Davison, J. (1989) Strife begins at 40 for the jaded package, *Sunday Times*, pA11, 3 September.

Davison, J. and Welsh, E. (1989) Chaos in the air – nightmare on the ground, *Sunday Times*, pA14–15, 30 July.

Dearden, P. (1989) *Towards Serving Visitors and Managing our Resources*, Paper in Proceedings of a North American Workshop on Visitor Management in Parks and Protected Areas, Tourism Research and Education Centre, University of Waterloo, February 14–17.

Dearden, P. and Rollins, R. (1990) *Planning and Management of Parks and Protected Areas in Canada: The Future*, Paper delivered at the 6th Canadian Congress on Leisure Research, University of Waterloo.

De Kadt, E. (1979) *Tourism – Passport to Development*, Oxford University Press, New York.

Denis, D. H. (1989) *Attitudes towards Holiday Destinations*, Unpublished paper, College of Commerce, University of Saskatchewan.

Derek Murray Consulting (1985) *Tipperary Creek Conservation Area Heritage Attraction*, Tourism Impact Study undertaken for Meewasin Valley Authority, March.

Derounian, J. (1987) Rebuilding hope in an untamed country, *Sunday Times*, pF3, 5 June.

Dhall, N. and Yuseph, S. (1976) Forget the product life cycle, *Harvard Business Review*, January/February pp. 102–112.

Douglas-Hume, M. (1989) Trust fights against 'plague on landscape', *Independent*, p7, 14 January.

Doxey, G. V. (1975) *A Causation Theory of Visitor-Resident Irritants; Methodology and Research Inference*, Paper given at San Diego, California, The Travel Research Association Conference no. 6, TTRA, pp. 195–198.

Duffield, B. S. (1982) Tourism: the measurement of economic and social impact, *Tourism Management*, vol. 3, no. 4, December, pp. 248–255.

Durrell, G, (1988) Impressions in the sand – Corfu, *Sunday Times Colour Magazine*, 2 July.

Dybka, J. (1988) Overseas travel to Canada – new research on the perceptions and preferences of the pleasure travel market, *Journal of Travel Research*, vol. 26, Spring, pp. 12–15.

Ecumenical Coalition on Third World Tourism (1986) *Third World People and Tourism – Approaches to a Dialogue*, ECTWT.

Edgington, J. and Edgington, A. (1986) *Ecology, Recreation and Tourism*, Cambridge University Press, London and New York.

Edwards, J. (1987) The UK heritage coast – an assessment of the ecological impacts of tourism, *Annals of Tourism Research*, vol. 14, no. 1, pp. 71–87.

Edwards, J. (1990) Tourism and recreation in the national park and other protected areas on the mainland of Portugal, *Journal of Parks and Recreational Administration*, vol. 8, no. 1, pp. 9–22.

Elias, D. (1987) Tourism in the balance, *The West Australian*, 11 November.

Elliot, H. (ed.), (1974) World Conference on National Parks – proceedings, IUCN Morges, New York.

Elroy, J. and Alburqueque, L. (1986) The tourism demonstration effect in the Caribbean, *Journal of Travel Research*, vol. 25, no. 2, pp. 31–34.

Elson, R. (1976) Activity space and recreational spatial behaviour, *Town Planning Review*, vol. 47, pp. 241–255.

Emery, F. (1981) Alternative futures in tourism, *International Journal of Tourism Management*, March, pp. 49–67.

English Tourist Board (1978) *Planning for Tourism, Planning Advisory Note*, ETB, London.

English Tourist Board (1988) *Visitors in the Countryside*, Proceedings of Conference on Rural Tourism, English Tourist Board, London.

Fagan, D. (1989) Cheap, exotic outpost of '70s, Phuket now a tourist hotspot, *Toronto Globe and Mail*, pB23, 19 December.

Farvar, M. T. (1984) The careless technology: ecology and international development – record of the *Conference on the Ecological Aspects of International Development* convened by the Conservation Foundation and the Centre for Biology of Natural Systems, Washington University, December 8–11, Airlie House, Warrenton, Virginia.

Fennell, D. and Eagles, P. (1990) Ecotourism in Costa Rica: a conceptual framework, *Journal of Parks and Recreational Administration*, vol. 8, no. 1, pp. 23–34.

Fesenmaier, D. (1985) Modelling variation in destination patronage for outdoor recreation activity, *Journal of Travel Research*, vol. 24, no. 2, pp. 17–22.

Festinger, L. (1957) *A Theory of Cognitive Dissonance*, Stanford University Press, Stanford, California.

Festinger, L. (1962) Cognitive dissonance, *Scientific American*, vol. 107, no. 4, pp. 16–21.

Fines, K. D. (1968) Landscape evaluation: a research project in east Essex, *Regional Studies*, vol. 2, pp. 41–55.

Fishbein, M. (1963) An investigation of the relationships between beliefs about an object and attitude toward that object, *Human Relationships*, pp. 232–240.

Fishbein, M. (1967) *Readings in Attitude Theory and Measurement*, John Wiley and Sons, New York.

Foote, Cone and Belding Communications (1987) *A Guide to the FCB Grid*, Foote, Cone and Belding Communications Inc, 101 East Erie Street, Chicago, Illinois.

Foxall, G. R. (1980) *Consumer Behaviour – a Practical Guide*, Croom Helm, London.

Fussell, P. (1982) *Abroad: British Literary Travelling between the Wars*, Oxford University Press, New York.

Gall, W. (1990) Restoration of an urban green space. In *Green Cities – Ecologically Sound Approaches to Urban Space*, ed. David Gordon, Black Rose Books, Montreal.

Gearing, C. E., Swart, W. and Var, T. (1974) Establishing a measure of touristic attractiveness, *Journal of Travel Research*, vol. 12, no. 1, pp. 1–8.

Geshekter, C. (1978) International tourism and African underdevelopment; some reflections on Kenya. In *Tourism and Economic Change*, Zamora *et al.* (eds), College of William and Mary, Williamsburg, pp. 57–88.

Getz, D. (1983) Capacity to absorb tourism – concepts and implications for strategic planning, *Annals of Tourism Research*, vol. 10, pp. 239–263.

Godbey, G. (1990) *Leisure Policy in the 1990s*, keynote address, 6th Canadian Congress on Leisure Research, Ontario Research Council on Leisure, pp. 6–12.

Goodden, S. (1989) Strollers in a peanut economy, *Independent*, p37, 7 January.

Goodwin, N. (1982) *Complete Guide to Travel Agency Automation*, Merton House Pub. Co., Wheaton, Illinois.

Graburn, N. H. H. (1983) Tourism and prostitution, *Annals of Tourism Research*, vol. 10, pp. 437–443.

Granger, W. (1990) Naturalizing existing parklands. In *Green Cities – Ecologically Sound Approaches to Urban Space*, ed. David Gordon, Black Rose Books, Montreal.

Green, P. E. and Rao, V. R. (1971) Conjoint measurement for quantifying judgemental data, *Journal of Marketing Research*, vol. 8, August, pp. 355–363.

Greenwood, D. J. (1972) Tourism as an agent of change, a Spanish Basque case, *Ethnology*, vol. 11, no. 1, pp. 80–91.

— (1977) Culture by the pound: an anthropological perspective on tourism as cultural commidization. In *Hosts and Guests: An Anthropology of Tourism*, V. Smith, University of Pennsylvania Press, Philadelphia.

Gregory, C. (1989) Life-blood of the nation's treasures, *Independent*, 13 May.

Groves, J., Moore, B. and Ryan, C. (1987) *Staunton Harold Hall: A Study of Traffic Flows and Visitor Activities*, Tourism and Recreation Studies Unit, Nottingham Business School, Nottingham Polytechnic.

Guest, P. (1988) The American Dream that came true – at a price, *Independent*, 24 December.

Guitart, C. (1982) UK charter flight package holidays to the Mediterranean – a statistical analysis, *Tourism Management*, vol. 3, no. 1, March, pp. 16–39.

Gunn, C. (1972) *Vacationscapes: Designing Tourist Regions*, Bureau of Business Research, University of Texas at Austin.

Gunn, C. (1979) *Tourism Planning*, Crane Rusak, New York.

— (1982a) *A Proposed Methodology for Identifying Areas of Tourism Development Potential in Canada*, Canadian Government Office of Tourism, Ottawa, Canada.

— (1982b) Destination zone fallacies and half truths, *Tourism Management*, vol. 3 no. 4, December, pp. 263–269.

Guy, B. S. and Curtis, W. W. (1986) *Consumer Learning or Retail Environments: A Tourism and Travel Approach*, Conference Paper, ed. W. Benoy Joseph, Academy of Marketing Sciences, Cleveland University.

Gyte, D. M. (1988) *Repertory Grid Analysis of Images of Destinations; British Tourists in Mallorca*, Trent Working Papers in Geography, Nottingham Polytechnic.

Gyte, D. M. (1989) Patterns of destination repeat business: British tourists in Mallorca, *Journal of Travel Research*, vol. 28, no. 1, Summer, pp. 24–28.

Hair, J. F., Anderson, R. E. and Tatham, R. L. (1987) *Multivariate Data Analysis – With Readings*, Collier Publishing Co., London, American Publishing Co., New York.

Hall, E. T. (1984) *The Dance of Life: The Other Dimension of Time*, Doubleday, New York.

Hallenstein, D. (1989) Scientists wring their hands as algae tide grows, *Sunday Times*, pA21, 16 July.

Hamilton, A. (1988) Tourist had 500 lizards in his luggage, *Independent*, 17 December.

Hammitt, W. E. and Cole, D. N. (1987) *Wild-life Recreation: Ecology and Management*, Wiley Interscience, New York.

Hanna, M. (1976) *Tourism Multipliers in Britain*, English Tourist Board, London.

Harrison, J. and Saare, P. (1975) Personal construct theory in the measurement of environmental images, *Environment and Behaviour*, vol. 7, pp. 3–58.

Haug, C.J. (1982) *Leisure and Urbanism in Nineteenth Century Nice*, The Regents Press of Kansas Lawrence, Kansas.

Haywood, K. M. (1986) Can the tourist life-cycle be made operational? *Tourism Management*, vol. 7, no. 3, September, pp. 154–167.

Helm, S. (1987) Local people 'left out' by Docklands boom, *Independent*, 7 December.

Henry, W. R. (1980) Patterns of tourist use in Kenya's Amboseli National Park: implications for planning and management, Quoted by Lea, J. *Tourism and Development in the Third World* (1988), Routledge, London.

Henshall-Momsen, J. (1986) *Recent Changes in Caribbean Tourism with Special Reference to St Lucia and Montserrat*, Trent University Occasional Paper no. 11, Ontario.

Heron, R. P. (1989) *Community Leisure and Cultural Vitality*, Stichting Recreatie, Rotterdam.

— (1990) *The Institutionalisation of Leisure: Cultural Interpretation*, Paper given at 6th

Canadian Congress on Leisure Research, Ontario Research Council on Leisure, South Ontario, Canada.

Hewison, R. (1987) *The Heritage Business*, Methuen, London.

Hewson, D. (1989) The crackdown on the costas, *Sunday Times*, 18 March.

Hibbert, C. (1987) *The Grand Tour*, Channel 4 TV Thames Methuen, London.

—— (1989) *Venice: The Bibliography of the City*, Norton, London.

HMSO (1987) A vision for England, *Employment Gazette*, May, pp. 233–237.

Hoosie, L. (1990) Gringos in paradise, *Business Magazine, Toronto Globe and Mail*, February, pp. 65–70.

Horsnell, M. and Johnson, B. (1988) Flight chaos will continue for years – CAA caught on the hop, *The Times*, p1 16 July.

Howard, J. A. and Sheth, J. N. (1969) *Theory of Buyer Behaviour*, John Wiley and Sons, New York.

Hoyland, P. and Smith, M. (1988) Pressure on to free airways for August, *Guardian*, 19 July.

Hudson, K. and Pettifer, J. (1979) *Diamonds in the Sky: A Social History of Air Travel*, BBC Books, London.

Huff, D. L. (1966) A programmed solution for approximating an optimum retail location, *Land Economics,* vol. 42, pp. 293–303.

Hughes, H. (1987) Culture as a tourism resource, *Tourism Management*, vol. 8, no. 3, September.

Hunt, J. D. (1975) Image – a factor in tourism, *Journal of Tourism Research*, vol. 13, no. 3, pp. 1–7.

Institute of Management Studies (1988) *Productivity in the Leisure Industry*, Institute of Manpower Studies, London.

Iso-Ahola, S. E. (1982) Towards a social psychology of tourism motivation – a rejoinder, *Annals of Tourism Research*, vol. 9, pp. 256–261.

Iso-Ahola, S. E. and Meissinger, E. (1990) Perceptions of boredom in leisure; conceptualisation, reliability and validity of the leisure boredom scale, *Journal of Leisure Research*, vol. 22, no. 1 pp. 1–17.

Jackle, J. (1985) *The Tourist, Travel in Twentieth Century North America*, University of Nebraska Press, Lincoln.

Jackman, B. (1988) Quality of the North Sea coastline, *Sunday Times Colour Magazine*, 11 June.

Jackson, E. (1990) Variations in the desire to begin a leisure activity – evidence of antecedent constraints, *Journal of Leisure Research*, vol. 22, no. 1, pp. 55–70.

Jackson, E. and Dunn, E. (1987) *Ceasing Participation in Recreation Activities; An Analysis of Data from the 1984 Public Opinion Survey*, Alberta Recreation and Parks, Edmonton, Alberta.

—— (1988) Integrating ceasing participation with other aspects of leisure behaviour, *Journal of Leisure Research*, vol. 20, no. 1, pp. 31–45.

Jafari, J. (1981) *The Unbounded Reaches of Leisure, Recreation – Tourism in the Paradigms of Play*, AIEST, vol. 22, Berne, Switzerland.

—— (1982) Understanding the Structure of Tourism. In *Interrelation between Benefits and Costs of Tourism Resources*, AIEST, vol. 23, St Gallen, Switzerland.

Johnson, R. (1974) Trade off analysis of consumer values, *Journal of Marketing Research*, vol. 11, May, pp. 251–263.

Jones, D. R. W. (1982) Prostitution and tourism. In *The Impact of Tourism Development in the Pacific*, ed. F. Rajotte, Environmental and Resources Studies Programme, Trent University, Ontario.

—— (1986) *Prostitution and Tourism*, Occasional Paper no. 11, Department of Geography, Trent University, Ontario.

June, L. P. and Smith, S. L. J. (1987) Service attributes and situational effects on customer preferences for restaurant dining, *Journal of Travel Research*, vol. 26, no. 2, pp. 20–27.

Kariel, H. G. and Kariel, P. E. (1972) *Explorations in Social Geography*, Addison–Wesley Publishing Company, Reading, Mass. and London, UK.

Kay, T. and Jackson, G. (1990) *The Operation of Leisure Constraints*, Paper given at 6th Canadian Congress on Leisure Research, Ontario Research Council of Leisure, Ontario.

Kelly, G. A. (1955) *The Psychology of Personal Constructs*, Norton, New York.

Kendall, K. and Booms, B. (1989) Consumer perceptions of travel agencies, communications, images, needs and expectations, *Journal of Travel Research*, vol. 27, no. 4, pp. 29–37.

Kennedy, L. (1989) Victims of a bogus Elizabethan invasion, *Independent*, 11 January.

Kidd, K. (1989) Thunder Bay consumers move south, *Toronto Globe and Mail*, pB1,B3, 4 December.

Kinnell, H. (1989) *Prostitutes, their Clients and Risks of HIV Infection in Birmingham*, Occasional Paper, Central Birmingham Health Authority, Birmingham.

Knox, J. M. (1982) Resident and Visitor Interaction, a Review of Literature and General Policy Alternatives. In *The Impact of Tourism Development in the Pacific*, ed. F. Rajotte, Environmental and Resources Studies Program, Trent University, Ontario, Canada.

Krippendorf, J. (1987) *The Holidaymakers*, Heinemann, Oxford.

Kruskal, J. B. (1964) Multidimensional scaling by optimising goodness of fit to a nonmetric hypothesis, *Psychometrika*, vol. 29, no. 10, pp. 1–27.

— (1965) Analysis of factorial experiments by estimating monotone transformations of the data, *Journal of the Royal Statistical Society*, Series B, vol. 27, pp. 251–263.

LaForest, M. J. (1989) Boating compromise reached, *Star Phoenix*, Saskatoon, pA10, 3 June.

Lamb, S. (1989) *The Meewasin Valley – Concepts and Implications for Tourism*, unpublished paper, University of Saskatchewan, Saskatchewan, Canada.

Lambert, A. (1989) Blighting the sights, *Independent*, 13 May.

Lane, B. (1989) Tourism; like junk food for the mind, *Independent*, 13 May.

Lea, J. (1988) *Tourism and Development in the Third World*, Routledge, London.

Learman, J., Stewart, T. and Presteman, J. (1989) International travel by US conservation groups and professional societies, *Journal of Travel Research*, vol. 28, no. 1, pp. 12–17.

Leopold, D. (1969) Landscape aesthetics, *Natural History*, vol. 78, pp. 36–45.

Lever, A. (1987) Spanish tourist migrants – the case of Lloret de Mar, *Annals of Tourism Research*, vol. 14, no. 4, pp. 449–470.

Lewis, B. and Outram, M. (1986) Customer satisfaction with package holidays. In *Are They Being Served*, ed. Brian Harris, Philip Allen, London.

Lily, T., Griffiths-Jones, R., Highet, B., Johnson, W. and Godfrey, J. (1984) Image and images – tourism in industrial England, *Tourism Management*, vol. 5, no. 2, June, pp. 136–149.

Liu, J. C., Sheldon, P. and Var, T. (1986) *A Cross-cultural Approach to Determining Resident Perception of the Impact of Tourism on the Environment*, Conference proceedings, ed. W. Benoy Joseph, Academy of Marketing Science, Cleveland State University.

Loukissas, P. J. (1982) Tourism's regional development impacts: a comparative analysis of the Greek islands, *Annals of Tourism Research*, vol. 9, no. 4, pp. 523–541.

Lovingood, P. E. and Mitchell, L. S. (1978) The structure of public and private recreational systems: Columbia, South Carolina, *Journal of Leisure Research*, vol. 10, pp. 21–36.

Lundberg, D. E. (1976) *The Tourist Business*, CBI Publishing, Boston, Massachusetts.

Lundgren, J. (1986) *Circumpolar Tourist Space – Comparative Reflections*, Occasional Paper no. 11, Department of Geography, Trent University, Ontario.

Lyon, A. (1982) *Timeshare – the Decline*, Unpublished thesis, Nottingham Business School, Nottingham Polytechnic.

McCannell, D. (1976) *The Tourist – a New Theory of the Leisure Class*, Schocken Books, New York.

McGirk, T. and Whitaker, R. (1988) Chaos looms as air-traffic controllers quit work, *Independent*, 13 July.

McIntosh, R. W. and Goeldner, C. R. (1986) *Tourism, Principles, Practices, Philosophies*, 6th edition, John Wiley and Sons Inc., New York.

McKenzie, C. (1989) Yellowstone – green once more, *Toronto Globe and Mail*, Toronto, 21 October.

McKinnon, I. (1988) Air holiday chaos 'will get worse', *Independent*, p1 4 July.

MacNaught, T. J. (1982) Mass tourism and the dilemmas of modernisation in Pacific Island communities, *Annals of Tourism Research*, vol. 9, pp. 359–381.

McPheters, L. R. and Stronge, W. B. (1974) Crime as an environmental externality of tourism, *Land Economics*, vol. 50, pp. 288–292.

Mader, U. (1988) Tourism and the environment, *Annals of Tourism Research*, vol. 15, no. 2, pp. 274–277.

Maloney, J. C. (1961) Marketing decisions and attitude research. In *Effective Marketing Coordination*, ed. G. L. Baker Jr, American Marketing Association, Chicago.

Marling, S. (1986) Cultural exploitation is part of the tourist package, *The Listener*, pp. 7–8, 21 August.

Marsh, J. S. (1986) Advertising Canada in Japan and Japanese Tourism in Canada. In *Canadian Studies of Parks, Recreation and Tourism in Foreign Lands*, Department of Geography, Trent University, Ontario.

— (ed.) (1986) *Parks, Recreation and Tourism in Foreign Lands*, Department of Geography, Trent University, Ontario.

Marshall Macklin Monoghan Consulting Group (1980) *Tourism Development Strategy – Collingwood-Midland-Orillia Zone*, Ontario Ministry of Tourism and Recreation, Toronto, Ontario.

Martin, C. and Witt, S. (1987) Tourism demand forecasting models: a choice of appropriate variable to represent the tourist's cost of living, *Tourism Management*, vol. 8, no. 3, September, pp. 233–246.

— (1988) Substitute prices in models of tourism demand, *Annals of Tourism Research*, vol. 15, no. 2, pp. 255–268.

— (1989) Forecasting tourism demand: a comparison of the accuracy of several quantitative methods, *International Journal of Forecasting*, vol. 5, no. 1, pp. 1–13.

Martin, W. H. and Mason, S. (1987) Social trends and tourism futures, *Tourism Management*, vol. 8, no. 2, June, p. 112.

Maslow, A. (1943) A theory of human motivation, *Psychological Review*, vol. 50.

Mathieson, A. and Wall, G. (1982) *Tourism, Economic, Physical and Social Impacts*, Longmans, Harlow, Essex.

Mayo, E. J. and Jarvis, L. P. (1981) *The Psychology of Leisure Travel*, CBI Publishing Co., Boston, Massachusetts.

Mayo, E. J. and Jarvis, L. P. (1986) *Objective Distance vs Subjective Distance and the Attraction of the far off Destination*, Paper presented to Academy of Marketing Sciences Conference, Cleveland State University, Ohio, ed. W. Benoy Joseph.

Mazanec, J. (1981a) *The Tourism/Leisure Ratio: Anticipating the Limits to Growth*, Paper presented to AIEST Conference, Cardiff, Wales.

—— (1981b) The tourism/leisure ratio: anticipating the limits to growth, *Tourist Review*, vol. 36, no. 4, pp. 2–12.

Mead, W. E. (1989) *The Grand Tour in the Eighteenth Century*, Ayer Co. Publishing, New York.

Medlik, S. (1985) *Productivity and Tourism*, Study for the Confederation of British Industry, CBI, London.

—— (1988) *Tourism and Productivity*, BTA/ETB Research Services, London.

Meewasin Valley Authority (1987) *Meewasin Valley Authority Development Plan*, 1987–1992, MVA, Saskatoon, Saskatchewan.

Meidan, A. and Lee, B. (1982) Marketing strategies for hotels, *International Journal of Hospitality Management*, vol. 1, no. 3, pp. 5–7.

Meidan, A. and Lee, B. (1983) Marketing strategies for hotels – a cluster analysis approach, *Journal of Travel Research*, vol. 21, no. 4, pp. 17–22.

Middleton, V. T. C. (1988) *Marketing of Travel and Tourism*, Heinemann Professional Publishing, Oxford.

Mill, R. C. and Morrison, A. M. (1985) *The Tourist System: An Introductory Text*, Prentice Hall, Englewood Cliffs, New Jersey.

Milligan, J. (1989) *Migrant Workers in the Guernsey Hotel Industry*, Unpublished thesis, Nottingham Business School, Nottingham Polytechnic.

Milliken, R. (1989) Sun, sand and sewage at Australia's most famous playground, *Independent*, 14 July.

Milman, A. and Pizam, A. (1988) Social impacts of Tourism on Central Florida, *Annals of Tourism Research*, vol. 15, no. 2, pp. 191–205.

Miossec, J. M. (1976) Un modèle de l'espace touristique. Quoted in *Tourist Development*, D. Pearce, 1981, Longman, Harlow.

Morisita, M. (1957) A new method for the estimation of density by the spacing method, *Seiro-seita*, vol. 7, pp. 134–144.

Morris, J. (1987) Sick of the tourist roller-coaster, *Independent*, 9 December.

Morritt, J. B. (1988) *The Grand Tour*, Century, Hutchinson, London.

Moynahan, B. (1983) *Fool's Paradise*, Pan Books, London.

Murphy, P. E. (1978) Preferences and perceptions of urban decision-making groups: congruence or conflict? *Regional Studies*, vol. 12, pp. 749–759.

— (1983a) *Tourism in Canada – Selected Issues and Options*, Department of Geography, University of Victoria, British Columbia, Canada.

— (1983b) Perceptions and attitudes of decision making groups in tourism centres, *Journal of Travel Research*, vol. 21, no. 3, pp. 8–12.

— (1985) *Tourism – a Community Approach*, Methuen, New York.

Myers, N. (1972) National parks in savannah Africa, *Science*, vol. 178, pp. 1255–1263.

Niedercorn, J. H. and Bechdoldt, B. V. (1966) An economic derivation of the 'gravity law' of spatial interaction, *Journal of Regional Science*, vol. 9, pp. 273–282.

Nightingale, M. (1985) The hospitality industry: defining quality for a quality assurance programme – a study of perceptions, *The Service Industries Journal*, vol. 9, no. 1, pp. 9–22.

North, R. (1988) Classical Toytown takes over the City, *Independent*, 7 March.

— (1989a) Commission sets out policy for developing rural areas, *Independent*, p7, 28 June.

— (1989b) Polluted Water supplies are blamed for sickness, *Independent*, p3, 22 February.

— (1989c) Scorched earth plan to get back to nature, *Independent*, p11, 23 January.

Nova (1990) *Poison in the Rockies*, Transcript from PBS, Program broadcast 29 May 1990.

Nunnally, J. C. (1967) *Psychometric Theory*, McGraw Hill, New York.

O'Brien, S. and Ford, R. (1988) Can we at last say goodbye to social class?, *Journal of the Market Research Society*, vol. 30, no. 3, pp. 289–332.

O'Grady, R. (1981) *Third World Stopover*, World Council of Churches, Geneva.

Okotai, R., Henderson, C. and Fogelberg, F. (1982) The cultural impact of tourism – art forms – revival or degradation? In *The Impact of Tourism Development in the Pacific*, ed. F. Rajotte, Environmental and Resources Studies Program, Trent University, Ontario, Canada.

Olsen, J. E., MacAlexander, J. H. and Roberts, S. (1986) *The Impact of the Visual Content of Advertisements upon the Perceived Vacation Experience*, Academy of Marketing Sciences Conference, Cleveland State University, Ohio, ed. W. Benoy Joseph.

Papson, S. (1979) Tourism, world's biggest industry, *Futurist*, vol. 13, no. 4, pp. 249–257.

Parasuraman, A., Zeithaml, V. A. and Berry, L. L. (1983) Service firms need marketing skills, *Business Horizons*, vol. 26, no. 6, November–December, pp. 28–31.

— (1985) A conceptual model of service quality and its implications for future research, *Journal of Marketing*, vol. 49, no. 4, Fall, pp. 41–50.

— (1988) SERVQUAL: A multiple-item scale for measuring consumer perceptions of service quality, *Journal of Retailing*, vol. 64, no. 1, Spring, pp. 12–37.

Parker, S. (1971) *The Future of Work and Leisure*, Praeger, New York.

— (1975) Evolution and trends in work and non-work time in Great Britain, *Society and Leisure*, vol. 1, pp. 73–88.

Patrick, M. (1973) *The Analysis of Personal Travel Demand – a Behavioural Approach*, Department of Civil Engineering, Carleton University, Ottawa.

Pearce, D. G. (1981) *Tourist Development*, Longmans, Harlow,

Pearce, P. L. (1982a) Perceived changes in holiday destinations, *Annals of Tourism Research*, vol. 9, no. 2, pp. 145–164.

— (1982b) *The Social Psychology of Tourist Behaviour*, Pergamon Press, Oxford.

— (1988) *The Ulysses Factor – Evaluating Visitors in Tourist Settings*, Springer-Verlag, New York.

— and Moscardo, G. M. (1984) Making sense of tourists' complaints, *International Journal of Tourism Management*, vol. 5, no. 1, pp. 20–23.

Pennings, J. (1976) *Leisure Correlates of Working Conditions*, Unpublished paper, Graduate School of Industrial Administration, Carnegie-Mellon University, Pittsburgh.

Pettifer, J. (1987) *Diamonds in the Sky*, Channel 4 TV, The Fragile Earth.

Pfafflin, G. F. (1987) Concern for tourism: European perspective and response, *Annals of Tourism Research*, vol. 14, pp. 576–588.

Phillips, A. (1988) *The Countryside as a Leisure Product*, Proceedings of the Conference in Rural Tourism, English Tourist Board, London.

Pielo, E. C. (1959) The point-to-point distances in the study of patterns of plant populations, *Journal of Ecology*, vol 47, pp. 607–612.

Pienaar, J. (1989) Fears grow that rural areas may be spoilt, *Independent*, p6, 28 June.

Pithers, M. (1987a) Pressures on Lakes landscape brings international warning, *Independent*, p4 30 December.

— (1987b) Popularity of Lakeland forces planning curbs, *Independent*, 29 March.

Pitts, R. and Woodside, A. (1986) Personal values and travel decisions, *Journal of Travel Research*, vol. 25, no. 1, pp. 20–25.

Pizam, A. (1978) Tourism impacts: the social costs to the destination community as perceived by its residents, *Journal of Travel Research*, vol. 16, no. 4, pp. 8–12.

— (1982) Tourism and crime – is there a relationship?, *Journal of Travel Research*, vol. 20, no. 3, pp. 7–10.

— and Pokela, J. (1985) The perceived impact of casino gambling on a community, *Annals of Tourism Research*, vol. 12, pp. 147–166.

Plog, S. C. (1977) Why destinations rise and fall in popularity. In *Domestic and International Tourism*, E. M. Kelly, ed. Institute of Certified Travel Agents, Wellesley, Mass, pp. 26–28.

Poon, A. (1988) Innovation and the future of Caribbean tourism, *Tourism Management*, vol. 9, no. 3, September, pp. 213–220.

Quayson, J. and Var, T. (1982) A tourism demand function for the Okanagan, BC, *Tourism Management*, vol. 3, no. 2, June, pp. 108–115.

Ragan, L. (1989) Despair in the dales on visitor onslaught, *Yorkshire Evening Post*, p8, 28 March.

Ramblers Association, (1988) *Pesticides: Waging War on our Countryside*, The Ramblers Association, London.

Reibstein, D. J., Lovelock, C. H. and Dobson, R. (1980) The direction of causality between perceptions, affect and behaviour: an application to travel behaviour, *Journal of Consumer Research*, vol. 6, March, pp. 370–374.

Reilly, W. J. (1931) *The Law of Retail Gravitation*, Putnam Press, New York.

Renton, A. (1989) At loggerheads with the turtle, *Independent*, p39, 5 August.

Reusberger, B. (1975) Elephant survival: two schools of thought, *Wildlife*, vol. 17, pp. 104–107.

— (1977) This is the end of the game, *New York Times Magazine*, vol. 40, (3), pp. 38–43.

Richards, G. (1972) *Tourism and the Economy – an Examination of Methods for Evaluating the Contribution and Effects of Tourism in the Economy*, Unpublished thesis, University of Surrey, Guildford, England.

Rigby, M. and Rufford, N. (1988) Tourists hit by air chaos, *Sunday Times*, p1 3 July.

Riley, S. and Palmer, J. (1975) Of attitudes and latitudes: a repertory grid study of perceptions of seaside resorts, *Journal of the Market Research Society*, vol. 17, no. 2, pp. 74–89.

Ritchie, J. R. and Zins, M. (1978) Culture as a determinant of the attractiveness of a tourist region, *Annals of Tourism Research*, vol. 5, pp. 252–270.

Rivers, P. (1974a) *The Restless Generation: A Crisis in Mobility*, Davis Pointer, London.

— (1974b) Unwrapping the African tourist package, *Africa Report*, vol. 19, no. 2, pp. 12–16.

Rodale, R. (1989) Editorial, *Prevention*, vol. 39, September, p. 27.

Rolfe, E. (1964) Analysis of a spatial distribution of neighbourhood parks in Lansing: 1920–1960, *Papers of the Michigan Academy of Science, Arts and Letters*, vol. 50, pp. 479–491.

Ropponen, P. J. (1976) Tourism and the local population. In *Planning and Development of the Tourist Industry in the ECE Region* pp. 104–109, Economic Commission for Europe, United Nations, New York.

Ropponnen, R. (1968) *Die Kraft*, Russlands, Helsinki.

Rothman, R. A. (1978) Residents and transients: community reaction to seasonal visitors, *Journal of Travel Research*, vol. 16, (3) pp. 8–13.

Ryan, C. (1989a) Trends past and present in the package holiday industry, *The Service Industries Journal*, vol. 9, no. 1, pp. 61–78.

— (1989b) *Attitudes towards Tourism by Nottingham Citizens*, Report for Nottingham Tourism Development Action Programme, Nottingham Business School, Nottingham Polytechnic.

— and Connor, M. (1981) *Tourism in Market Harborough*, East Midlands Tourist Board, Lincoln.

— and Groves, J. (1987) *Attitudes of Cruise Line Holidaymakers*, Working Paper, Nottingham Business School, Nottingham Polytechnic.

— and Richardson, M. (1983) *The use of Swimming Pools in Broxtowe – an Application of Gravitational Theory*, Unpublished paper, Nottingham Business School, Nottingham Polytechnic.

— and Wheeller, B. A. (1982) *Visitors to Nottingham Castle*, Report for Nottingham City Council, Nottingham Business School, Nottingham Polytechnic.

Saaty, T. L. (1980) *The Analytical Hierarchy Process: Planning, Priority Setting*, McGraw Hill, International Book Co., New York.

Saleh, F. and Ryan, C. (1990) *Service Quality in Hotels – Servqual Revisited*, Paper presented for Tourism Research in the 1990s, University of Durham, Durham.

— (1991) Analysing service quality in the hospitality industry using the Servqual model, *Service Industries Journal*, to be published in vol. 11, no. 3, July.

Samuelson, A. (1989) The rip-off merchants of Venice, *Independent*, p29, 24 June.

Sarbin, H. B. (1981) *The Traveller: 1981 and Beyond*, Published remarks before the World Hospitality Congress, Boston, Mass, 11/3/81.

Sax, J. L. (1980) *Mountains without Handrails: Reflections on National Parks*, University of Michigan Press, Ann Arbor, Michigan.

Schul, P. and Crompton, J. (1983) Search behaviour of international vacationers – travel specific lifestyle and socio-demographic variables, *Journal of Travel Research*, vol. 22, no. 2, pp. 25–30.

Schwaninger, M. (1984) Forecasting leisure and tourism, *Tourism Management*, vol. 5, no. 4, December, pp. 250–257.

— (1989) Trends in leisure and tourism for 2000–2010. In *Tourism Management and Marketing Handbook*, ed. S. Witt and L. Mountiho, Prentice Hall, Hemel Hempstead.

Scott, D. R., Schewe, C. D. and Frederick, D. G. (1978) A multi-brand attribute model of tourist state choice, *Journal of Travel Research*, vol. 17, no. 1, Summer, pp. 23–29.

Seabrook, J. (1989) A dying fall in the valleys, *Independent*, 15 July.

Searle, R. (1989) Banff National Park, *Borealis*, Spring, vol. 1, no. 2, pp. 9–12.

Seely, R. L., Iglash, H. J. and Edgell, D. (1980) Utilising the Delphi technique at international conferences, a method for forecasting international tourism conditions, *Travel Research Journal*, vol. 1, pp. 30–36.

Sessa, A. (1988) The science of systems for tourism development, *Annals of Tourism Research*, vol. 15, no. 2, pp. 219–235.

Shackleford, P. (1987) Global tourism trends, *Tourism Management*, vol. 8, no. 2, p. 101.

Shackley, M. 1989, *The Impact of Tourism on Bradford*, Unpublished paper, Nottingham Business School, Nottingham Polytechnic.

Shaw, S. (1990) *Where has all the Leisure Gone? The Distribution and Redistribution of Leisure*, Keynote paper presented at the 6th Canadian Congress on Leisure Research, pp. 1–4.

Sheldon, P. and Mak, J. (1987) The demand for package tours – a mode choice model, *Journal of Travel Research*, vol. 25, no. 3, pp. 13–17.

Shepard, J. M. (1976) A status recognition model of work-leisure relationships, *Journal of Leisure Research*, vol. 6, pp. 58–63.

Sheridan, M. (1989) Emergency status for Italy's algae problem, *Independent*, 19 July.

Shimizu, J. K. (1988) *Tourism Forecasting and the Delphi Technique: a Case Study*, Unpublished MA thesis, University of Waterloo, Ontario.

Silman, L., Ben-Akiva, M. and Baron, R. R. (1981) *Forecasting Tourism Demand by Modelling Individual Choices*, 31st AEIST Conference, Cardiff, 13–19 September.

Sinclair, M. T. (1981) *The Theory of the Keynesian Income Multiplier and its Applications to Tourist Expenditure in Malaga*, Unpublished Ph.D thesis, Reading University.

— and Sutcliffe, C. M. S. (1982) Keynesian income multipliers with first and second round effects: an application to tourism expenditure, *Oxford Bulletin of Economics and Statistics*, vol. 44, no. 4, pp. 321–338.

Smallwood, J. (1973) The product life cycle; a key to strategic marketing planning, *MSU Business Topics*, Winter, pp. 29–35.

Smith, M. (1988a) More night flights only offer temporary respite, *Guardian*, 19 July.

— (1988b) Plastic enemy within the sea, *Independent*, p17 14 November.

Smith, S. L. J. (1983) *Recreation Geography*, Longmans, Harlow.

— (1989) *Tourism Analysis – a Handbook*, Longmans, Harlow.

Smith, V. L. (1977) Eskimo tourism: micro models and marginal men – in *Hosts and Guests: The Anthropology of Tourism*, The University of Pennsylvania Press, Philadelphia, pp. 51–70.

Somers, M. S., Barnes, J. G., Stanton, W. J. and Futrell, F. (1989) *Fundamentals of Marketing*, McGraw Hill Ryerson Limited, Toronto.

SRI International, (1989) *The VALS^{TM} 2 Typology*, SRI International.

Stankey, M. (1981) Integrating wildlife recreation into decision making – pitfalls and promises, *Recreational Research Review*, vol. 32, no. 9, pp. 31–37.

Stewart, J. Q. (1948) Demographic gravitation: evidence and applications, *Sociometry*, vol. 11, pp. 31–58.

Summary, R. (1987) An estimation of tourism demand by multivariate regression analysis – evidence from Kenya, *Tourism Management*, vol. 8, no. 4, December, pp. 317–322.

Sutherland, J. (1988) Turtle and tourist at loggerheads, *Sunday Times*, pF2, 24 April.

Taylor J, (1987) *Urban Planning in Nottingham*, Paper delivered at Trent Polytechnic Nottingham in Open Lecture Series, Nottingham.

Tiechk, G. and Ryan, C. (1990) *The Attitude of Japanese Tourists to Canada*, In preparation, University of Saskatchewan/Nottingham Business School.

Toffler, A. (1970) *Future Shock*, Random House, New York.

Toffler, A. (1981) *The Third Wave*, Benton, New York.

Toh, R., Kelly, M. and Mu, M. (1986) An approach to the determination of optimal fares – some useful insights on price elasticities, monopoly power and comparative factors, *Journal of Travel Research*, vol. 25, no. 1, pp. 26–33.

Tourism and Recreational Research Unit (1981) *The Economy of Rural Communities in the National Parks of England and Wales*, TRRU Research Report no. 47, TRRU, University of Edinburgh, Edinburgh.

Tourism Canada–Tourisme Canada, (1988) *Pleasure Travel Markets to North America – Switzerland, Hong Kong, Singapore – Highlights Report*, March, Prepared by Market Facts of Canada, Tourism Canada, Ottawa, Ontario.

— (1989) *Discussion Paper on a National Tourism Strategy*, Tourism Canada, August, Ottawa, Ontario.

Tourism Ecumenical Network (1986) Third World People and Tourism – ECTWT and Third World Tourism Ecumenical European Net, Tonbridge, Kent.

Tourism Steering Group, Stratford-upon-Avon (1978) Report to Stratford-upon-Avon District Council.

Travis, A. S. (1982) Physical impacts: trends affecting tourism – managing the environmental and cultural impacts, *Tourism Management,* vol. 3, no. 4, December, pp. 256–262.

— (1984) *The North West Leicestershire Tourism Potential Study*, Leicester County Council, Leicestershire.

— (1989) Tourism destination area development (from theory into practice). In *Tourism Marketing and Management*, eds S. Witt and L. Mountiho, Prentice Hall, Hemel Hempstead.

Turner, L. and Ash, J. (1975) *The Golden Hordes: International Tourism and the Pleasure Periphery*, Constable, London.

Tuting, L. (1989) Trekking Tourism in Nepal, translated by Rainer Heard from 'Tourismus und Ökologie' *Ökozid 5* Focus Verlag, Giessen (ed.) Claus Euler.

Uysal, M. and Crompton, J. L. (1985) An overview of approaches used to forecast tourism demand, *Journal of Travel Research*, vol. 7, pp. 7–15.

Valenzuela, M. (1988) Spain, the phenomenon of mass tourism. In A. Williams and G. Shaw (eds), *Tourism and Economic Development*, Belhaven Press, London.

Vandermey, A. (1984) Assessing the importance of urban tourism, *Tourism Management*, vol. 5, no. 2, pp. 123–135.

Vaughan, D. R. (1986) *Estimating the Level of Tourism-related Employment – an Assessment of two Non-survey Techniques*, BTA/ETB Research Services, Thames Tower, London.

Vaughan, R. and Long, J. (1982) Tourism as a generator of employment: a preliminary appraisal of the position in Great Britain, *Journal of Travel Research,* vol. 21, no. 2, pp. 27–31.

Voelkl, J. and Ellis, G. (1990) *Use of Criterion Scaling in the Analysis of Experience Sampling Data*, Proceedings of 6th Canadian Congress of Leisure Research, Ontario Research Council on Leisure, Ontario, Canada.

Waiser, B. (1989) *Saskatchewan's Playground*, Fifth House Publishers, Saskatoon.

Wall, G. (1983) Cycles and capacity: a contradiction in terms?, *Annals of Tourism Research*, vol. 10, pp. 268–270.

Wall, G. and Barai, B. (1986) *Socio-economic Variations in the Use of Leisure; An Indian Example*, Occasional Paper no. 11, Department of Geography, Trent University, Ontario.

Wallace, A. F. C. (1956) Revitalisation movements, *American Anthropologist*, vol. 58, p. 265.

Walter, J. A. (1982) Social limits, *Leisure Studies*, vol. 1, September, pp. 295–304.

Ward, L. M. and Russell, J. A. (1981) Cognitive set and the perception of places, *Environment and Behaviour*, vol. 13, pp. 610–632.

Weaver, P. A. and McCleary, K. W. (1984) A market segmentation study to determine the appropriate ad/model format for travel advertising, *Journal of Travel Research* vol. 22, no. 1, pp. 12–16.

Welsh, E. (1988) Tackling the effluent society, *Sunday Times*, pF2 24 April.

— (1989) National parks pave the way, *Sunday Times*, pH3 9 April.

Weyerhaeuser Canada Limited (1989) *Forests for Everyone; Today and Tomorrow*, Weyerhaeuser Canada's 20 Year Management Plan, Prince Albert, Saskatchewan, Canada.

Wheeller, B. A. (1983) *Recent Trends in UK to USA and UK to Florida Tourist Flows*, Unpublished paper, Nottingham Business School, Nottingham Polytechnic.

— (1990) *Alternative Tourism*, Paper presented at the Tourism Research into the 1990s, University of Durham, Durham.

White, P. E. (1974) *The Social Impact of Tourism on Host Communities: a Study of Language Change in Switzerland*, Research Paper 9, School of Geography, Oxford University, Oxford, England.

Whysall, P. (1974) *The Changing Pattern of Retail Structure of Greater Nottingham*, Unpublished Ph.D thesis, University of Nottingham, Nottingham.

— (1989) Commercial change in a central area – a case study, *International Journal of Retailing*, vol. 4, no. 1 pp. 45–61.

Williams, A. and Shaw, G. (eds) (1988) *Tourism and Economic Development – a Western European Experience*, Belhaven Press, London.

Wilson, R. (1989) *Changing Markets of the English Seaside Resort*, Unpublished thesis, Nottingham Business School, Nottingham Polytechnic.

Witt, S. (1978) *The Demand for Foreign Holidays*, Unpublished Ph.D thesis, Bradford University, Bradford.

— (1980a) An econometric comparison of UK and German foreign holiday behaviour, *Managerial and Decision Economics*, vol. 1, no. 3, pp. 123–131.

— (1980b) An abstract destination mode-abstract node model of foreign holiday demand, *Applied Economics*, 12, 16 June, pp. 163–180.

— and Buckley, P. (1985) Tourism in difficult areas: case studies of Bradford, Bristol, Glasgow and Hamm, *Tourism Management*, vol. 6, no. 3, September, pp. 206–215.

— and Martin C. (1987) Deriving a relative price index for inclusion in international tourism demand estimation models, *Journal of Travel Research*, vol. 25, no. 3, pp. 38–40.

— and Mountiho, L. (eds) (1989) *Tourism Management and Management Handbook*, Prentice Hall, New York and London.

— and Martin, C. (1989) Forecasting tourism demand: a comparison of the accuracy of several quantitative methods, *International Journal of Forecasting*, vol. 5, no. 1, pp. 1–13.

Witt, C. and Wright, P. (1990) *Tourism Motivation, Life after Maslow*, Paper from Tourism Research into the 1990s, Department of Economics, University of Durham, Durham.

Woodside, A. and Ronkainen, I. (1984) How serious is non-response bias in advertising conversion research? *Journal of Travel Research*, vol. 22, no. 4, pp. 34–37.

World Tourism Organisation, (1980a) *Consultation and Cooperation Agreement*, WTO, Madrid.

— (1980b) *Physical Planning and Area Development*, WTO, Madrid.

— (1982) *Review of Governmental Policies on Environmental Impacts of Tourism*, WTO, Madrid.

— (1983) *Workshop on Environmental Aspects of Tourism*, WTO, Madrid.

— (1985) *The State's Role in Encouraging the Development of New Destinations and Ensuring Balanced Distribution of Tourist Flows and Regional Economic and Social Developments*, WTO, Madrid.

— (1988) *Workshop on Environmental Aspects of Tourism*, WTO, Madrid.

Wright, P. (1988) *On Living in Another Country*, Verso, London.

Wyer, J., Towner, J., Millman, R. and Hutchinson, R. (1988) *The UK and Third World Tourism*, TEN Publications Third World Tourism European Ecumenical Network, Tonbridge, Kent.

Yamba, B. (1988) *Swedish Women and the Gambia*, Conference on Anthropology of Tourism, Froebel College, ed. Tom Selwyn, London.

Yardley, J. (1990) *The Role of Mood in Measuring Levels of Satisfaction with Recreational Participation*. Paper at the 6th Canadian Congress on Leisure Research, University of Waterloo, South Ontario, Canada.

Yong, Y. W., Keng, K. A. and Leng, T. L. (1989) A Delphi forecast for the Singapore tourism industry – future scenarios and marketing implications, *International Marketing Review*, vol. 6, no. 3, pp. 35–46.

Young, B. (1983) Touristization of traditional Maltese fishing-farming villages, *Tourism Management*, vol. 4, no. 1, March, pp. 35–41.

Young, S., Ott, L. and Feigen, B. (1978) Some practical considerations in markets segmentation, *Journal of Marketing Research*, vol. 15, August, p. 408.

Zeithaml, V. A. (1988) Consumer perceptions of price, quality and a means ended model and synthesis of evidence, *Journal of Marketing*, vol. 52, no. 3, July, pp. 2–22.

Zipf, G. K. (1946) The P1P2/D hypothesis: an inter-city movement of persons, *American Sociological Review*, vol. 11, pp. 677–686.

Zuzanek, J. and Mannell, R. (1983) Work leisure relationships from a socio-logical and social psychological perspective, *Leisure Studies*, vol. 2, September, p. 327.

Name index

Subject index